# THEORISING MEDIA

MANCHESTER
1824

Manchester University Press

# THEORISING MEDIA

## Power, form and subjectivity

*John Corner*

Manchester University Press

Published by Manchester University Press
Altrincham Street, Manchester M1 7JA, UK
www.manchesteruniversitypress.co.uk

*British Library Cataloguing-in-Publication Data is available*

*Library of Congress Cataloging-in-Publication Data is available*

ISBN 978 0 7190 9656 3 paperback

First published by Manchester University Press in hardback 2011

This paperback edition first published 2014

The publisher has no responsibility for the persistence or accuracy of URLs for any external or third-
party internet websites referred to in this book, and does not guarantee that any content on such
websites is, or will remain, accurate or appropriate.


Printed in Great Britain
by TJ International Ltd, Padstow

*For Denise*

# Contents

# Acknowledgements

The chapters in Part I are new work, although a section of Chapter 3 draws on and develops material which first appeared in the commentary piece, 'Debating Culture' in *Media, Culture and Society*, 16.1 1994, 141–8.

The Items in Part II have been previously published, sometimes in different versions, as follows: Chapters 4, 5 and 6 in *Media, Culture and Society*, 29.4 (2007); 23.4 (2001) and 31.1 (2009) respectively; Chapters 7 and 8 in *Studies in Documentary Film* 1.1 (2007) and 3.2 (2009) respectively, and Chapter 9 in Jostein Gripsrud (ed.) (2010) *Relocating Television*, Routledge, 41–54. I thank the publishers, Sage. UK, Intellect Books and Routledge for permission to use the material in Part II.

I am grateful to the many referees involved in providing advice in development of the draft material in Part II as well as the relevant editors, including particularly Raymond Boyle, Deane William and Jostein Gripsrud.

I also thank my colleagues at Liverpool University, particularly Kay Richardson and Katy Parry, and at Leeds University, particularly Stephen Coleman, David Hesmondhalgh and David Morrison, who have influenced some of the ideas and the writing in Part I. I also want to acknowledge the contribution made by Peter Dahlgren of Lund University in direct comment on my writing, in broader conversational exchanges and more generally in the richly suggestive example of his work on many of the themes addressed in this volume.

# Introduction

'Theorising' is used in this book to indicate the activity of trying to reach adequate conceptual terms for understanding media structures and processes. It is therefore rather different from, if necessarily related to, the idea of 'media theory', the body of published explanations and propositions about the media that has developed from different fields of study. Both have their place in what follows, but primacy is given to the former. Later in this introduction, I discuss definitional matters concerning the 'theoretical' a little further.

Part I of this book explores three aspects or dimensions of media structure and process that are central to any understanding of how the media work. Part II consists of a number of more focused analytic commentaries and case studies which both draw upon and contribute to conceptual discussion and development regarding these aspects. Each of the aspects is broad and rather loose in definition, but the identifying terms themselves – power, form and subjectivity – are essential categories for enquiry, whatever the internal differentiations that are then made within them and the linkages and overlaps identified both between the three and across other categories and terms.

'Power' is of course the long-standing principal theme of media research, sometimes employed directly, sometimes through ideas of 'influence' and of 'effect' and also of 'policy'. Attempting to understand, and perhaps to contest, the way in which the media are placed within flows of political, social and cultural power, acting both to relay power and as distinctive sources of power themselves, has been an aim of most media research internationally and the main aim of a great variety of enquiries. Changes both in political systems and media systems, including changes in economics, technology and conventions of practice, have shifted the terms on which power questions need to be asked, even though there are also important continuities with an older agenda.

The notion of 'power' covers extensive territory as a way of framing theoretic and analytic concerns. 'Form' has an expansive ring to it too, although by pointing to questions about the communicative organisation of media artefacts and performances it suggests distinctive points of focus. 'Form' can be studied with exclusive, ground-level attention to specific media products, or it can be explored with an interest in making connections with other aspects of media organisation and process. The recent tendency has been towards the latter, particularly towards the tracing of the formal aspect of the linkage between aspects of media production and consumption, attempting to explore the 'vocabularies of value' which feed into perception and judgement here. Study of media form has drawn heavily on the Arts and Humanities strands of media enquiry, including those strands that fed into the development of Cultural Studies as an academic field. In work on media from Social Science perspectives, the relative neglect of formal questions (including questions of aesthetic organisation) is acknowledged to have constituted something of a regular 'blind spot', and the possibilities for greater cross-disciplinary awareness and contribution here are strong.

'Subjectivity' is a term that has only more recently gained general usage in media research, although it has been employed as a significant category in cognate areas, including literary, film and feminist studies, for some time. This growth follows recognition of the complexity and importance of questions about identity and the 'self' in any attempt to engage with how the media operate within contemporary society. It is not as if the term highlights an area which was previously in darkness. A concern with how individuals, and the organisation of individual perceptions, relate to media activities is traceable from the very start of systematic research into media. However, the term 'subjectivity' collects together an agenda of issues about the formation of selfhood, the construction of identity and the dynamics of consciousness that places new emphases and poses new questions. This immediately extends to questions about power and about form, including ones to do with the generic character of our experience of the media, the way in which this experience is organised in relation to quite specific and different kinds of product rather than being essentially a matter of general orientation.

To select these three categories for discussion might justly raise the question of 'why these?' and perhaps also 'why not others?' My answer here, effectively restating the claim of my opening sentence, is that power, form and subjectivity, although they are by no means the only major terms we need, provide us with a very productive route for reflection and audit at the present moment. Together, they run through some broad, varied and also changing terrain, both empirically and conceptually. All three indicate areas in which engaging new work has been produced, sometimes at the most general level but also within more tightly localised settings. They are headings under which we can confidently expect much activity in the future. In my first three chapters I hope to have shown, not just by assertion but by example, how deeply interconnected they are, matters of power essentially turning on issues of form and subjectivity; the study of form intimately connected with subjectivity and, frequently, to power; the whole area of subjectivity raising questions about formal factors and about power relations.

Before describing in a little more detail the structure of the book and the organisation of the accounts within it, I want to touch on two other points which deserve mention as part of these preliminaries. First of all, I want to make a few remarks about the nature of 'theory' in media and cultural research, and the changing theoretical profile which the area has displayed, particularly since the 1970s.

Theory is essential to most academic enquiry because it indicates a level at which evidence, analysis and concepts are connected together to form a generalised explanatory account, however provisional and partial, which can be applied to a given range of phenomena and conditions. Theory can be highly formalised, as for instance in the hypothesis systems often used in the natural sciences as well as elsewhere, or it may take on a rather more casual character, as it does in some theorising about art, including literature. It may have a strong interest in causal relations and in the making of predictive claims (climatology might quickly, and problematically, come to mind here) or it may be causally restrained, and hold back from strong predictive statements. Across most areas of academic activity there has been a strengthening recognition of the difficulties in the way of talking about causality and of making claims about predictability. This recognition has gone along with increased caution about the ways in which data are collected and about the application of schemes of analysis in relation to the framing ideas which guide enquiry. In the humanities, a much broader and stronger scepticism about the stability and integrity of established forms of academic knowledge and modes of knowing has followed the influence of postmodernist commentary, causing continuing debate (see Sim, 2004 for perspectives across diverse fields of study).

Media research has a spectrum of theoretical ambition which runs from the attempt to offer a tight account of causal relations with optimum predictability, right through to more gestural, suggestive notions about the character of artefacts, circumstances, processes, relationships and interconnections. Research that is funded by public and corporate bodies in order to find out things about the consequences of particular media policies or media content, for example, may often, and quite understandably, be required to arrive at firmer propositions than research which is entirely academically oriented and intent on exploring a particular area of media operations against a number of conflicting ideas.

I have discussed elsewhere (e.g. Corner, 1999) the way in which media research is one of those areas in which 'theory' is sometimes used interchangeably with 'ideas' in a way that is not always helpful, although perhaps hard to avoid. To have an idea about something, say for instance new tendencies in reality television, is certainly to work at a level of abstraction above the particular instances and analyses that have informed the idea. We may justly describe it as 'theorising'. However, whether this idea could justly be called a 'theory' about the new tendencies would, I think, depend very much on its intellectual character. If it involved suppositional linkages and relationships between the different aspects identified that could be stated in the form of a proposition (as it certainly might do), then it would be useful to call it a theory. If it was just one speculative notion about a single aspect, for instance that observational sequences were being edited at an increasingly rapid pace, the notion of theory might seem misleading and pretentious. The widespread use of 'theory' outside of specialised academic contexts to indicate all that which is not 'practice' (for instance, as part of the UK driving test!), has helped to loosen usage within academic circles and, here, each discipline area has developed its own internal pattern of conventions, formal and casual.

Media research does not have much disciplinary tightness as a field of enquiry. The category of 'media studies' provides what is now an international core of work dedicated to the study of media systems, but a whole range of disciplines, including sociology, psychology, political studies, history, linguistics and literature, either continue to pursue their long-standing interest in aspects of media processes, or have recently developed such an interest. This means that, both theoretically and methodologically, the area is much more various (or messier) than many other fields of enquiry which have developed more coherently as relatively unified projects within a given disciplinary frame. We have to accept this as being in the nature of the focus of study. Attempts at 'tidying up' would be futile and often intellectually reductive, although the regularly heard call for more engagement across the different sub-specialist and discipline-oriented lines of approach is still worthy of further heeding.

Theory can be developed simply by critically examining other theories, perhaps in terms of their logical coherence and consistency, but a central route for its generation in many disciplines has been through evidence and analysis. Without subscribing to naïve ideas about the readiness with which 'confirmation' and 'proof' can be obtained, it can be seen that in most cases it is through testing theories against kinds of data that the most productive line of development lies. When the usage of 'theory' slips close to becoming a posh synonym for 'hunch' or 'viewpoint', this approach is, clearly, not so relevant. Hunches and viewpoints can be usefully exchanged and debated, but they usually lack the necessary degree of firmness and clarity to be tested until they have been formulated more fully. Viewpoints are also explicitly subjective, perhaps as the basis for further conceptual development, so exchange regarding them (valuable in itself) is often one around normative criteria and parameters for judgement, rather than about evidence. Here, we touch on a quite central difference between theories as working propositions (or more formally, hypotheses) made prior to analysis and theory as 'built' from a phase of enquiry. Theory prior to enquiry may be confirmed, questioned or usefully modified by theoretical exchange and debate. However, in most cases, it is a mistake to confuse it with theory that has emerged from enquiry. This is to blur together two distinctive relations of conceptualisation to reality. It makes no sense at all to lose the distinction between that which is hypothetical and that which is offered as the product of enquiry since, despite the necessary interconnections and interaction between them, the attitude we take towards each needs to recognise its specific status in order to allow relevant modes of critical response and use.

For some time now, media research internationally has been a lively, one might say hectic, area for theoretical activity. In addition to lower-level theorising, a whole sequence of high-altitude '-isms' have passed through the area, rearranging the intellectual landscape in often significant and sometimes confusing ways. Within this context, a number of thinkers have been found widely suggestive. Of these, perhaps Jürgen Habermas, Michel Foucault and Pierre Bourdieu can be seen as exerting the strongest influence across the broadest swathe of study, although most specialist and sub-specialist areas have their own key theorists, sometimes offering perspectives showing not only variation but also conflict.

Given this conceptual landscape, it is not surprising that the business of 'theoretical orientation' has taken on a distinctive character within research and debate. 'Beaming down' from high-level theories in ways that are productive for middle-level conceptualisations and for analytic frameworks has posed challenges, some of which are familiar from other fields and some of which follow from the distinctive constitution of the media and cultural studies area. Making extrapolations from higher-level propositional claims that actually work for lower-level enquiry is often more difficult than it might appear. Similarly, taking the findings of enquiry 'back up' so as to modify previous theory in ways that are coherent and productive for overall research goals can be difficult, too. The danger of placing grand theoretical pronouncements alongside analysed instances in a relationship of suggestive correlation is evident. Research may simply be used to 'illustrate' selected aspects of theory in ways which preclude both serious critique and cogent confirmation and which lack the evidential/argumentative force to develop knowledge further, whatever the 'progress' suggested by its manner of presentation. Attempts to produce composite theoretical perspectives by selective borrowing across the range may ignore the real obstacles to coherence which would exist were the theories to be engaged with fully in their own terms. In going beyond the provocative assembly of selective quotation from several sources, the amount of original work needed to produce new and useful theoretical propositions from the elements of different bodies of previous thinking can be easily underestimated.

Although 'high theoretical' ambition rightly continues to be one marker of international work in media and cultural research, it is now clear from the monograph and journal literature that a stronger strand of empirical investigation and of lower-level development in relation, for instance, to the refinement of analytic vocabulary and of problem-framing has established itself. The continuation of the more stratospheric levels of conceptualisation attracts debate, but with less sustained intensity and often with more concern to connect across to work in adjacent areas and 'down' to the results of specific enquiry and to arguments around particular instances, including comparative instances. This has produced what can be seen as a fresher climate for theoretical development, reducing tendencies towards the dogmatic and the repetitive and making theoretical matters more exciting and exploratory again.

My second preliminary point can be handled more briefly. It concerns my use of the term 'the media' and, at points, the idea of 'mediation'. Just what is included and what not in any use of 'the media' varies considerably. As the term has increasingly taken over from the usage of 'mass media', and before that of 'mass communication', largely perhaps because of the negative political, social and cultural assumptions seen to be bundled into these terms (see Corner, 1979 on this issue), it has retained the focus on central media structures, institutions and processes while extending beyond these to connect selectively with a variety of other practices and representational modes. So, for instance, the study of cinema is certainly study of a medium, but cinema will often not be included within the category of 'the media' as this term is currently employed in academia, a fact largely due to the legacy of 'mass media' as indicating, primarily if not exclusively, the activities of press and broadcasting. Some parts of popular literature can be subsumed under the dominant idea of 'the media', and so can some parts of popular music, but again, within academia, the earlier association of 'mass media research' with largely sociological kinds of enquiry into the major institutional systems of public communication is likely to inhibit this. The arrival of what is still called 'new media' over the last two decades has, it is clear, quite radically changed the agenda of 'media studies', with the newer technologies, applications and contexts taking their place, sometimes slowly and awkwardly, alongside 'old media' within the core definition. Nick Couldry has recently noted (Couldry, 2009) some of the conceptual and analytic implications that have followed from this expanded sense of what is now an extremely varied and rapidly changing field of cultural practices, with the very idea of '*the* media' (often rendered as a singular noun) providing an often highly imprecise focus for investigation and debate, one open to confusion and to suspect generalisations.

Given my themes and interests, I have chosen to focus principally on press, broadcasting and 'new media', with only occasional references to cinema, music and literature. However, questions concerning the varying boundary-lines which the category 'media' now displays, the criteria for boundary-drawing and the pattern of usage of the term across different areas of enquiry and argument (including those outside of academic settings) deserve continuing attention.

Related to this is the notion of 'mediation'. I have used it at points in what follows to indicate that which is produced through media practice and which is both an artefact or a communicative event of one kind or another. Following the discussion above, I realise that this could apply to a painting, a song, a novel or a film as well as a television programme, a newspaper photograph or a webpage. My usage here is meant to be essentially descriptive rather than analytical, although I am aware that the term 'mediation' (like the idea of 'representation') can carry with it certain assumptions about communicative practice, its referents and its functions, that are very much open to question. I hope that the more detailed contexts in which I use the word encourage the reader to pursue such questions.

## THE STRUCTURE OF THE BOOK

Part I of the book is organised as three large chapters that audit the themes that I have chosen to discuss. Each chapter is in part a review of relevant ideas in circulation and debate, often working across both the arts and the social studies perspectives which have been applied, but I also want it to be a fresh, clarifying and provocative engagement with the primary term itself and also some of the conditions and practices it has been used to identify and to investigate. Citation is necessarily highly selective and used primarily to indicate points that I judge to be of principal interest, rather than to document what is sometimes the extensive literature that has developed around them. I have moved around quite freely, both laterally, across the chosen areas, and vertically, in engaging issues at different levels of generality and in discussing examples. A number of my examples could have been used as illustrations in more than one chapter, since they span the principal categories. Some are familiar from the research literature, others less so. My approach assumes a reader who has some familiarity and engagement with media research as an academic area but it does not assume the specialist knowledge that might be expected, for instance, by the reader of a journal article. This means, I hope, that without having the formal organisation and style of 'textbook' writing, the accounts will be found useful by different kinds of student reader, particularly those on more advanced programmes. The field of media research is one that draws on an extensive multi-disciplinary literature where levels of mutual awareness are often low. There are some issues and themes around which a degree of field-wide agreement can be agreed as to terminology, criteria of significance and the agenda for further enquiry. However sub-specialism when combined with different disciplinary orientations inevitably means that many topics show a literature extensively fragmented in perspectives and approaches and often disinclined to take seriously, or even to notice, work on a related topic coming from an academic location perceived as 'other'.[1] For a writer attempting a general survey, this brings with it heightened risks of navigation, as references that another writer would emphasise may simply be mentioned in passing and attention given to ideas that would, in another book, hardly merit a mention. What I have wanted to do will always show its origins in my own view of media research, shaped by a specific, sometimes strongly directed but often quite accidental, sequence of academic events, encounters and teaching and research commitments making up my career over 35 years. However, I would like to think that it also displays some sensitivity to the wider profile of publication and debate as this has shaped the steady institutional growth of the area as a recognised site of international scholarship.

Part II of the book is made up of selected material from essays and articles that I have published in the last decade and which variously pursue issues related to the three main themes. Each is accompanied by a short note of commentary which, among other things, connects them within the wider thematic setting that I have established. They all address a general readership interested in media research, despite some of them having origins in specialist papers. Their thematic relevance is a consequence either of their conceptual focus (for instance, the recurring issues of 'ideology', of 'propaganda' and of the 'public') or an application to selected instances in which the primary emphasis is not so much on the substantive critical assessment of the specific items as on broader questions concerning dimensions of power, formal structures, the diversity of communicative processes and the challenges of analysis. More on the character of Part II is given in a short note that precedes it.

## NOTE

1    The precise pattern of mutual recognition and mutual interest across the different types of inquiry gathered around specific themes concerning media is worthy of closer attention. Although there is undoubtedly an inclination towards greater interdisciplinary engagement, it is not surprising that the economics and organisation of academic research have helped preserve and even strengthen a degree of 'balkanisation' and subsequent blinkering in areas which would benefit from a more open and regular dialogue. An example here would be research from within political studies and from within cultural studies on the mediation of politics and on popular perceptions of political power (discussed at points throughout what follows, particularly in Chapters 1 and 3).

# PART ONE

# 1

## *Power*

In this chapter I want to explore a selection of the numerous and wide-ranging issues that are to do, directly or otherwise, with the 'power' of the media. Research into the various aspects of power, and arguments about it, have always been at the centre of academic interest in media. Sometimes, the focus has been on 'influence and effects', a concern with the measurable consequences of output for the perceptions and attitudes of media readerships and audiences. This is the strongest strand of international research, operating across a wide variety of often contesting theoretical and methodological approaches, and it is certainly one that has been continuously well-funded, including by governments and by corporate enterprise. However, the concern with the power of the media goes beyond the specific research objectives of 'influence and effects' research, even if it is regularly returned to them in one form or another. It is present, for instance, in much content and textual analysis, it is often the central issue underlying production studies, and it is a principal theme in work on history, policy and, with an obvious directness, on media–political relations.

In my discussion I shall attempt to differentiate the most important aspects of thinking about media power, including those strands of work which serve to connect ideas about power to specific, researched instances and examples as well as to broader theorisations about social and political organisation. I shall look at some of the terms which have regularly been used in writing about power and examine what possibilities there are for revising and developing our ideas around the issues that they seek to identify and, often, to engage with critically. One recurring theme will be the extent to which, in any given theoretical account or offered example, media power is seen to be 'bad', something which our politics and our culture would be improved by having less of. A recurrent assessment here is that it is 'power without responsibility', to use a resonant phrase from the writings of Rudyard Kipling which provides the title of a major, long-standing textbook in media studies (Curran and Seaton, 2009). As in many debates about power in other contexts, the idea of 'good power' is often rather elusive, although the necessity of power itself is an implicit premise of any political and social order. It is interesting here, and relevant to some of the work elsewhere in this book, to reflect on the way in which the term 'powerful', when used of a specific programme, film or printed item, is nearly always a term of approval. Such usage is essentially about the 'strength' of the work so described, variously aesthetic or thematic. Saying that a programme was 'powerful' is at some distance from general claims about the 'power of the media', but the degree of descriptive continuity with the larger claim and what is often the evaluative contrast with it are revealing of the complexities underlying ideas of media power at the level of the artefact (where individual critical appreciation is projected in the judgement) and then of the 'system' (where an unacceptable degree of subordinate social relations may appear to be involved).

Another recurring theme is the way in which the powers of the media are perceived to be in various degrees of alignment or disjunction with other agencies and institutions of power in society. In some cases, this amounts to seeing media organisations not as exercising power 'of their own', but acting as a relay or conduit for sources of power external to them, most often the state or major corporate bodies. They can thereby be perceived, in at least part of their functions, to transform political or economic power into forms of cultural power through the legitimising visibility they give it across a range of generic types. Indeed, as Dahlgren (2009) points out, the principal issue then becomes that of 'power *over*' the media rather than the more familiar 'power *of*' question, although typically both become combined, since anxiety about the former is largely grounded in assumptions about the latter. In other cases, tensions and even conflicts can be observed between given media organisations and governmental agencies, companies or entire commercial sectors, a situation sometimes reflected openly in media content, thereby complicating, perhaps radically, the profile and flows of 'relayed power'.

The capacity of the media to contribute to the 'way things are' in society, to circumstances and events, as a result of the perceptions they encourage, the information they provide and the feelings they generate, whether directly or in combination with other factors, is essentially a form of 'soft' power. It does not have the physical, possibly coercive, dimension that, for instance, military power, police power and aspects of economic power, including the power of labour relationships, can and do have in many countries. As a form of 'soft' power, the measurement of its causality and its consequences in any particular instance presents difficulties and generates dispute. The final focus of most debates about media power concerns the transfer or generation of meanings and of value. These debates are essentially (if not always explicitly) about conditions of subjectivity, of awareness, knowledge and affective orientation. Even if the primary evidence of media power is present in given economic circumstances (as in the structure and pattern of information and entertainment distribution) or in institutional scale and prominence (as in the relative dominance of given media providers within a national or international area), the final consequences, and then the arguments about these, may largely turn on the impact of such arrangements upon the terms of individual perception, knowledge and feeling and the conditions for behaviour which these provide. In that sense, the arguments are about symbolic and cultural aspects of power.

It is worth noting that it is now a routine assumption in most societies that the media *do* have power. The strength and direction of it (and even the definition used to identify it) may be subject to heated dispute, but most public and commercial organisations carry out their work, most obviously their publicity work, with the premise that media outputs can exert a significant degree of power over both public and corporate perceptions and therefore bring about changes to the 'action frames' within which they operate. This power is perceived as providing the grounds of opportunity, perhaps bringing state, corporate or broader public benefit (it is power worth courting), but there is also a perceived risk of getting caught up in media power flows which may be harmful. The harm may relate to specific news stories or to particular characterisations and themes in entertainment and fiction, but it is often thought to require clear strategies of avoidance and, where encountered, of damage control. The whole, fraught debate about the kind and level of regulation to apply to the media system is essentially one concerning the different kinds of 'benefit' and of 'harm' to which the powers of the media can contribute, if not solely bring about. Both organisations and individuals are implicated, as is clear from the way in which entry into the highly mediated celebrity sphere, even for a temporary period, can bring fame, wealth but also a sometimes disastrous transformation of the terms of 'private' living for many of those involved (Marshall, 2006 provides an exploration of diverse media–celebrity relations).

## THEORISING POWER IN SOCIAL RESEARCH

Before exploring in more detail the character of media power and some of the more disputed aspects of our attempts to understand it, it might be useful to consider briefly the conceptual problems posed by thinking more generally about power as a factor in politics and social order. One very good, if by no means comprehensive, way to do this is by looking at the key arguments in Lukes (2005), a book which offers a revision of his classic work of thirty years earlier (Lukes, 1974). This revision has special interest for media researchers, since it is informed by the author's reading of the two theorists whose ideas of power have been referenced most often (if not always with the clearest outcomes) by writers in media and cultural studies – Pierre Bourdieu and Michel Foucault. Not all parts of Lukes' scheme of conceptualisation have relevance for media, but a great deal of it is suggestive, particularly where questions of systemic power relations involving other sources of power (the subject of my next section) are concerned.

Lukes organised his original account around three 'dimensions of power'. The first was the dimension of formal (and 'official') decision-making, and the social actors identifiably involved in this. The second was the less definable routes and processes of agenda-setting, by which certain issues attained public visibility, and were given prominence within a ranking, or were perhaps marginalised or excluded altogether, without this being made fully explicit and accountable. The third was power through almost entirely unacknowledged modes of domination, in which a strongly hegemonic relationship produced deep levels of compliance through intensive socialisation. It was this last dimension of power which, in 1974, Lukes saw as requiring the most attention, since it seemed so central to the way in which political and social order was maintained in many countries, and yet it so frequently escaped from those 'audits' of power carried out through the empirical investigations of political scientists. In many countries, the media have been seen as decisively operative in all three dimensions, either in a relationship characterised by (selective) relay from other, more established, sources of power, or in ways that have introduced quite distinctive power elements (for instance, that of the projected personalities of the powerful) into the dynamics of political and social organisation.

In his commentary of revision and development, Lukes makes a number of general points about power that have implications for any approach to the study of the power of the media. These include:

1. Power is a capacity or ability to bring about a specific effect or consequence. It can be identified in its potential agency as well as in its realisation.
2. Power needs to be thought of in relation to the potentially positive, affirming, enabling idea of 'power to' as well as the dominative, negatively constraining idea of 'power over'. (We can note the widespread use of the term 'empowering' here to describe an increase in power for individuals and groups previously having marginal scope for emancipation, self-definition and social action).
3. The possession of the capacity for power and the exercising of such capacity are not dependent upon 'intentions', although motives and strategies should be taken into account in power analysis.
4. Following Foucault (for example in the work collected in Foucault, 2002), power needs to be engaged with in its close and crucial relationship with forms of knowledge and the distribution of knowledge.[1]
5. Following Bourdieu (for example in Bourdieu, 1992), forms of power may work through symbolic means, including strategies to achieve and sustain control that can in their strongest articulations be called forms of 'symbolic violence'.[2]

Certainly, the powers of the media have frequently been regarded within recent debate as working to 'constrain' rather than 'enable' the interests of the majority of the people, although throughout this chapter I will want to make connections with both kinds of judgements, sometimes to be found in uneasy combination. In this respect, the economic 'freedom' of the press to operate with minimal public regulation has often been regarded as allowing, in practice, limitations to be imposed on the wider political and cultural freedoms of citizens to enjoy a diversity of views and opinions (Baker, 2002 and Splichal, 2002 discuss this fully). One of the reasons that debate about media power is distinctive is that it concerns the major agencies of popular knowledge and of cultural engagement and reproduction, whose growth and social permeation have produced a situation where degrees of 'media-dependency' (a reliance on media sources) are the norm, whether or not this is finally assessed as constituting a form of domination. Like other forms of political and social power, the power of the media can be met by expressions of criticism and of personal rejection and opposition but it is only really countered by kinds of practical intervention.

Increased scope for effectively placing a check on mainstream media power can follow from democratic public policies in which there are built-in channels of proper responsiveness to public dissatisfaction, codes of public representation and the development of the media in the public interest (this last term being, inevitably, subject to definitional debate; see Chapter 6). On the other hand, it can be the result of direct action to provide independent alternatives to established production and circulation. This is a strand of work with a strong record of commitment, effort and imagination, but one perennially limited by the economic requirements for becoming a successful media 'player', even at local levels (see Atton, 2001 on the history and varieties of the 'alternative media' perspective).

It is beyond dispute that media activities are deeply implicated in the broader pattern and profile of power in a society, particularly where the distribution of knowledge and the according of values are concerned. Indeed, their positioning and function here exceed the significance accorded to them in Lukes' suggestive account, a common enough kind of oversight in accounts from political sociology and political theory. In addition to advancing a framework for engaging with the symbolic dimension of media, Bourdieu has also influentially used the idea of 'field' to explore the broader interconnections of the different domains of social and cultural production, providing degrees of both autonomy and interdependence (including economic and political) for specialist practices (see Bourdieu, 1993 and the discussions in Benson and Neveu, 2005 and Couldry, 2007). However, the most comprehensive and influential framework for thinking about this issue of the broader societal linkage of the media has centred on the idea of the 'public sphere' as developed by the critical social theorist, Jürgen Habermas (see Chapter 4). Habermas (particularly Habermas, 1989) presents what has become a persuasive narrative of how 'good' media power, the power to resource and circulate deliberation about political and social matters, a power which appeared to provide the basis of a public, critical rationality and thereby held the hope of being an agency of democratic progress, transformed itself. It became, by contrast, an increasing constraint on this development, aligning with dominant economic power blocs and shifting its primary imperative from one of providing open information and argumentation across contesting positions to one of commercial profit and the reinforcement of established authority. In these narrowing circumstances, retaining the space for a public sphere separate both from the state and from purely corporate interests has become increasingly difficult even to envisage, let alone achieve.

Habermas's writings on this theme, including later ones in which the precise terms of the critique and the prognosis are subject to revision, remain a key reference point for a wide range of international media studies (for examples of diverse approaches, see Calhoun, 1993; Garnham, 2000; McKee, 2005; Couldry, 2010; and Chapter 4 of this volume). Given the continuing vulnerability of the 'public' idea and continuing perceptions of commercial distortion and elite alignments within the media system, the references are likely to grow. It is to issues of alignment that I now turn.

## MEDIA AND SYSTEMIC POWER

I have suggested that there are very good reasons, historical, political and sociological, for seeing media institutions and processes as exercising their powers *systemically*, that is to say within the terms of a broader pattern of determining relationships with other sources of power, the vested and often elite interests of which they routinely serve to maintain, whatever the localised tensions and questioning that might also occur. It is clear that the systems within which the media are placed, and against which any general claims for the independence of media organisations have to be judged, vary greatly across national settings, even though strong elements of internationalisation have become evident at the level of media markets and media products. These systems also show the transitions of historical change and development, sometimes in gradual and uneven transformation, but also in rapid and radical shifts, such as those brought about widely by the new media technologies of the last twenty years and by the forms of 'free market' thinking about the media economy that have extended across Europe and beyond, often revising or displacing older models (Baker, 2006 provides a useful synopsis).

It is without doubt the kind of 'fit' that the components of the media system have with the political system that has produced the most anxiety and received the most attention over the years. Here, the connection with external power relations is frequently made explicit, perhaps in formal, even constitutional, arrangements between political and media institutions. However, in many countries this kind of recognition of the media's placement within the political system has been considerably modified, as indicated above, by an emphasis on the media's location within the system of market economics, at its loc⁻˙ national and globalised levels. China is an obvious example with countries in Eastern Europe, but subtler shifts have occurred in many national systems across the world. The kinds of power relationship involved here are unlikely to be openly proclaimed and may not be immediately identifiable. Nevertheless, the impact upon the economic organisation of everyday life and upon forms of consciousness and value (including political value) has often been judged to be pervasive and deep across a diversity of suppliers and kinds of media goods and services.[3]

Where tendencies and orientations in the political system and the economic system are in broad harmony, then the expectation of a strong 'power reinforcement' role by the media, embracing different technologies, modes of funding and both formal and informal controls, seems justified, and research would expect to discover this. Where there is some distance, and even tension or conflict, between the two, then the possibility of a more complicated pattern, one in which a degree of 'power-questioning' occurs, emerges. Outright opposition to the policies and actions of dominant power formations may be articulated, either within the terms of an already formed political or economic elite that is a subordinate power formation (e.g. a parliamentary opposition), or within the terms of an emerging group (e.g. a political party or a campaigning body) which is perhaps attempting to become such a formation. Elite dissensus, a split about ends or means within the sphere of those already possessing 'political capital' (see Davis, 2010 on use of this term, taken from Bourdieu), is a point of significant development, even of crisis, in the history of many countries, often interconnecting their political, economic and media systems, and bringing about decisive shifts.[4] The emergence of new groups wishing to develop or even to 'seize' power through routes of corporate and/or public approval, and having realistic chances of doing so is, of course, also of great significance for media institutions and practices. Their response to such emergence is crucial for any analysis of just *how*, and with what predictability, they are systemically connected to broader patterns of elite economic and social management and to the dynamics of change in these patterns.

When addressing questions about the levels and kinds of power relationship that elites have with the media, and exercise *through* them, it is important to note that neither history nor contemporary analysis provide us with clear examples of a political or social system in which elites *do not* seek to exercise a degree of control over media activities and particularly over what 'gets said' by the media. We can trace this through historically from the tight management of religious and monarchic bodies to various kinds of secular state regulation and covert interventional strategies, sometimes supported by alliance with corporate elites and sometimes not. The amount of 'communicative space' that various kinds of elite have allowed for non-elite contributions to circulate and be open to debate has varied considerably. Many countries have been through periods in which the nature of the elite itself has undergone a rapid transition. However, perhaps more recognition that an inequality between the relationships which elites have with media, and those which 'ordinary people' enjoy, is the historical and international norm could be helpful. It might check the tendency towards shocked indignation (indicating surprise) that is sometimes a feature of academic commentaries. It should certainly not check the desire to investigate and criticise, identifying deficits and campaigning for change, but it would provide such activities with what is an often missing degree of historical realism about the exercise of power. It might also bring into sharper focus the challenge of imagining kinds of alternative, 'non-elite' structures and processes that could work effectively within the forms of existing or of possible systems.

We cannot properly consider questions of media power without addressing the issue of how these questions might be distributed across the different media. Such distribution might show wide variation. In many societies, it is clear that anxiety about the 'power of the press' was overtaken some time ago by concern about the power of television. This is not only because of the distinctive capacities of television as a means of illustration and persuasion, but because television has in many societies become the most popular media form, one with unparalleled political, social and symbolic centrality within the space of the nation, and the press has correspondingly declined in its salience or been further differentiated across discrete market segments, certainly in the newspaper sector but also in the expanding magazine sector too. This has not stopped sectorial anxieties emerging (for instance, about tabloid coverage of celebrities or about particular kinds of teenage magazine) but these have been different from the broad 'aggregational issues' (for example, about distortion of public knowledge and the undercutting of national moral values) that have characterised much debate about television. Concern about cinema continues too, but this has also, for some time, been largely displaced by attention to the domestic medium. Cinema's identity as involving media performances which you pay to go out to see, rather than access through transmission into the home, together with its emphasis on fictional rather than factual materials, has often been a modifying factor in discussion of the kind and strength of the systemic power it might relay and the character of its impact upon civic space.

It is interesting to place radio within this context of comparative media concern. In many countries, it is only quite recently that deregulation has produced a situation in which 'radio power' has become an issue, surrounding, for instance, popular music playlists or the attitudes and behaviour of talk-show hosts, although in countries where radio is still the primary systemic medium, many of those concerns which, internationally, we see surrounding television (including those of bias and misinformation) are to still to be found strongly active. In Britain from the 1920s through to the 1950s, radio was a key medium of state and corporate promotion (including of wartime propaganda), having the advantage, that was then extended to television, of being received 'privately' in the home and of not, unlike a newspaper, requiring literate engagement (for detailed accounts here, Briggs, 1985 and Scannell and Cardiff, 1991 are invaluable).

The latest medium around which ideas of power have been debated, extensively and sometimes heatedly, is self-evidently the web. Often regarded initially as a non-systemic, indeed an anti-systemic, agency of communication, it has increasingly become obvious that significant connections both with corporate and even with state power are features of the web's global profile as an informational and cultural tool, even if its very nature encourages stronger patterns of diversity than previous media, across both the content range and the origins of provision. Not surprisingly, it is principally the 'libertarian' properties of the web that have been seen as potentially dangerous by many of those wishing to emphasise the negative character of its power just as they been a key point of reference for those celebrating its political and social promise (see the discussion in Chapter 3). In particular, the circulation of pornography and the encouragement of children into kinds of social danger through networking sites and, differently, through gaming, have been the subject of much debate and research (a recent survey is Livingstone, 2009). To this has been added concern over the integrity of that which is offered as information and knowledge on the web. Such concern replicates some aspects of the long-running anxiety about press and television as sources of social knowledge but the focus is, as yet, less on the possibilities of macro-systemic influence and more on the activities of fringe and 'extreme' groupings, and 'deviant' individuals, who are now able to use the web as a public communicational platform (Cammearts, 2008 examines aspects of this through case studies).

## MEDIA POWER AS A PROBLEM

Even in those societies in which media power is seen as problematic, it is not usually found to be so across all of its dimensions and instances. Where the interests of the state are served well by media systems, this function is unlikely to be seen as an issue by governing elites, whatever concern for the 'public interest' and for the independent integrity of journalism they might continue to express. Similarly, corporate interests using the media successfully both as direct channels for advertising and (through news and other programme formats) as an agency for the 'quieter' forms of routine, promotional activity, have no reason to see such power as being in need of correction. Health education initiatives, many poverty and disaster action projects, charities of all kinds and special interest groups would similarly regard the exercising of media power, both in the impact of the coverage of issues and events and the capacity to act as a means of persuasion in changing attitudes and in raising money on their behalf, as largely benign. It is likely that, in many societies, a substantial majority of people not directly involved in such media use would nevertheless regard it as largely positive too. It would be viewed as essentially 'pro-social' in character. What are the factors, then, that lead certain kinds of media power to be regarded as excessive or misdirected, or somehow undesirable?

Nearly all ideas of 'bad' power have their grounding in perceptions about the distortion to either knowledge or values, or both, which the media introduce into general consciousness through their part in constructing the symbolic environment. This is an environment in which people develop as gendered and ethnically various citizens within the framing terms of economic inequalities and opportunities. The distortions can be seen as a matter of undue *passivity*, the uncritical reflection of established realities as acceptable and even natural, or as more *active*, the strategic reproduction of dominant assumptions and ideas in ways which exclude others. There can be an interplay between these rather different 'distortive' tendencies. Some of these critical perceptions are primarily *structural* in character, that is to say they identify distortion as following from aspects of the systemic relationships I discussed above. Others are primarily *discursive*, regarding distortion as essentially a product of the particular modes of knowing and of feeling that the media encourage through their distinctive uses of language and image. Many ideas of the 'badness' of the media, or of a particular part of the media, combine structural and discursive elements, but the question of where the emphasis is placed is nearly always a significant one in pursuing enquiry and debate.

## THREE MODES OF STRUCTURAL DEFICIT

It is possible to identify three different routes through which arguments about the structural deficit of the media are advanced. Again, even though they often occur in combination, the kind of emphasis each is given has important consequences for what is being claimed as the existing situation and put forward as the way or ways in which this situation might be changed.

### Elite dominance

Ideas of structural deficit can work with the notion, discussed earlier, that the linkage between political elites and the media is too direct and strong. This linkage can be a formal and largely explicit arrangement (as it is, for instance, in China at the moment, although even here the situation is subject to change[5]), or it can be informal and largely denied (as it is, for example, in many Western countries). An important part of any analysis would be evidence of the extent to which significant parts of the media, if not the media system as a whole, worked to support the views of the political elite against alternative and perhaps critical perspectives (Hallin and Mancini, 2004 is an outstanding attempt to plot international patterns, richly suggestive for further work). Quite crucial here is the matter of where to define the contours of the 'elite perspective'. This is particularly an issue where a national political system includes different political parties competing for publicity and power by pursuing distinctive economic and social programmes. Such a situation involves a degree of inter-elite conflict, most obviously during election periods, in relation to which the media can align itself with varying degrees of partisanship or proclaimed 'objectivity'. Certain media elements, including perhaps both major and minor players within the system, might position themselves behind existing governmental perspectives and priorities, while others might become strong agencies of critique and articulation of the need for change. Just what the overall pattern is across broadcasting and the press (where some affiliations will be explicit and others will go undeclared or denied) has to be a key focus for developing any argument about structural deficit of this kind.

However, some critics would want to argue that pursuing the argument through inter-elite relationships, and the factional tensions occurring here, is essentially beside the point and that it is the broader relation between the elite groupings as a whole and the media that needs primary if not exclusive attention.[6] Logically, this requires that the differences between elements of the elite (including government and opposition and/or major political parties) be seen as less important than the overall homogeneity of the elite grouping. There are likely to be considerable differences both in the real and the perceived levels of elite homogeneity, relating to the profile of economic and political views within a given national system at a particular time. For instance, if a broad commitment to capitalist development were taken as a marker of elite commonality, then it would be very difficult to find in Europe any 'elite' elements that depart from this position, whatever the marked variations in economic and social policy concerning its pursuit. It is therefore not surprising that anti-capitalist views, along with outlined alternatives to capitalism, are not a strong feature of mainstream European media content, however much the financial crisis of 2008–9 has generated commentary and opinion pieces which connect with an extended range of economic thinking. However, if foreign policy were taken as a marker, it would be possible in many European systems to find a range of significantly different views about national, European and US policy, and a range of media positions taken up in relation to these (although not always mapping neatly on to the broader political pattern). As questions of social policy, including health and welfare policy, become more pressing in many countries (including, as I write, in both Britain and the USA), it is possible to find a range of different perspectives among political elites here too, a range which could be seen as showing significant levels of diversity by most applied criteria even if it was also possible to identify muted and excluded positions. Again, this goes along with variations, however skewed, within the pattern of media coverage. Such coverage both reflects and encourages inter- and intra-elite dispute, with only detailed research being able to establish the relationship between these two dynamics and to evaluate the extent to which given phases of policy dissensus were media-led or media-reinforced.[7]

Sustaining the 'elite dominance' argument at the most general level, the level above inter-elite (and intra-elite) disagreements, risks losing a degree of cogency in the terms in which political deficit is identified, particularly in respect of those countries where lively and sometimes substantial inter-elite contests occur and receive a diverse (if finally 'unbalanced') profile both of media advocacy and critique. It risks generalising the charge of deficit to one of broadly reflecting (and thereby perpetuating) the outer parameters within which the state and its economic and cultural institutions frame their judgements and actions. This is not an insignificant charge, certainly (see Slavoj Zizek's recent account (Zizek, 2010) of the need to think 'outside the box' politically, including in relation to the current, framing terms of liberal democracy) but it has a degree of obviousness to it, one that needs to be recognised within normative perspectives on media–political relations that seek to inform attempts at specific measures for change. It also risks conflating situations in which the media reflect the perspectives of an internally varied and quite loosely defined 'elite' and those in which they reflect a highly unified and possibly sharply demarcated one. Such a conflation has been made explicit in some commentary. Indeed, in pursuit of arguments in favour of the 'propaganda model' (Herman and Chomsky, 1988, and see the discussion of this term in Chapter 4), it has often been suggested that inter-elite contest is not only of secondary significance but is often itself a device of strategic deception, one by which the political system, especially as reported in the media, can seem to be more open to alternatives than it really is (Klaehn, 2002 provides an example of this argument). This view risks underrating the real importance of inter-elite conflict in the historical development of many political systems, as well as overestimating the level of direct management which most political elites can exert even over those parts of the media system which share their values. Of the available elite controls, forms of censorship, information concealment and other kinds of official and unofficial secrecy (see Chapter 4) still constitute a core area of public information management, although it is one now prone to various kinds of leak and investigative revelation.[8]

Agencies other than those which are directly and openly political are obviously at work in resourcing media accounts. Educational, health, military, legal, historical and, importantly, commercial institutions feed into what is written, said and shown across the generic range. Some of what is provided here is elite both in origin and in strategic design, and some of it is positioned less clearly in relation to existing structures of power and to forces of change. Advertising has received particular attention within media studies (among the huge range of recent publications, see McFall, 2004 for a clear overview of the issues), since part of the steady permeation of social life by the media ('colonisation' is a term with a more critical edge) is often seen to have been achieved through the amplification and aesthetic projection of prescriptive notions of 'life' and of 'living', however fanciful and possibly harmful, by those with something to sell. However, in the formation of the ideas and perceptions of gender, ethnicity and class in public circulation (the last category routinely subject to blurrings and denials in recent British mediation, the other two now more available for 'identity debate' after years of suppression by dominant perspectives), the links between media and many other, diverse, parts of the political and social system are active and significant. These links are reflective, working with what is already there, but constitutive too, working as resources for the production of future realities. As later chapters will variously show, the 'reflective/constitutive duality' affects nearly all attempts to identify (or assert) the character and consequences of specific media representations. Either one side or the other is given (perhaps exclusive) emphasis or ideas about the proportions of each involved in combination are the subject of enquiry, dispute (and sometimes confusion).

What about non-elite perspectives? How do they get selected for an airing? Do they have any chance of becoming 'elite' themselves, even if only as a relatively minor formation in a heterogeneous elite sphere? Can they retain at least some of their characteristics as 'ordinary' and yet still be regularly accessed and circulated alongside elite accounts in ways that are practically meaningful for deliberative engagement and action by the society as a whole? This question is central to any sense of the media as using their power, or allowing their power to be used, democratically, and I will address it under the separate heading of 'diversity'.

## *Levels of diversity*

Diversity is seen to be a good thing within many accounts of media power, working to reduce power abuse and to enable the media–political relationship to be a more democratic one. However, diversity of outlets by itself is no guarantee of diversity of coverage and of opinion, and there is an increasing recognition of the hollowness of ideas of 'choice' when these are simply part of the ideology of an increased market competition, often resulting either in more ways of obtaining the same thing, or the restriction of optionality to a privileged few. That said, the dynamics of consumer choice continue to be a dominant part of British political life, as I write this in 2010.[9]

At one level, diversity is simply a function of market conditions, of how many different products can be profitable within the same segment, or into how many separate segments the market (its users, audiences or readerships) can be divided. Diversity at this level may certainly open up better conditions for political diversity than are offered by intensive concentration but it by no means entails these. I noted above that where the political elite consists of distinctly different groups, with agendas that both overlap but also contrast, it is likely that a diverse market of outlets will reflect some of this variation. It will do so through the separate lines of influence and perhaps sponsorship that sections of the elite variously have with broadcasting and press activities.

For only one elite group to find its views articulated through the media in a situation where established elites were in formal rivalry would not be impossible, but it would be most likely to occur in a transitory stage, perhaps for instance in the attempted suppression of a rising non-dominant elite group or groups. Again, there are many international examples, historical and contemporary, varying in the speed and scale of transition. We must remember that the dominant elite (usually represented formally in the government) will almost certainly have the advantage of being fully and immediately accessed to the news media to explain its views and actions, even if these views and actions are subject to a critical exploration which is also reported in, and perhaps partly conducted by, the media. The way in which the media relate to, and report, the business of government is an issue of major importance in any discussion of 'dominance', one where possibilities for reform and alternatives need continuing attention (Schlesinger *et al.*, 2001 provides an illuminating study of a new system and its problems). Although changes to current practice here are often highly desirable if not urgently necessary in many national settings, the continuation of some kind of inequality in the primary media access made available to elites (and/or 'appropriated' by them) as against other possible contributors will, I think, be hard to avoid.[10]

But how are non-elite ideas and interpretations fed into the media pattern or (with varying degrees of intent) kept out of it? An important factor here is the scale of established support for non-elite ideas when compared to the support for ideas within the elite frame. Measuring this support through public opinion research is controversial (not least because of the nature of a proportion of this research as a promotional tool for elites), but the existence of an emerging (or residual) body of non-elite thinking might be seen as a precondition for media coverage, let alone the possibility of some level of media alignment. Such a profile of coverage and alignment can be subject to quite radical shifts, such as those which occurred in the last decade in the international coverage of climate change (with dramatic reversals following the 'Climategate' events of 2009[11]) and are currently occurring in Britain around military involvement in Afghanistan and (very differently) around the payment of expenses to Members of Parliament.[12] What can happen here is that non-elite ideas grow to the point where their articulation in the media leads, along with other factors, to their taking up (albeit with revision) by groups within the elite, followed by their appearance within inter-elite debate and perhaps finally within dominant elite policy.

However, national systems are not by any means fully 'open' in the way this might suggest, and many non-elite ideas do not make it any further than the minority groupings, and related media outlets, within which they are developed. Could a strong, even majority-endorsed, non-elite view be ignored by the media in their orientation towards accessing elite views and giving privilege to elite frameworks? The scale of the British protest marches against the imminent invasion of Iraq in 2003, together with measurements of public opinion at the time (see Robinson *et al.*, 2010), indicate how it is possible for political elites finally to make decisions going against strong indicators of dominant public attitude. However, sections of the media supported the anti-war position (some, right through the military campaign itself) and the decision to go to war has since become strongly controversial within the elites of all major British political parties, including among politicians holding governmental office at the time. Widespread non-elite perceptions of the risks that the war entailed did not stop the war, but they were re-activated when two things that those supporting the invasion used as justifications for their actions did not happen: the finding of weapons of mass destruction, and a relatively rapid transition to a stable civil society in Iraq.[13]

Behind the interplay between the various media, elite and non-elite formations, there is the long-running question of the extent to which the media act not so much as resources of public opinion but as shapers of it. If the view is taken that the media are primarily shapers of public opinion, then the fact that non-elite views are not held on any significant scale by the general public simply becomes a truism. Citing this as any kind of justification for the relative ignoring of non-elite opinion is unacceptable. But at the same time, as suggested above, blaming the media for an under-representation of views outside those of elite groups lacks a degree of cogency if appropriate evidence of the existence of these views among the general population is not forthcoming. Not surprisingly, this question of the available, relevant evidence is a continuing focus of research and debate, just as what we might call 'talking up' or 'talking down' the level of underlying popular dissent surrounding the decisions taken by the political elite has been a feature of media and cultural studies for some time, especially in its more polemical moments. In the 'talk up' approach, emphasis is placed on the strong levels of resentment and resistance to dominant views which exist, mostly unreported by (and therefore unreinforced by) media coverage. Within this perspective, considerable support for new kinds of media–political relationship, for new kinds of politics and of political communication, is seen to be already apparent but routinely overlooked. In the 'talk down' approach, the emphasis is placed on the efficiency with which the articulation of dominant perspectives across the media has suppressed and neutralised popular critical scrutiny and dissent. Here, a far stiffer challenge is posed for any shift away from existing elite dominance, since the grounds of dissatisfaction have yet to establish a firm popular presence and articulation.

These questions have been explored by studies making close empirical examination of people's subjective relationships to the terms of power their focus rather than making claims about these relationships at a higher level. For instance, Kevin Barnhurst (1998) finds that young citizens perceive a 'powerlessness' at the more general (indeed, Foucauldian) level of the comprehensive permeation of elite power flows into multiple aspects of their everyday lives, rather than at the limited, formal level of self-conscious citizenship within a political system. The question of how power is experienced personally and locally (within what Barnhurst calls the 'fine meshes'), including the sense of the insufficiency of that which is available to the self, is an important complement to other kinds of analysis and it is one which inevitably connects with the performance of the media, which variously might be seen to be reinforcing or, with varying degrees of effectiveness, helping to counter, any perceived forms of coercion, subjection and exclusion. Of recent studies, Couldry, Livingstone and Markham (2007, revised 2010) is an impressively comprehensive examination, both quantitative and qualitative, of how the private and the public world relate, the forms of 'disconnection' that occur between them and the central role of the media in generating ideas of involvement or of a routine indifference (sometimes accepted, sometimes regretful and sometimes resentful). The extent, across the various demographic groups, to which it is the media system or the political system which is seen to be primarily at fault in sustaining high levels of disconnection, and in what combination they are seen to work, provides an important question for future enquiry. This raises issues that lead on to my third element of structural deficit – deception.

## Deception

Elite dominance need not necessarily lead to, or be supported by, deception in any useful sense of that word, except insofar as by accepting (even if resignedly) the perspectives and accounts of those with an agenda grounded in sector and class privilege, the majority are implicated in the media's perpetuation of a hierarchy of power relations that may not align with their own best interests or, indeed, with ascertainable 'real circumstances'. That said, elite dominance will almost certainly use a variety of approaches to controlling aspects of the flow of public knowledge, particularly in areas (such as foreign and defence policy) where secrecy has long carried official legitimacy, even if there have been regular debates about its scale and nature. However, most accounts of elite power have included ideas and evidence about forms of deception practised self-consciously as an ingredient of strategic communication, directly and through the media (Corner, 2010a looks at political publicity in relation to this question). These have varied from what are sometimes relatively simple ideas of 'propaganda' as a flow of calculated lies, exaggerations and highly selective information designed to mislead the public as to what is happening, often 'in their name' (see Chapter 4), all the way through to the most complex theories of ideology as a regulator of imagination, consciousness and subjectivity of a far more subtle kind, not needing routinely to descend to the level of direct falsehoods (reviewed in Chapter 5). In his general account of power, discussed earlier, Lukes (2005) sees this kind of 'power over' as working through internal constraints placed on people's resources for understanding and on their capacities for judgement.

The idea that strategies of deception are a pernicious element of media power (and of political power, too) relates to a wide range of international evidence concerning the difference between what politicians say (and the media often uncritically report) and the verifiable facts of the situation as established by a number of other agencies, sometimes only later. In certain areas, statistically based claims and counter-claims are open to debate. In others, the precise patterns of motive and intent at work are impossible to gauge. However, in a large number of instances what has been 'officially' claimed to be the case can be shown with reasonable firmness not to be so or not to have been so. In a smaller number of these cases, it can also be satisfactorily demonstrated that the political claims (and perhaps the media reporting of them) were made in full knowledge of their questionable character, if not of their complete falsehood (once again, the political and media uses made of the data from military intelligence assessments prior to the invasion of Iraq in 2003 have provided a strong, recent example).[14]

Accompanying this primary level of deceptive communication, there is a secondary level consequent upon it. This is the level of denials. Deniability has become in many countries a routine political practice, often resorted to in the face of accusations regarding, for instance, policy goals, the integrity of specific political programmes or kinds of involvement (especially 'deals') with other members of the political or corporate elite nationally and internationally. In particular, denying 'knowledge of' something (perhaps at a decisive moment in the past), as part of a claim of innocence in respect of what has become a controversial issue, is a familiar move. It is important to note here how, in many national contexts, the media have effectively helped to increase the frequency of denial through their intensive coverage of politicians in relation to breaches of integrity and abuses of power, often reported within the 'scandal' frame (on this, see Thompson, 2000). Although the pattern varies considerably, we could see this as an example of the media's 'good power', flushing out what are often low credibility responses to cogent charges of bad political practice. The pattern, across any national media system, of mediations that work in support of political deception and those which seek to expose political deficits, including deception (often generating a series of 'denials', variously convincing or otherwise, in so doing), is obviously a significant feature of the more general profile of media–political relations.

The practices of deception in politics, both those which have been long-established and those of more recent origin, clearly follow, in good part, from the belief that telling the public the truth on a given issue or in respect of a particular event would undercut the interests of the dominant political elite and its allied groups. In a limited number of instances, justification of deception may also be attempted in relation to the 'public good' (national security is the paradigm case, including that during wartime, but with the principle now being applied much more generally and routinely around the threat of terrorism). Deception is a way of securing higher levels of acceptance or acquiescence and reducing political damage, including damage to plans still in formation. However, as I observed, its increased use often brings with it an increased risk, since the 'scoop' value of political scandal is strong and, in certain circumstances, its market worth can outweigh the established journalistic tendencies towards supporting the politically powerful.

The perceived boundaries of 'acceptability' in deception are also a contributing factor in any given political use. This acceptability, the terms of which can change quickly over a short period, relates first of all to reference within the political class (are other people doing it?) and then to the general public (what kinds of deception are tolerated, even if resignedly, here? What is considered unacceptable deception, deserving of sanctions or punishment?). Certain low levels of deception may become 'naturalised' both within the political system, the media system and even by the general public. To some extent, on both sides of the Atlantic, the practice of 'spin' (a practice often extremely unclear in definition – see Andrews, 2006) has become absorbed into political routine in this way. Nevertheless, at higher levels of frequency, intensity and scale, deception can become a strong political story in its own right, one in which there is often much at stake. This happened at various stages of the British Labour governments after the election in 1997 through to 2010, leading to the rather odd situation in which fear of government manipulation of the media became itself a major media story, leading among other things to acute problems of credibility even for those political initiatives and pronouncements that might have been generated with a good measure of political integrity. At the highest level, emerging news stories around 'deception', particularly those in which a charge of 'lying' can be sustained, have the potential to become headline items in mainstream outlets and to threaten individual political careers and party fortunes (again, continuing coverage of the circumstances leading to the invasion of Iraq in 2003 is the obvious British example).

The debate and the ongoing research about deception as an area of 'bad' media power is interconnected, as we have seen, with broader debates about the character of deception within politics. Many commentators, adopting what they regard as a 'realist' position, have noted the endemic nature of forms of deception to the practice of politics, particularly where political activity involves taking a competitive stance against other factions of the political elite (not always the case) or involves strategic attempts to address the interests of very different constituencies with positive accounts of what is happening and what is planned or negative accounts of what competitors are doing and planning (on this issue see, for instance, Runciman, 2008 and Newey, 2009). The emphasis is then on those instances of deception which go beyond what is judged to be conventional in publicity and governing practice and become serious breaches of public trust and accountability. How well or not do the media perform in these instances? How good are they at recognising or marking the normative limits to 'acceptable' deceit? These are questions that need to remain firmly on the agenda of research and debate and to be a marked feature of enquiries that seek to provoke discussion beyond the academic sphere.

A comment on 'cynicism' may be useful here: since although the cynical orientation can be seen as a partial antidote to political and media deception, it is also widely regarded as a problem in its own right. If cynical attitudes about public life become extensively developed, then this is likely to reduce an interest in public and political participation and also to reduce the chances of good initiatives finding firm support. Cynicism is certainly no solution either to deficits in politics or in mediation. It is not surprising that in the debate about the growth of cynicism in many countries, particularly among young people, the negative terms of much media coverage of politics have been seen by some to be the primary cause of disaffection, while others, including many media professionals, have regarded the 'badness' of the situation to be largely a product of a crisis in public trust following a decline in standards within the political class (Lloyd, 2004 provocatively outlines the case for seeing the media to be a significant part of the problem). In Britain, the 2009/10 'scandal' of Members of Parliament's expenses, referred to above, would be a case in point. Even here, where financial deception was found to be present on a previously unrecognised scale, distorted reporting by the media was sometimes argued to be a factor in producing the public outrage and anger that resulted (Raban, 2009 offers an account advancing this view).

## DISCURSIVE DEFICIT

Many ideas about media power have a 'structural' component. However, they frequently have a 'discursive' component too, and sometimes this carries the stronger emphasis. Here, it is the communicative characteristics of the media that are given focus and the way in which these characteristics carry implications (usually negative ones) for the resources out of which a society's politics and culture are built, sustained and transformed.

Although a long history of anxiety has developed around print media (an anxiety recently refreshed by the key functions that textual components perform within websites), a great deal of modern concern about media power has been about orality and its visuality. It has been about the talk that the media carry and about the images they show. The division between knowledge and emotions does not directly map on to differences of media form, but quite frequently the movement towards spoken and visual modes of mediation has been judged as a shift away from the potential that print carries for critical rationality and informational precision.

It is, of course, television that, since the 1950s, has most often been the primary focus of anxiety about the discursive power of the media. The formal features of television are referred to extensively throughout this book, particularly in Chapters 2 and 3 but also selectively in those that follow. Here, we can identify four constitutive elements (within a vast literature of commentary, a perceptive general review is provided in Bignall, 2007 and aspects of current change are explored in

Gripsrud, 2010). First of all, there is the personable nature of television, allowing its talk to make forms of appeal not available in print communication. Related to this, there is its much-discussed domestic character, entering the home and the times and spaces of the evening (and now of the daytime too) in a way that develops further the intimate communicative permeations of radio. Thirdly, there is its obvious visual profile, the commitment to 'show' where at all possible by resort to a wide range of documentary and theatrical approaches. Finally, there is its cross-generic commitment to time-based narratives, often placing emphasis on a rapid pacing of development and action (see Chapter 9). In different permutations, these four factors have combined to produce what is a continuing sense of television as a medium carrying the potential to weaken 'public reason', even in countries like Britain where public service commitments have been strong. We are not yet at a stage in the convergence of television with the internet, at levels of cultural production and of use, where this long-standing concern has been subject to serious revision.

Television has often been regarded as having both a power of diversion (taking the attention away from much that is important) and of trivialisation (transforming into simple and frequently entertaining terms that which is serious and multi-faceted). When combined with variants of 'structural' power as discussed above, it is not surprising that such properties have been seen as profoundly political in character.

Of all the factors regarded as suspect in the implications that television carries for the exercise and development of public reason, the deployment of moving images has been the most frequent point of reference. As well as providing the basis of its character as a cultural diversion from the serious and the important (Postman, 1985 is a classic account), this aspect of 'show business' (in a richly dual sense of the term) has made television a strong and pervasive agency of representational naturalism, of that which is self-evidently so. Thus, in some views, it is an agency of systematic misrepresentation, a vehicle of ideology that is in alignment with the tendencies towards illusion and deception by elites noted earlier (Regis Debray's idea of the 'videosphere' presents a strong version of this position, recently discussed in Collins, 2010). While print media and even radio provide a degree of declared or 'open' authorial sourcing for the descriptions and evaluations they offer, whatever the strategies of covert persuasion also being pursued, television routinely grounds its accounts in the innocence of its 'showings', in relation to which its spoken accounts are often presented as merely elaborative and interpretive, rather than constitutive.

Not everyone has taken this negative view of television's discursive capacities and potential, although the dominant tendency has been towards caution and ambivalence at best. Very few have followed the broadly benign assessments of Marshall McLuhan in seeing television as exemplifying the 'wholeness, empathy and depth of awareness' (McLuhan, 1973: 13) which electronic technologies bring by virtue of their being offered as 'extension' of our bodies. McLuhan's profoundly *sensory* engagement with media still has the imaginative and conceptual originality to inform our thinking about mediation beyond the level of specific content, but it routinely postpones, or displaces, nearly all questions of social and political power. Seeing media as such totalising, transformative agencies of culture and consciousness, does not help us much in identifying their specific *uses* as agencies of governance and social order, uses which show more continuities with the past than McLuhan's apocalyptic apprehension of change allows for. Certainly, the way in which television escapes, even more emphatically than radio, the restrictions of literacy, presenting its wide repertoire of audio-visual appeal with an 'easy' sensory accessibility, is widely recognised, opportunistically so by those in power. However, rather than being unproblematically viewed as part of the good news about television, this very availability and charm, with its unprecedented social reach, has frequently been regarded by some social groups and commentators as a key part of the problem of fitting television 'properly' into politics and into culture (see, again, Postman, 1985 and the more recent arguments of Putnam, 2000).

## RESEARCHING POWER

First, another point about definitions. I have discussed above how media power, across its various structural and discursive dimensions, is frequently seen as a 'bad' thing, a source of anxiety and of regulatory concern. I have also pointed to those instances where the media's capacities to communicate and persuade widely and effectively, to shape the symbolic environment and therefore the conditions of action, are regarded as benign and welcome. One such example was public health information, another the appeals made on behalf of charities. Pushing out further, I suggested that the general, journalistic power of the media to inform large populations with increasingly updated information about 'what is going on' was often and unsurprisingly regarded as having a dominantly positive character. Indeed, strong recognition of the productive contributions of journalism to the development of civic culture was frequently made in the eighteenth and nineteenth centuries, whatever the perceived failings and exploitative sensationalism of particular newspapers. More recently, in many countries, celebration of journalism's contribution to political and social development and of its potential for helping to bring about pro-social and pro-democratic change has been checked, to different degrees, by growing perceptions of its deficits. As some of my examples above have shown, the seriousness of these deficits, economic, institutional and professional, and the possibilities for remedying them, have been regular points of reference both inside and outside academic enquiry.

However, there is another reason, alluded to earlier, why ideas of 'good media power' come through less clearly than the opposite view. This is because 'good' instances of mediation are often not really regarded as instances of 'power' at all and therefore are not seen to provide proper counter-examples. One assumption at work here is that media power has an essential manipulative component and that it necessarily involves a persuasive force (advertising is a paradigm example) seeking to bypass individual rationality and thereby aiming to 'impose' its meanings upon readerships and audiences, rather than to provide a social and individual resource for them to use. To work with this assumption quite obviously skews the fundamental perception of what media power is and the kind of debate that can be had about it. If taken to be a suspect attribute for the media to possess, power can only be described and assessed negatively, within a normative scheme that can logically admit no positive exemplars. It is a position that marginalises any recognition of media as variously and routinely 'powerful' in their role as providers of many different kinds of knowledge with a very wide uptake. Such a role may be seen more in terms of 'communicative capacity' than of 'power', downplaying the sense of its shaping impact. However, such terms encourage too reduced a sense of the force of mediation within contemporary society and politics. This is an issue to which I return to in Chapter 3, regarding ideas about 'influence'.

We can identify some of the very different lines of power that centre on the media, rather than simply involve them, by taking an example that might not seem an obvious choice by which to develop a discussion of this kind – football in the UK. Football is a sport that retains strong continuities, in its rules and in its 'culture', with its long history as both a sport to watch and a sport to play. However, it is also a sport that we might quickly agree to have been transformed by the media, most obviously by television, which among other things radically changed the terms of being a fan (for a comprehensive review, see Boyle and Haines, 2004).[15] What are the diverse 'power effects' which television has exerted upon the game?

1. The economic power of television has had a huge impact on football finances, both for live and for recorded transmission. This carries massive benefits for clubs in a 'premium' position to sell, independently or collectively, television coverage of their games. It also brings risks too, as was clear in the UK recently when the collapse of certain TV operations and the deals struck with them had a dramatic effect on a number of clubs operating below the level of international visibility.

2. The availability of 'live' coverage, in homes, pubs and clubs across the country and internationally, has extended the fan base for football, bringing it to many people who, for a variety of reasons, including geographic distance, would not normally attend at a football ground. Not only the size but also the make-up of fan culture, involving factors of gender and of class, has therefore changed. Since television allows supporters to follow the fortunes of several clubs, including foreign clubs, an extension of fan engagement well beyond a single focus for support has also occurred.

3. On the basis of the new visibility of football and its expanded supporter/fan base, many clubs are able to significantly increase their terms of corporate sponsorship and their income from club-related merchandise. Sponsorship indicators (e.g. on players' shirts) and ground-based advertising become fully incorporated into the terms of television's advertising and promotion.

4. Another consequence of the higher visibility of football and its new sources of revenue is that footballers have become 'stars', able to support star life-styles and to generate stories, including gossip, within the framework of celebrity journalism. Both newspapers and magazines, with their own economic interests sharply in focus, give increased attention to the footballer star, who develops as a stock figure within the international celebrity system, often transcending the particular sporting prowess on which their reputation is built and making strong connections with other parts of that system, including popular music and show business generally.

5. The dynamics of the footballer celebrity system, combined with the new, spectacular aesthetics of football as a televisual event, encourage a wider sphere of football-related consumer culture,

including books, clothes, films, television programmes and games, sometimes on an international scale.

6. Clubs often develop their own extensive publicity, certainly extending to websites and often to television channels. As well as relating as news sources and as 'clients' to existing mainstream media, there is thus a significant extension into media production, seeking direct and more controllable channels through which to achieve heightened cultural visibility.

7. In some clubs, tensions arise between emerging patterns of ownership and decision-making within a new corporate frame, on the one hand, and the traditional fan base on the other. Tensions within fan culture sometimes reflect the differences between regular attendance and the more casual kinds of engagement offered by television. The media, at a fundamental level one source of 'the problem', also become involved in the reporting of club disquiet as yet another kind of 'strong story' about football. More generally, with the growth of the football economy, coverage of a specialist kind is found more often in business as well as in sports sections of broadcast, press and web news output (see for instance, the regular updates on http://footballeconomy.com). In Britain recently, Liverpool Football Club and Manchester United Football Club have, among many other clubs in 2010, faced major problems over ownership and borrowing. In some cases, clubs with far less revenue potential, like Portsmouth Football Club, have been brought into receivership (their administration temporarily taken over by the state, through legal process, as they are declared bankrupt).

Together, the power relations at work in the above examples display many different characteristics, sometimes operating in combination, and would require different approaches to investigate. The correlation of statistics would identify the impact of the media upon revenue streams and upon the growth in merchandising and in transfer fees and players' wages. Viewing figures would establish the dramatic expansion of spectatorship. However, changes in the nature of football culture, and shifts not just in the scale but in the values associated both with the game and with the 'brand' of certain top clubs would require a more qualitative engagement. Just how persuasive, and in what ways, have different kinds of media coverage been in 'warming up' the image of football, taking it away from the associations with risk, violence and bad behaviour with which it was strongly identified in the 1980s? How deep, or shallow, is the new cultural positioning of the sport, how far is it susceptible to further shifts in its mediation? Both these questions raise issues around cognition, emotional engagement and attributions of value that would require forms of audience research, as well as analysis of media output, to explore fully. What is obvious, across several indicators, is that there is a high degree of media-dependency now installed within the professional game, strongly linked not only to the economic conditions for further growth but also to the conditions for survival.

How far is it possible to debate the values that the media transformation has brought? Well, for those in the top clubs, the position seems broadly positive, although the level of borrowing often required in funding operations at this level brings its own problems, as the general financial crisis of 2008 and its aftermath sharply exposed. Access to the game as a live action experience has undoubtedly been judged as a benefit by many who would previously have only followed it, if at all, through recorded highlights and clips on sports news. Regular supporters at football grounds also have had their experience enriched by the televisual opportunity to watch games other than those they attend. As indicated, however, some fans and commentators identify shortcomings in the change of priorities, and dislike many aspects of the shift of football's economy and culture from its basis in localised allegiance to a basis in the world (quite literally) of its mediated and marketised projection.

We can take another example, this time one that is much more familiar from the media research literature and touched on at points earlier in this chapter and developed further in Chapter 3. How do media, and media power, affect 'political culture', the pattern of knowledge, values and dispositions that constitute the context for political action, including that within the professional political sphere?[16] Here, the situation if anything becomes more various and complex than with football, as well as finally much more important. We can look at some of the possibilities:

1. By acting as a major producer and distributor of regularly updated knowledge about circumstances and events and of news about the sphere of professional politics, the established media largely work to provide the essential primary conditions for democratic citizenship. This is the (at least potentially) benign power of the media, one that is often woven into accounts of modernity and democratisation with varying degrees of hope for the future and of qualification regarding the present.

2. By acting as an agency supportive of elite interests and elite frameworks of interpretation, the established media largely work to

produce acquiescence for dominant political viewpoints and for the larger power system. They do this by excluding or marginalising accounts that cannot easily be fitted into the dominant perspective, by presenting dominant views as 'natural' and by employing a range of tactics of deception in order to secure for these dominant views the widest possible acceptance. This is the malign power of the media, variously identified, with different inflections and strengths, in accounts of ideological management and in the 'propaganda' perspective on media–society relations. Much work on the impact of the internet has seen it to be a potential, and partly realised, check on this established power (e.g Hermes, 2006; Dahlgren, 2009; Coleman and Blumler, 2009), while other commentators have suggested, by contrast, that its overall trajectory is broadly in alignment with elite frameworks (e.g. Miller, 2007 and Cammearts, 2008).[17] I discuss this further in Chapter 3.

3. By reflecting, albeit selectively, the range of views and values in the wider culture beyond the elite, the established media are an important part of a 'democratic conversation' on these views and values. By bringing such material to the attention of the political class, sometimes in the form of popular protests and campaigns that may receive editorial support, they also act as a check on forms of elite hegemony and, more specifically, on 'bad policy'. This is another example of benign power, giving more emphasis than item 1. above to opinion, rather than just information.

4. By being located within increasingly strong market contexts, the established media have a diminishing sense of responsibility towards the public they serve and a stronger commitment to increasing the commodity value of their products at the lowest possible production cost. The effect of this, intentional or not, is to make them agencies for the reproduction of existing inequalities. This is another variant of malign power, stressing economic rather than directly political linkage, although including the latter in its reach. The extent to which, and the way in which, media products are 'commodities', items whose identity is essentially fixed by their market, rather than their social, value, remains a regular point of dispute, lurking underneath many commentaries that might not address it explicitly. One argument might be that it moves media operations towards greater alignment with elite political power, but another would be that, precisely by making primary a profitable connection with satisfying perceived demand, it opens up

lines of connection with popular experience and values that depart from, and sometimes conflict with, elite frameworks.

Research on the impact of the internet, referred to above, has seen the relative freedom from direct market influences and the unprecedented responsiveness to user demand as key factors in the political importance of web use, especially when combined with what is, in many contexts, the even more significant relative freedom from direct state control.

Across all of these possible lines of power, the full generic range of the media, as well as their internal variability, needs to be borne in mind. That is to say that drama and comedy may be more important than news services in respect of much of what is going on in the making of political meanings (a point that media research has been rather slow to recognise) and that significant differences within the same medium and then across diverse media and their institutions are likely to occur. Although there is a vital economic component to media–political relations, most of the forms of power I have indicated above turn on questions, first of all, about identifiable patterns of output and then about the impact of such patterns upon political consciousness and action. This raises different issues of conceptualisation and evidence, although (as I shall examine more fully in Chapter 2) the use of analysed output as an indicator of impact is a long-standing, regular feature of media research and in its more exploratory modes is hard to dispense with.

A 'black box' often lies at the end of power questions, an opaque space, social and psychological, in which the precise relationships between (and relative strengths of) the consequences of media activity and the consequences of all the other significant factors bearing on consciousness and action are played out. As a realm for analysis, 'political culture' is distinct from my earlier example in a number of ways. Among these is the relative ease with which it is possible to define for research purposes the boundaries of 'football culture', not to underestimate the difficulties posed even here. Just how far the boundaries of the 'political' extend culturally, what forms of thought, emotion and activity the term can be used to describe beyond those practices explicitly established as political, is a question underlying, and sometimes troubling, much current work into media and politics (see, for instance, Brants and Voltmer, 2010). The dangers of too tight a definition, foreshortening politicality around its formal dimensions and ignoring its social extent (including what Peter Dahlgren calls the spaces of the 'proto-political' and the 'pre-political'),[18] are joined by those of too inclusive an approach, in which the specificity of the political as a quite distinctive dimension of the social is at risk of being dispersed. Again, this issue is addressed further in Chapter 3.

Engaging with the contemporary and changing variants of the media's involvement in structures and flows of power has presented a challenge to research, requiring revision of the questions to be asked and innovation in addressing them. Among the many researchers to perceive the need for fresh conceptual and methodological tools to engage with this challenge is Nick Couldry, whose writing is distinctive for its attention to shifts in the character of the media's symbolic power combined with innovative empirical approaches to assessing how power-relations work at ground level. His writings offer a useful example for comment in any review of how ideas of power can be applied, and taken forward, in the analysis of the media.

Couldry's empirical research has primarily taken the form of a strong development of media sociology, particularly of the ethnography of media use. Some of his work (for instance, Couldry, 2000) has concerned itself with the 'spaces' of media power, characterised by him as lying beyond the traditional focus of 'texts and audiences' (2000: 8). He acknowledges the influence on his work of a critical engagement with the historical and phenomenological framework developed by Paddy Scannell in his exploration of broadcasting's character as a constitutive element of everyday life (see, for instance, Scannell, 1996 and the discussion in Chapter 2). He also connects strongly with Roger Silverstone's anthropological emphasis on framing ideas of 'medium' (as opposed to discrete texts) and on the pervasiveness of contemporary forms of 'myth' (see particularly Silverstone, 1994). The stated goal is the exploration of how 'the media world' and the 'ordinary world' operate with a clear division between them but also, grounded in this division, a relationship that involves specific forms of intersection and of dominance. Emile Durkheim's concern with the distinction between the sacred and the profane as a pivotal point in the operation of symbolic power in traditional societies is an explicit reference point and a guide in this project (specifically, Durkheim, 1995/1912).

In the course of analysing the different ways in which the media work to constitute the social order, naturalising this effect in the process of performing it, Couldry gives emphasis to their framing of events. By this he means, not the specific narrative and normative parameters which the media routinely place on their accounts, but the more inclusive shaping of the contours of 'social reality' that mediation processes introduce. In the case studies of Couldry (2000) this shaping is explored closely through respondent accounts around particular instances of 'media' and 'ordinary' coming into close proximity in specific places. Principally, these are the place of the television studio tour (Granada TV in Manchester), giving the public a chance not just to see but to inhabit television's creative spaces, and the place of a public demonstration 'covered' by the media, in which geographic space, becoming the socialised space of a group protest, exists alongside mediated space, the space of a 'media event'. What kind of orderings, namings and imaginings does mediation construct around these places and spaces, and how does this symbolic activity impact upon the experience and understanding of those from the 'ordinary world' involved, temporarily, in the 'media world'? What kinds of disalignment and disruption occur alongside the various attempts at harmonious interrelations? What are the consequences of these encounters for participants' broader and longer-term view of their position in an 'ordinary world' which is extensively constructed from the materials of mediation? Couldry's exploratory approach to ideas of symbolic power is coupled with his careful, ethnographic documentation to develop our sense of the terms and the contours of media engagement and of media domination. In doing this, they avoid both the tendency towards top-heavy theorisation, collapsing variation and complexity, and that towards a dense empirical engagement which declines to work through conceptually the implications of its data and local analysis.

In more recent studies, Couldry has pursued these strands of thinking about power (see for instance Couldry, 2006a, 2006b and 2008). He has re-stated the need for a deconstructive analysis of the media's modes of naturalisation, giving focused attention to questions of 'ritual', questions which have remained a key part of his research agenda. By 'ritual' he means the symbolic spaces and practices that are opened up in height-ened moments of media – ordinary relations, moments that are part of the 'ceremonial' interconnection of the media world on the one hand, projecting its confident sense of socio-symbolic 'centrality', and the ordinary, everyday routines of living on the other.[19] This theme connects back to his earlier case studies of place and space. In Couldry (2008) he gives the example of the final night of a *Big Brother* series, but also a range of more mundane encounters that have a 'ritualised' element, involving a pleasurable engagement with anticipated spectacle, the satisfactions of a familiar order of language and, reflexively, an enjoyment of the performance of the role of spectatorship itself, perhaps as a fan. Ritual relations imply co-ordination and subordination (albeit a subordination perceived as 'freely given') and Couldry argues that a contesting of the media power that produces such relations is a necessary part of any significant opposition to dominant economic and political power more generally. He also points to the need for more research on alternative media, on different ways of producing spectacle and of relating to it, perhaps of using forms of mediated ritual to different social and political ends.

Couldry's accounts will undoubtedly be a useful reference point for future research and debate on media power, if not at the level of structures then certainly at the level of processes. Although he is right to warn about the dangers of over-concentration on texts and audiences in media research, moving too decisively away from attention to forms of textuality, understanding and use would seem to be unwise. The localised dynamics of form and interpretative practice still figure importantly within power flows and should continue to be one focus for making further conceptual and methodological progress. However, addressing the relationship of mediated to lived realities within a more expanded sense of the modes of symbolic management that the media introduce is undoubtedly a gain, particularly insofar as it involves the collection of varieties of evidence, rather than simply speculation. The connection back to the 'sacred' and 'profane' and the renewed emphasis on 'ritual', although they are suggestive, might also bring problems of definition and application if they are brought too centrally into the research frame (on this question, see the debate in Cottle, 2006 and Couldry and Rothenbuhler, 2007). Their rich metaphoric resonance as terms, their strong echoes of traditional social orders, can inhibit adequate recognition of the full range of constituents now at work in everyday cognition and feeling.[20] That said, Couldry's writing has caught the 'boundary work' performed by contemporary media with a useful clarity and illuminating detail. His current development of the idea of 'voice' (Couldry, 2010) in analysing the deficits in the range of speakers, terms of speaking and practices of listening evident in much contemporary democratic culture suggests further routes into the analysis of the present profile of power and the delineation of its alternatives.

I have developed a synoptic account which has pointed not only to the very different ways in which the media are implicated in power relations, directly and indirectly, but also to the ubiquitous nature of questions about power in all areas of media research. Recently, these questions have become more complex in their asking. This is, first of all, a result of the increasingly wide range of media practice now apparent, often within changed economic and technological contexts. Secondly, it follows wider recognition, across the arts and social sciences, of the subtlety and stealth of many power relations alongside those which are more direct and explicit. Continuing work, for instance, on ethnicity and on gender, brings this out sharply (for instance, see Downing and Husband, 2005 and Gill, 2006 respectively).

Researching power will remain a top priority for international media enquiry, both in respect of the media as themselves powerful in various ways and as they reinforce or undercut the power of other agencies (acting as kinds of power broker). Theorising about media power would benefit from a phase of critical consolidation in which key approaches and models are given further, comparative attention, with their points of convergence and divergence worked through in debate. In particular, I have suggested there is a need for a sharper focus on the overall pattern indicated by the different accounts we have of the relations between kinds of knowledge, modes of knowing and modes of power. Inspiration can come from better dialogue across disciplines with an interest in media but also those (like History and, very differently, Psychology) having a concern with dimensions of power. Beyond the academic sphere, there will be continuing issues raised about how the media might perform 'better' were there to be changes in their structures and practices. It would be good to think that the enquiries and assessments of scholars could make a contribution here. Both in academic and more broadly public initiatives it will always be useful and often necessary, when engaging with contemporary instances, to keep in mind the long history of richly various, heated and sometimes confused debates about the kinds of power that the media might possess.

## NOTES

1    Lukes himself goes on raise some difficulties with the relationships between 'power', 'rationality' and forms of political and social compliance that Foucault suggests across different texts (Gordon brings some of Foucault's writing on the topic usefully together in Foucault and Gordon, 1980). These relationships have been at the centre of debate about Foucault and about the kind of politics that might be derived from his thinking. Paras (2006) is a recent discussion.

2    'Symbolic violence' occurs in a number of the works, with Bourdieu and Passeron (1977) being an important, early commentary. The usage is partly metaphorical but is also meant to indicate an equivalence to physical aggression and harm not generally recognised in conventional discussion of cultural structure and process.

3 The media's role in the processes of 'commodification', whereby personal values as well as a range of public values increasingly conform to the terms of economic exchange within different types of market, is widely discussed. See Mosco (1996) for a general review and Hearn (2008) for an account based on recent research.

4 European, African, Asian and Latin American examples have all been drawn on to explore this aspect of systemic media–political shifts. For an early and extensive review of the situation in Eastern Europe, see Sparks and Reading (1998).

5 Among recent commentaries about shifts and continuities in Chinese media–political relations, see Tilt and Xiao (2010) and Tong (2010).

6 Those working within Herman and Chomsky's 'propaganda model' (1988) often take this view.

7 See Piers Robinson (2002) on how the play-off between media reporting and elite policy-making figures in the context of foreign policy involving military interventions.

8 As I write, a huge range of leaked documents concerning US activity in Afghanistan, put online by the organisation WikiLeaks, is receiving major mainstream media headlines and will doubtless impact upon future discussion of policy and possibly on policy-formation. See for instance, the multi-page feature in *The Guardian*, 26 July 2010.

9 The rhetoric of 'choice' is enjoying a resurgence in the context of a further wave of privatisation of public sector provision, carried out in the stated interests of 'deficit management'.

10 An obvious point here is the significance accorded by media to governing elites as initiators of political action, which is then a necessary reference point for any development, critique or opposition. In those cases where an elite is placed in a reactive mode, responding to events or to the political strategies of those outside its sphere, the access differential may not be so marked, although the newsworthiness attributed to its reactions may confer a visibility quickly equalling and perhaps surpassing that of initiating groups.

11 The dispute about integrity in the measurement of global warming following the hacking of emails from climate scientists working at the University of East Anglia became a major international story, the effect of which may have been to refigure the way in which climate change is reported by journalists in the foreseeable future.

12 The conduct and cost of the Afghanistan campaign and an expenses scandal involving Members of Parliament were both major news stories in Britain for large parts of 2009/10. The latter was widely considered to have caused the most serious breakdown of public trust in Westminster politics of modern times.

13 In summer 2010, the evidence being given to the Iraq Inquiry under Sir John Chilcot was part of the regular weekly news agenda of press and television, feeding into public discussion a number of questions about

the integrity of individual politicians, notably Tony Blair, as well as of governmental structures and processes.

14    The range of analytic accounts continues to develop, but Danner (2006) brings together material both from US and British sources.

15    In relation to what follows, I should add that the sports pages of the UK press during the period 2008–10 are a rich source of further data concerning specific clubs as well as the general situation.

16    Among key texts here are Street (1997); Corner and Pels (2003); van Zoonen (2005) and Jones (2010), along with an increasing range of articles, mostly in media and cultural studies journals.

17    The suggestive ideas of Daniel Dayan (2009) about 'monstration' as an emerging mode of public representation, involving internet activities in their varying relationship with mainstream media, and the kinds of centre/periphery roles thereby taken up, are relevant here.

18    For example, in Dahlgren (2009). I engage with Dahlgren's work further, along with definitions of the 'political', in Chapter 3.

19    Couldry has identified the way in which the media project themselves as socially and culturally 'central' and noted some of the ideological consequences of the priorities and emphases this introduces (see Couldry, 2003). Of course, one source of the socio-centrality of the media in a country like Britain follows from their strategic use by the principal institutions of political, social and cultural power.

20    'Ritual' has regularly been brought into discussion of media process, including by James Carey (see, for instance Carey, 1989) as well as by anthropologically oriented writers like Roger Silverstone, mentioned earlier. It is a useful counter to overly rationalistic accounts of how the media play into public life, but it sometimes raises questions concerning forms of self-consciousness and of orientation to context not sufficiently pursued in analyses employing the term.

# 2

## *Form*

Whereas 'power' is a term taking us immediately to the contested centre of media research and debate, including that conducted outside the academic sphere, the notion of 'form' is far less certain in its indications. To talk beyond the academy, and even at points within it, about enquiry into form is to invite a degree of suspicion. Around the notion of form in respect of the media there is often the sense of something elusive and possibly of secondary significance to what really needs to be known more about. Formal analysis suggests a carrying over of concerns from literary and visual arts scholarship, with a tendency towards a finessing of points about aesthetic organisation that might be judged as only of marginal, elaborative interest on an agenda defined by political and sociological investigation, some of it carrying a sense of urgency. There is no doubt that certain treatments of media form have encouraged this view, although making connections with approaches to form in critical discussion of the arts more broadly should be a part of any application to media. Drawing on a strong and intellectually various lineage of work, one showing many recent developments of importance, I want to consider formal issues as pivotal for media research and to lend support to the view that a continuing address to concepts and methods for analysing them is of the utmost importance for progress in understanding how the media work.

First, I want to look at how form figures in the broader context of media theory and research, particularly in regard to ideas of 'medium' and of 'content'. This will provide a basis for assessing formal relations, the ways in which questions of formal organisation and function compare across different media and connect with the higher-level formal categories of narrative and genre and with ideas of realism.

I suggested that 'form' can seem an airy, gestural notion, not one made easily subject to robust empirical analysis. The Concise OED provides some indicators that help get matters of definition just a little sharper: '1a ... an arrangement of parts: b. the outward aspect or shape of a body ... 2b the mode in which a thing ... manifests itself.'

I see media form as being essentially a matter of three different dynamics, those of organisation, those of articulation and those of apprehension. *Organisation* raises questions about the production of form but also about its 'objectified' deployment as a necessary constituent of discursive and aesthetic artefacts. *Articulation* raises questions about form as performance, giving to the term a marked sense of process and practice. *Apprehension* gives emphasis to engagement with form by viewers and readers, the dynamics by which formal factors become active in the production of knowledge and emotions, in the complex, subjective interactions of our media encounters which are part of our larger, continuous immersion in mediation. I acknowledged in the Introduction that the term 'mediation' has been employed in rather different ways in the research literature, and that here I am using it broadly to indicate the practices, processes and products of using media systems to craft and distribute different kinds of communicative performance or artefact. I would want to suspend the suggestion of 'go-between' and of intervention that the word carries in other contexts not to do with the media, although in some cases these associations would clearly be appropriate too.

Considerations of form that become detached for too long from matters of 'content' (for example, looking at the narrative structures of reality television without regard for *what* is being depicted and represented) are likely to seem unhelpfully abstract, although there is a long tradition in media research of examining content without much attention, if any, to formal factors. The prominent strands of analysis known collectively as 'content analysis' are evidence of the strong content-orientated tendency at work internationally, although not all such work ignores formal issues (see Krippendorff, 2004 for a comprehensive account and Deacon et al., 2007 for a useful overview). Precisely where the boundaries might be drawn between the manner and organisation of saying or showing something, on the one hand, and what is being said or shown, on the other, will be in many cases unclear and so the division between 'form' and 'content' cannot be a matter of neatly defined boundaries. Nevertheless, however problematic both terms might be, sometimes suggesting other possibilities by way of alternatives (e.g. 'style' for 'form' and 'theme' for 'content'), my view is that the form/content duality is a productive one for media research to work with. The uncertainty it carries does not inhibit analysis but acts as a useful reminder of the real complexity of the interplays and fusions at work in communication.

A primary justification for close attention to form in media research is not, as it is in much humanities commentary on the arts, the intrinsic interest of exploring expressive creativity, 'how pleasing things are done', but a recognition that form is necessary to an understanding of the media's sociality, of its constitutive connections with individual conscious-ness and with social and political order. It is this emphasis that has been a prominent factor behind the growth of 'textual analysis', in all its vari-ants, as a significant feature of humanities-oriented media research. With some simplification, we can say that insofar as the study of output features in international media research, 'content analysis' has been the favoured social science approach and 'textual analysis' the favoured approach from arts and humanities perspectives. The idea of 'text' itself already positions the focus of study as an object of analysis, drawing on the long-standing usage of literary criticism (crudely put, ordinary people read novels and poems, students of literature consider 'texts'). This positioning brings advantages, certainly, but it introduces the problem of a potentially fore-shortened and over-stabilised view of a work's full identity and dynamics of meaning. The application of the term to audio-visual production can also carry over literary assumptions (for instance, about narrative, about genre, about the relationship of an artefact to its contexts of production and distribution) in ways that may pass unexamined and quietly distort how formal factors are addressed. One further consequence here, again of potential value but also carrying risks, is the easy shift from 'text' to 'read-ing', where the latter term is used to describe a whole range of modes of sonic/aural and visual engagement and processing which are very differ-ent from the construing of print upon a page.[1]

The problem, a continuing one, with not bringing matters of form properly into media analysis is that of sliding into seeing mediation as a process in which determinate materials ('content') are transmitted with varying degrees of efficiency, rather than a process in which meanings are generated by intersecting dynamics, including those at work in what I have called above acts of 'apprehension'. A content-based approach to media products finds it much harder to engage closely with the range and variability of media output as generators of meaning and value and also with the nature of professional media practices as essentially *creative* (rather than as 'technical', a matter essentially of *relay*). Seeing media production as the exercising of creative skills, even in cases where what is produced is found variously deficient, extends an awareness of diver-sity and possibility in mediation. It also allows a proper consideration of technology both as a key factor in the availability and application of the formal options with which producers work, and a factor defining the nature of mediation as an *experience* for readers and viewers, through various devices of domestic and personal delivery.

Some of the above points can be brought together within the working idea that theorising and analysing matters of form in media research is best done when the media are seen to be deeply cultural as well as political and social agencies. The title of Raymond Williams' classic text, *Television: Technology and Cultural Form* (Williams, 1974) gives the emphasis with a fine directness, arresting in its originality at the time. However, there are still parts of the field in which a sense of the cultural is foreshortened in ways that restrict attention to how the media operate. Until recently, the study of political communication was particularly prone to this foreshortening, although a marked shift is now discernible here (see, for instance, Bennett and Entman, 2001; Corner and Pels, 2003; van Zoonen, 2006; and Jones, 2010 for examples of the cultural placing of the political).

The diverse work of writers in Cultural Studies has helped to extend a cross-disciplinary sense of the importance of the 'cultural context' for many areas of social enquiry which have previously worked within a narrower framework of what is relevant and what is not. At the same time, the relative looseness of formulation found acceptable by some cultural researchers, and the tendency towards an extensive reliance on methods drawn from the openly subjective interpretative schemes of arts 'criticism', has often produced a defensive reaction from researchers in the social sciences.[2]They have wanted to make the case for continuing and revising established ideas of scholarship in their area and for more tightly specifiable, empirically accountable and, often, more 'quantitative' practices of enquiry. This has often resulted in kinds of uneasy stand-off, perceivable for instance in the differences between conference programmes on the same or similar topics and between journal identities in the same broad area as well as in the range of criteria used by the various schemes for research funding (in the UK, the differences between the Arts and Humanities and the Economic and Social Science research councils in their approach to media projects would be pertinent). The study of media form has often been caught up in these divisions and tensions. However, there are signs that a stronger 'sociology of culture' is emerging (the new journal *Cultural Sociology* is a significant indicator here), one in which cultural studies and anthropological perspectives are being brought together, not without a degree of lingering mutual suspicion, with those from political science and sociology. Already, this has had implications for the kind of attention given to media form, and development is likely to continue (for example, some very different lines of convergence around form and production are taken in Born, 2004; Calhoun and Sennett, 2007; Hesmondhalgh, 2007a; Caldwell, 2008 and Cottle, 2008).

I want to pursue the question of the relations at work within media form by taking the broad and distinctive areas of sonic form, visual form and forms of writing as they cut across the different media. This allows connections as well as differences to appear more sharply than might occur by working immediately under specific medium headings (e.g. television, the press). Despite the frequency of their appearance as a point of reference in academic enquiries, the basic formal characteristics of the media as the materials of creative practice and of diverse cultural satisfactions seem to me to deserve further attention in terms of their historical and cultural 'remarkableness'. By this I mean a registering of their terms of *appeal* (a word carrying relevant senses both of a kind of address and of attractiveness) as a preliminary to making conceptual and analytic progress.

In two further sections, I then want to consider the higher-level descriptive/analytic categories of narrative and genre, in which different formal elements are active, including varieties of those modes of representation designated as 'realist'. There are other categories of significance, but these two have a particularly strong application across nearly all of media culture and they bear directly on questions both about media production and media consumption.

## COMPARATIVE FORMAL RELATIONS: SOUND, IMAGE, WRITING

### *Sonic/Aural form*

Sound recording (sometimes called 'phonography') comes just a few decades after photography in the history of the various ways of achieving a mechanical, electrical, electronic and now digital 'record', ways that constitute the modern media through its various phases of development and change. However recorded sound, whether of voice or of music, works to provide a sense of *performance* and, importantly, of a performance *experienced*, that photography, whatever its evocative power, cannot generate. It does this as a result of its capacity to capture duration, the unfolding in time of a particular event, most often though not always an event that was intended to be communicative. By reproducing the primary experience of listening to people talk or play musical instruments, or the experience of listening to the sounds of purposive or natural action, it has the effect, to use a term from Giddens (1991), of 'disembedding' socio-sensory experiences from the contexts of their occurrence. Photography 'disembeds' too, but only, as I shall discuss later, through a process of 'stopping' time that provides the still image with rich, evocative qualities largely by marking its difference from the flows of reality. The reproduction of these flows in sound recording (and later, in film and television) carries huge consequences for the relationship between mediation and consciousness, with implications for the character of media artefacts as objects of perception and of individualised experience that have since become intensively developed within the cultures of media production.

The dramatic shift in the profile of mediation brought about by sound recording is not just an extension in the conditions of perception, and preservation, of sonic events, it is also a shift in the conditions of *sociality*. Voices can be heard, variously anonymous or named, speaking of many things in many different colloquial or formal ways to various kinds of specified or implied addressee, including those listening to the recording rather than to the original 'live' delivery itself. The transformative technology of radio makes extensive use of this facility but also adds to it the possibilities of 'liveness' itself being mediated, thus bringing together the reproduction of event flow and the effective co-temporality of the event and its hearing by a radio listener. It is hard to overestimate the change this brings to the character of mediation and to the options for media form. Among other things, it serves to reconfigure aspects of social power, including the power of political elites, as widely circulated forms of 'spoken power', rather than, when not experienced physically, forms of 'documented power' (power mostly read about in newspapers and official documents, for example, and only routinely 'heard' through its lower-level agents, like magistrates and police).

Historians of radio, and writers on radio formats, have been alert to the richness of address that the medium allows and to the social impact this carries. Among them Paddy Scannell, drawing extensively on the ideas of the philosopher Martin Heidegger, has best caught the extraordinary subtlety and depth of the social relations that radio speech generates, social relations which were subsequently carried over, and modified, in the development of television. He has presented his ideas in a number of publications, but Scannell (2000) offers a very clear account of his central insight:

> To whom, then, do the media 'speak'? Who do they address, and how? If, say, a television programme is watched by 15 million

people, how is watching that programme experienced by all those millions? Do they find that they are addressed as a multitude? As all those millions? As 'the masses'? The answer is surely, no. Each viewer finds that what they see and hear seems to speak to them directly and individually. If this is so, then broadcast programmes and daily newspapers appear to have a peculiar communicative structure. They are heard, seen and read by millions (by anyone and everyone) and yet, in each case, it seems, they speak to listeners, viewers or readers personally, as individuals. They are, it could be said, *for* me or anyone. I will call this a *for-anyone-as-someone* structure. (Scannell, 2000: 5)

He then describes the properties of 'for anyone' structures (which are what we might call 'open access' communications) and 'for someone' structures (which by contrast are specifically designated communications, personally addressed, if not always explicitly so). Broadcasting speech, he notes, frequently combines the two in an unprecedented way.

I want to keep the emphasis on talk, both on radio and then within the combined communicative profile of television, dealing with print a little later. However, we should remind ourselves that although there are some important connections across the experiences of engaging with the media, the reader of the newspaper or magazine is positioned very differently from the broadcast listener. The reader is not being addressed by talk, and the 'liveliness' of that form of engagement is therefore not at work in the management of the mediation process, which is temporally controlled by the reader and not by the material itself. This carries psychological and social implications to which I shall return.

Scannell's perceptive analysis of the way social subjectivity is constituted by broadcast talk, encouraging a particular sense both of individuality and of group membership, has consequences for the way we understand the different kinds of talking that gets done on radio and television as well as the essential social identity of these media. In particular, as he has pointed out in his own historical work (notably Scannell and Cardiff, 1991), radio allows a distinctive sense of informality and intimacy that was not available to public speakers prior to its development. What it brings about, rapidly in some areas, far more slowly in others, is a 'colloquialisation' of public speech, a tendency that affects the modes of formal speech, such as the established public oratory of politicians, as well as immediately being apparent in the many modes of 'ordinary talk', recorded and live, that radio in most countries quite quickly included in its programming. As I indicated above, this

introduces different assumptions about social distance and social relations than those of a culture grounded in print-based mediation. As
political and social claims-making, accountability and dispute become
increasingly performed through the spoken forms heard on radio and
then on television, the consequences grow in scale and significance.
There is what can be seen as a 'colloquialisation' of social relationships
and of power relations as well as of language (see Fairclough, 1995).

Scannell, although he includes in his influential analysis the ways in
which established power has used broadcasting, takes the view that its
distinctive uses of speech, and the characteristic forms of programme
design which have followed from these uses, have often had a socially
benign character. This is particularly so, he judges, when speaking has
occurred within the normative frame of public service broadcasting. The
mediation of voice, particularly within radio, has lent itself to an affirmative humanism, combining kinds of positive sociality with kinds of
positive individualisation. Matters of form as well as of content have
been crucial to this achievement. This is against the more sharply critical view, taken by some of the writers I cited in Chapter 1, that
communicative informality and what we might call the 'social warmth of
broadcasting' has worked chiefly in the service of ideological management, including the management of feeling, and to the furtherance of
established interests. In this view, it has been more a matter of strategy
than of attempts at democratic interconnection and mutuality. There is
a fundamental issue here about the relation between matters of form
and matters of social power, explored further later in this chapter.

Scannell is right to bring television into his argument about the
broadcast voice because it had the developed repertoire of radio talk
available for its use, albeit with adaptation, from its inception and it is,
of course, now the primary medium of mediated talk in many countries.
However, in what general ways might television's use of sound differ
from that of radio services?

First of all, it is clear that in many cases television does not have to
generate as much speech as radio, because in most of its generic forms,
looking at the pictures provides the information and lines of engagement
that radio would have to establish entirely through its speech and sound.
Secondly, the social spaces constituted by television talk will differ from
those of radio, insofar as unseen speakers will generally be referencing
much of what they say to the images over which their talk occurs, and
seen speakers will be established for us as physical beings in physical
locations, rather than as voices 'out of the air', requiring imaginative acts
to embody and place. The kind of intimacy and sociality encouraged by

television is thus different in important respects from that of radio. Allowing for generic variations, there is less intensity of focus on the speaking voice as this now connects and intersects variously with the plane of the moving visualisation. However, by frequently presenting the bodies and faces of speakers, sometimes in eye-contact with the camera and therefore the viewer, television is an even more directly 'personable' medium than radio, one whose repertoire of mediated sociality is extensive and vivacious. Plotting diverse aspects of its personable character has become a theme in many different types of analytic writing about television (see for instance the contributions to Allen and Hill, 2004).

Aurality in mediation is not, of course, confined to speech. From the earliest days of sound recording, it involved importantly the reproduction of music. Again, in a way that it is easy to underestimate in the context of the range of contemporary media options, it thereby transformed the whole nature of musical culture, bringing a wide accessibility to musical experience, and a degree of permanence to certain performances, that goes well beyond any idea of simply an 'extension' or a 'development' of the situation before. In another major step, radio took this possibility further forward, making the experience of music of different kinds a part of domestic life, subject to increasing levels of portability, only rivalled more recently by the possibilities afforded by tape, CD and MP3 technologies. Music was mediated into the 'routine', mundane world, its spaces and schedules. This has happened to such a point that it is now very difficult, within settings defined by digital technology both in production and consumption, to think about many aspects of the contemporary everyday without a musical element being caught up within them somewhere (on this, and the broader historical background of musical recording, see Chanan, 1997; Katz, 2004; and Morton, 2006).

The transformation of musical culture, across the spectrum of classical and popular, was the most obvious consequence of musical recording and then of radio's mediation of musical performance. But the inclusion of music as an element of dramatic performance was transformed too. Traditionally, this had been a 'live' accompaniment to varieties of theatre and cinema, a practice with a classical lineage and with opera as the international art form grounding itself in dramatic/musical combination. Radio and then sound cinema had the opportunity to use the communicative scope of music in their storytelling, giving narrative punctuation, emotional emphasis and an array of descriptive connotations to words and images through the selective use of musical phrases and scores.

Music added to the intensities of what was increasingly becoming, as Raymond Williams described it in relation to television, a 'dramatized society' (Williams, 1989/1974), one in which various enacted stories, often of other times and of kinds of life unfamiliar to the majority of the audience, circulated routinely. Music became a part of the mediation of socialised emotion (its varieties seen as appropriate to particular relationships, situations and events) and to the organisation of feeling in a whole range of cultural productions within the media. With its capacities for forms of aural identification and mood cueing, it quickly becoming essential to forms of promotion (including radio and television title sequences), to the development of advertising (most obviously, in the form of the 'jingle'), and in many countries it expanded beyond its early significance in cinema and then television fictions to become a stronger presence in material of a more factual kind, including news and documentary.

The recording and mediation of types of 'noise' seems less obviously an issue for analytic attention, although the capacity to let people hear sounds (e.g. of battle, of transport, of heavy industry, of animals, of natural phenomena) that in many cases they would never be able to listen to for themselves, was among the first novelties of recording apparatus and, deployed in different ways, it is a continuing focus for imaginative radio production as well as a necessary, if often background, element of film and television work. Whether accompanied by images or not, mediated noises are a powerful way of positioning the hearer's imagination in a physically distant world, whether in factual portrayal, realist fiction or in constructions more fancifully conceived, and thus they have always been a key feature of the media's capacity to 'disembed' and 're-embed'.

## Visual form

The transforming impact that recording and then radio broadcasting had on the world of sound was brought much earlier to visual culture by the development, and then increasingly popular availability, of photography (first to view, then to produce). However, whereas the sound recording had little or nothing by way of precedent in established culture, photography had drawing and painting. This was a limited line of precedence, given photography's shocking capacity to portray the objects in front of the camera using the light rays returning from the object itself as the source of the record. Nevertheless, at least for a while, there was a relationship of mutual adjustment between the kind of 'realism' that photography was able to produce and the kinds of 'realism' which certain schools of painting strove to achieve (for a discussion, see Nead, 2008). Both were forms of pictorial realism grounded in fidelity to appearance, but they involved different kinds of interplay between ideas of the apparent and the essential, between the physical world and the 'truth'. The 'truth' could be perceived, more passively, as to do with the properties of what was manifestly 'there' for the image to 'capture' or, more actively, as to do with what good work should, by its imaginative interventions, strive to 'reveal' and even to 'construct'.

The range of scholarly writing on the history and development of photography is huge and it has recently been given further focus and scope through the emergence of digital imaging (Trachtenberg, 1980 and Wells, 2003 offer useful collections for the non-specialist; see also the discussion of documentary images in Chapter 7 and the case study in Chapter 9). Digital applications have not only changed the fundamental character of production and distribution, with the web as a platform they have massively increased the presence of the still image in various kinds of context and within a range of novel formats (sometimes re-working earlier formats such as the 'slide-show' sequence which, accompanied by captions or spoken commentary, is now found on many websites, including those of newspapers). It is not an exaggeration to say that photography has gained a new cultural centrality as a result of these changes.[3] As with sound recording, however, the early history of photography encourages us not to underestimate the original cultural impact, the sensory and cultural thrill, of this now routine way of con-structing and preserving visual moments.

I remarked above on the relations between early photography and painting. Writing on photography, from its earliest days, places a strong emphasis on questions of form, quite often on the 'transformative' as well as the 'replicative' organisation of images. This emphasis is in some contrast with the later, more popular engagement with photography as essentially a matter of content, of *what* is shown, often with commemo-rative purpose (e.g. the holiday, the wedding, children at different stages of development, relatives and friends). With some simplification, the form/content split in discussion of photography can be seen as a split between photography considered primarily as a pictorial art form, as aesthetic *work*, and photography as a means of recording selected reali-ties, first of all in journalism and commerce and then more broadly, with the development of cheap cameras, within the practices of domestic and personal self-documentation. The spread of photographic activity throughout society brings with it a variety of interconnected visual realisms, many of them with low levels of artefactual self-consciousness but with a strong sense of mediating purposes and satisfactions. Meanwhile, fascination with the aesthetic possibilities of the photographic image, on it own and in multi-media combinations, continues and develops, often in alignment with broader tendencies in the visual arts (discussed in Cotton, 2009).

This split is not categoric but it is of importance in any assessment of photographic culture as a culture of mediation and it is interesting to note that it does not have a direct parallel in sound recording. This is to say that although radio broadcasting quickly shows a creative interest in using sound imaginatively and according to different aesthetic recipes (Scannell, 1986 discusses BBC experimentation in the 1930s), the principal forms of the medium are most often regarded as 'carriers' of content. If the content is, for instance, lines of poetry, a quartet by Beethoven or a dramatic production, then the recording or broadcast is framed as aesthetic but the radio form itself is not judged to be a primary factor in such framing.

In this connection, it is relevant to observe that although the idea of realism is widely used in relation to images, it is not often applied to the *primary* elements of phonography and radio outside of the context of broader programme structures and narrative design. To say of a particular recorded sound or act of mediated speaking that it was 'realistic' would seem an idle comment to make, given the character of its origins, whereas in relation to a specific piece of photography the implicit comparison with other possible modes of portraying the physical world, including those of fine art, allow the remark a degree of sense.

With the development of cinema and then of television/video, visual mediation acquires the capacity, there in sound recording and radio from their inception, to replicate the temporal sequence of events (as a happening, as a performance, as an active constituent of narrative) both through the primary process of recording and the subsequent processes of editing. This closer approximation to the event or action itself brings with it, as do sound recording and radio, a strong sense of experiencing that event or action rather than, with photography, of having it evoked. The addition to sound of sight constructs a viewing position of simulated or vicarious 'witness' in which the perceived difference between the time of the recording and the time of the viewing (considerable in the case of archive film, virtually non-existent in the case of live television) becomes, if only for the duration of the viewing, reduced if not altogether elided (Mulvey, 2005 provides a recent critical reflection on this and related issues). The continuing power of audio-visual forms clearly has something to do with this mixture of sensory impact and temporality, which brings an apprehension of 'world' to 'self' in seemingly direct, exciting and often provocative ways, with the actual work of mediation often 'disappearing'. It is a combination that significantly expands the grounds for using the term 'realism'. For as well as the depiction of physical detail, there is also the portrayal of action and process, of shifting spatial and temporal co-ordinates, to bring into any judgement as to the similarities between mediation and 'the real'. However, I want to pursue the idea, developed further below, that 'realism' is best seen as a term describing a 'real-seemingness' in that which *is known not be taken directly from the real* but known instead to be the product of artifice. In consequence, it is a term most productively used of fiction, including dramatic fiction, and indeed it has a long history of being so employed. That sense of 'real-seemingness' that non-fictional film and television portrayals of actions and events can carry as a result of the continuities of movement through space and time, produced by the editing of their distinctive materials, might better be called 'documentary naturalism' (see Chapters 7 and 8). Nevertheless, overlaps and confusions of terminology abound in this area.

One further point worth noting here is the extent to which the application of the varieties of moving audio-visual recording work to 'dramatise' what they show, whether or not they are self-consciously conceived as dramatic (and mostly thereby fictional) productions. They do this simply by virtue of their *showing* of people, events and circumstances, a showing that could previously only have been accomplished in forms of theatrical performance. This connection between theatre and the diverse factual as well as fictional formats of film and television has important implications for that 'dramatised consciousness' which Williams thought television had brought about (Williams, 1989/1974).

There is an extensive critical literature on the ways in which the power of audio-visual portrayal is exercised in the very different typical viewing contexts of the darkened cinema auditorium and the room at home (Ellis, 1982 is a lucid and influential account). In the latter case, although part of the effect is to 'pull one out' through the screen to the world, indeed to the various worlds, depicted upon it, another part is to 'carry the world into' domestic and personal space, a space (unlike the space of the cinema) that is strongly marked as a space for the self, a familiar and often fully visible context for the viewing experience. The particular combinations of 'pull out' and 'carry in' strategies are important elements in television's various modes of generic address, contributing to the specific form of what Scannell calls the 'for-anyone-as-someone' character of much of their talk. Another important, indeed defining, capacity of television, not available to cinema, is the possibilities for 'live transmission' that it offers across a wide generic range. Here, the perceptual and psychological sense of being co-present with an event unfolding on screen is reinforced by the fact that what is being watched is actually occurring at the same time as the watching. It is important analytically to distinguish this effect, of a literal immediacy given by the terms of transmission, from that sense of immediacy which is variously produced across the genres by a range of devices of visual construction and speech (again, the essays in Allen and Hill, 2004 show a range of approaches to this phenomenon, and see Scannell, 2009). Forms of live transmission have been important to television throughout its history. Initially a matter of technological necessity, they have become, within the routine contexts of pre-recorded production and, more recently, time-shifted domestic consumption, a regular marker of the continuing televisual capacity to connect engagingly with the ongoing real, whether in terms of a news report, a major public event or the routines of the *Big Brother* house (visual portrayal and time are discussed further in Chapter 9).

Questions of form become an 'obvious' issue for most of cinema and for at least certain generic areas of television because what is being watched is a fictional artefact, a self-declared product of imaginative creation. To engage with it even at the most casual conversational level invites talk of it alongside other recent productions of a comparable kind (gangster film, romantic comedy, situation comedy, police series), some assessment of how particular scenes worked, how actors performed, how satisfactory or otherwise was the ending. Consideration of media form here immediately becomes consideration of *art form*, whatever the diverse and perhaps casual vocabularies of criticism and criteria of judgement that are brought into play. However, other areas of film and (particularly) of television do not invite this kind of scrutiny. They do not present themselves as 'art' and their artefactual character (e.g. their combinations, elisions, compressions, expansions) are offered, often through modes of reportorial or presentational naturalism, as largely a technical and professional achievement, rather than one involving aesthetic design and the strategic organisation of the satisfying and the pleasing. This has posed a continuing challenge, both of approach and vocabulary, for the formal analysis of non-fictional television and particularly so for analysis that seek to be suggestive beyond the specialist sphere of media research, for instance in discussion of production values within the industry itself and in the development of public media policy.

## Forms of writing

As one of the oldest forms of mediation, sometimes seen to be in decline against the rise of audio-visual options but now being applied in a greatly extended range of possibilities through the development of the web, writing has a wide formal profile encompassing professional and ama-teur applications and radically diverse contexts. Lacking the direct sensuous replication of recording technologies or the primary human engagement of speech, writing as a medium is obviously linked to the competences of literacy. It is a form of annotation that requires a degree of technical skill not only a cultural awareness in its comprehension as well as its production. The distribution of this skill, at different levels, has been a major factor in political and social, as well as cultural, development. Its absence has been seen as a major limitation on social progress, often one requiring urgent educational initiatives (see Vincent, 2000 for a historical account).

Most serious discussions of writing quickly acknowledge how unparalleled a medium for detailed description, exposition and argument it is. The options that written languages offer for sustained discursive work and for high levels both of specificity and generality cannot be equalled by speech or by visual portrayal. What we might call the 'indispensability' of writing has sometimes been a controversial issue, particularly when placed against the democratic accessibility of the newer media forms and the lively orality that they permit, often alongside pictorial presentation. It is manifestly the case that a strong commitment to seeing writing and reading as 'core' social and civic practices has sometimes resulted in a failure to acknowledge the real achievement of work in audio-visual forms, for instance in broadcast journalism and television feature programming. At a grander level, literature is still widely taken to be a sphere of practice against which the creativity and imaginative qualities of cinema and of television have regularly to be judged and against which they will frequently be found wanting.[4] This 'literariness', along with notions from the established visual arts, sometimes contributes to a tension internal to the newer media, one between different genres and their placing within distribution and exhibition, relating to different audiences with diverse expectations of viewing.[5]

Nevertheless, the dominance of writing as a matrix and a datum medium for discursive and aesthetic practice of all kinds is likely to continue and indeed, with the web, to flourish, since modes of writing remain a core online form, given prominence by the practices of emailing and blogging alongside the basic informational requirements of website design, and unlikely to be displaced quickly, given their informational and expressive range. Just one example of writing's perceived indispensability as a component of successful communication might be taken from the extensive practice of accompanying many items of contemporary art, including gallery photography, by often lengthy and detailed caption notes on what the item is designed to be 'saying' and what the artist had in mind when creating it. This kind of practice trades on a play-off between the particularity and perceptual/sensory 'closeness' of the viewed art object, on the one hand, and the generality and distance of the related text on the other. In any particular case, the levels of independence of the artefact in relation to the text remains a matter of judgement, although the sense that a given work is offered as *only* open to proper appreciation through engagement with the terms of the written account which accompanies it is sometimes strong.[6]

'Distance', seen as not just a focal quality but also a feature of disposition towards the world, can be achieved in a variety of forms, including kinds of speech and image use, but there is no doubt that writing's approach to descriptive portrayal through its tightly localised processes of dissection and assembly allows for fine variations of distance, including rapidly changing ones. The fact that 'distance' is also often seen as a prerequisite for clear critical engagement connects back to the point made earlier about how writing and reading figure centrally in ideas of political and social order and how widespread competence in their application is considered essential to the practices of democracy.

Questions of accessibility often relate closely to questions of form. In writing, it is widely understood not only that different people will not want to read the same things but also that people *will not be able to read* the same things. Given inequality in educational opportunity, some people will find some writing 'too difficult' to comprehend. This is likely to be both a matter of vocabulary, of not knowing what certain words mean, and a matter of sentence organisation, including syntactical form and length. As the move towards the higher end of literary writing, including poetry, is approached, these difficulties are joined by more general problems with the organisation of narratives, and appreciation (in part, the comprehension) of the imaginative devices used to construct various 'literary' effects. There is a clear parallel here with 'difficulty' and 'access' in relation to the forms of visual and audio-visual expression. Designed to give pleasure by encouraging distinctive kinds of perception, such work may well cause frustration and anger in those who find themselves 'blocked' by the formal routes it takes.[7]

Differences of approach to written form, often with distinct audiences as well as purposes in mind, are evident across all the media employing writing. They are a key variable in website design, where precisely the question of attractiveness and accessibility for target groups is an issue (Who do we want to look at this page? Will they like its layout? Will they be engaged by, and understand, what is said there?), often one requiring frequent revision and updates in styling (Brugger, 2009 and Flavian *et al.*, 2009 provide detailed assessments).[8] The web as a medium is a carrier of writing, film, photography and sound, and cannot now be essentialised easily around any one communicative mode, even though new genres of writing and new ways of working with text have been among the most strikingly original achievements of web activity. It is precisely the combinatory aesthetics of the web, when linked to the unprecedented sense of live participation which accompanies its use, even as someone just 'looking', that is changing the broader terms of our relationship to media as one involving diverse formal encounters.

Layout, not just the writing itself, is also a major formal variable in magazine and newspaper design. It is there in the continuing division between the look of 'quality' daily newspapers, with their requirement to indicate different orders of significance across an extensive range and to provide detailed textual treatments, and the appearance of the popular tabloids, displaying a bolder approach to headlines, a less textually dense organisation of stories and a more immediate sense of what is on a page. The history of newspaper layout (discussed thoroughly in Barnhurst and Nerone, 2001) traces a line of developing visual design that has, in most cases, made papers 'easier' on the eye and allowed an increasing use of images and of attractive page composition within the column system.[9] In both these examples, websites and newspapers, questions of layout bring together matters of written form with broader matters of visual styling.

I want to move now to a more general level of discussion, examining categories which have proved indispensable, if problematic, in discussion of media form across very different kinds of practice.

## THE CENTRALITY OF NARRATIVE

Narrative is a category that has engaged analysis and theory across nearly all forms of mediation, an important one because spoken and enacted stories and the diverse forms of storytelling are central to what the media do in a range of generic frameworks and for a diversity of purposes. Common elements are the providing of engagement, the bringing out of significance and the generation of impact. Even where a narrative is not developed in a written, read or enacted account, media items often promote narrativised understanding in the minds of readers and viewers. Painting and photography frequently cue us towards a sense of the 'story behind' the image as part of the process of engaging with it and working upon it imaginatively to produce pleasure and knowledge.[10] Narrative analysis holds the promise of being able to provide at least some of the clues as to why certain media products work extremely well, developing a massive presence in cultural space, whereas others are marginal or fail despite their attempts to win popular attention by drawing on a high level of resources. There is also the question of how narrative form relates to the structure of ideas and values within a given item, a long-standing issue in respect of many traditional as well as modern media. Here, non-fictional forms, too, have been a focus for dispute, because the question of how much narrative shaping, and of what kind, should occur alongside (and perhaps interwoven with) exposition and argument is one that has frequently been raised. News stories and history programmes on television are two rather different examples of this (for example, see respectively Eldridge, 1995 and Bell and Gray, 2010). In both cases, there has been a perception that certain kinds of narrative structuring reduce the possibilities for thoughtful engagement and shift too heavily the orientation of the account away from critically framed knowledge (a knowledge that offers itself as accountable, as open to question).

One of the problems of discussing narrative in media research has been the tendency for the term to become unhelpfully expanded in its scope. At some point, almost all accounts can be deemed to have narrative elements insofar as they involve a development over time, a sequence of connected happenings. Some indication of the resonance of the term can be got from the fact that 'narrative' has become a favoured word in political and corporate planning, where it indicates the larger pattern to be given to events and to be projected in publicity. 'What's the narrative?', 'Do we have a narrative?' are questions asked in a way that illustrates the discursive premium now placed on being able to locate policy announcements and initiatives within a longer 'storyline' of achieved or intended outcomes. Such usage, with references back to literary and dramatic examples, is perhaps a symptom of the fear of being seen as too short-term or fragmented in approach. It appears to have grown out of an attempt to counter the tendency towards a popular scepticism about continuity in managerial vision. Although not primarily a matter of production within the media, it is worth noting how this usage is often about production *for* the media. It is about trying to manage the broader frameworks of significance in which discrete events attain public visibility and meaning

What is often suggested by a critically negative view of non-fictional narrative design is that the material under scrutiny uses 'too many' of the structural devices by which fictions are crafted, around generic clusters like the 'fairytale', the 'thriller', the 'mystery' and the 'farce'. A good narrative has a pleasing structure of development and suspense, little symmetries of circumstance, character twists, plot reversals and surprises. Propp's (1928) analysis of components of narrative design, although grounded in a study of folk-tales, remains instructive, with adaptation, for many contemporary instances, while Todorov (for instance, 1969) develops a more theoretically ambitious version of a narrative typology, with its characteristic phases of development. Narrative exerts a pull on the imagination and has a coherence and shape often making the account memorable. Non-fictional accounts may only be able to generate an approximation to this by fashioning their materials in ways that serve, whether intentionally or not, to misrepresent. They may misrepresent, for instance, the relations between real people, the time-scale of events and the range of factors bearing on particular conditions or incidents. All accounts are necessarily selective constructions of the realities they describe, but narrative forms, when applied to non-fiction, may often achieve their cultural attractiveness at the cost of introducing more drastic transformations of their materials than is good for the integrity of the knowledge that is being offered. This is likely to be a continuing point of anxiety and critique around media form, and central to the very notion of journalism as a kind of 'storytelling' within broad ethical and referential protocols, one whose 'balance' and attempted approximations to 'objectivity' have to involve some constraint on narrative options.[11] The challenge of proposing alternatives to present narrative usage and, more ambitiously still, of trying to implement them has been variously taken up (Frus, 1994 conducts an enquiry into established and emergent practices).

In relation to fiction, narrative is seen to be an essential feature of creative crafting rather than, in itself, a potentially suspect element. While the specific kind of narrative design employed is regularly the focus of critical debate in any appreciation of a written or audio-visual fiction, there has developed an extensive diversity of narrative models within whose terms authors, scriptwriters and directors can situate themselves through mixtures of imitation and originality. Across all media, a shift towards greater complexity, multiple layering (sometimes interwoven, sometimes not) and stronger play with ambiguity of character, action and implied values has been noticeable, although this varies with generic context and the demographics of audiences and readerships (the contributions to Herman, 2007 reflect these shifts in a broader historical context, while Nelson, 2007 is an excellent exploration of developments in television drama). The further changes that the web will bring to narrative fiction and the use of narrative more widely, both by linkage with film and television productions and within entirely web-based fictions, are likely to include many new possibilities for enrichment and complexity, both in narrative design and modes of viewer or reader engagement and satisfaction (Manovich, 2001 remains a key point of reference for analytic work here, but see also Bassett, 2007 for a recent, perceptive review).

How narratives end, and the evaluative implications these endings carry, have provided a regular focus of analysis (again, Allen and Hill, 2004 contains different approaches to this issue). Here, 'closure' has frequently been used as a negative term, indicating an aesthetic neatness in bringing the strands of a story together in 'resolutions' that perform distortive work on the real messiness and contradictions of living and of circumstance.[12] This criticism has been applied in different ways both to factual and fictional works and, in the latter case, particularly to works which carry the promise of a 'realist' engagement with characters, themes and situations. Here, certain forms of 'closure' have been seen to fail to provoke audiences and readerships to think further about that to which they have attended and about its implications for them and the political and social systems in which they are located. At their worst, they have been regarded as encouraging simplistic and mistaken perceptions, a point I attend to further in discussion of 'realism' in the next section. Insofar as journalism 'shadows' some of the formal devices of fiction and drama, its forms of closure too can be seen to displace accounts unacceptably far over into the realm of the imaginatively satisfying and, as with other aspects of narrative design in non-fiction, to do so at the cost of informational integrity and of a proper challenge to the thinking of audiences and readerships.

In the context of these critical perspectives, it is useful to note how a selectivity which is often fierce in its exclusions and its emphases is an accepted and widely enjoyed feature of most cultural production, including the production of 'strong endings'. Selectivity is one determinant of cultural quality. Grounded in a recognition of this, a sense of what is (or might be) excluded by the specific decisions entailed in making cultural artefacts is a familiar dimension of critical response. It involves speculation, for instance, as to what is 'out of the frame' (particularly as this applies to painting and photography) or indicated paradoxically only by signs of its absence (as in the literary critical idea of 'eloquent silences'). However, a problem emerges if the sense of omission and exclusion, rather than being specific, is seen to indicate some general discursive or aesthetic deficit, because it is clear that no piece of work, no 'text', can be 'open' in the sense of avoiding exclusions and suppressions, and that insofar as it tried to do so it would quickly become incoherent. This situation is close in some respects to that criticism of journalism or of documentary works that accuses them, in much-used phrases, of not 'giving the whole story' or the 'full picture', when it is obvious that no such project is possible and that the critical emphasis has to be placed on the specificity of what was omitted and its significance. Nevertheless, the promise of the 'open text', presenting optimal interpretative freedom to readers and viewers, seems to continue to be found attractive by some, although perhaps less strongly so than in previous decades.

There is a need for more research on the parameters of narrative acceptability as seen by diverse audiences across the generic range, perhaps research that makes use of short works devised especially for the purpose of such enquiry.[13] Since both journalistic and fictional forms are subject to continuing change (although not usually in the directions favoured by critics), and have become increasingly diversified across national as well as international production, enquiry would have to include several co-ordinates and variables in order to make significant progress. The connection between narrative forms and forms both of knowledge and of knowing deserves to be understood more fully (a point explored in Creeber, Tulloch and Miller, 2008). Knowledge of specific events or issues is, for many people, now formed from the combination of a wide range of mediated narratives, reportorial, expositional, testimonial and fictional, working within different kinds of generic model and carrying out different kinds of transformation, some self-conscious and some not, upon its materials.

To give an example, at the time of writing this chapter, the war in Afghanistan is receiving intensive and regular journalistic attention in Britain. To these mainstream flows of narrative, there is added a wide range of contributions coming in the form of testimony from the parents of those killed while serving in the armed forces, and much more than we have ever had before in the public domain, from those in the forces themselves, sometimes at a senior level. Emails and blogs have played a major part in this extension in scale and range of the narrativised mediations of the Afghanistan conflict (including most recently the online publication of a large number of highly sensitive leaked documents by

WikiLeaks – see Chapter 1, note 8). The personal stories, both in primary form and then perhaps as selectively relayed by press and broadcasting, have taken their place alongside the different journalistic approaches, including those which attempt to tell a story 'from the inside' or 'from ground level', using the special possibilities that follow from being embedded temporarily with troops. Over the full scope of these different kinds of narrative, with their diversities, overlaps and tensions, established ideas of 'heroism' and of 'sacrifice' – strong determinants of storytelling and of value from previous military conflicts – exert their influence.[14] However, the new dynamics at work in telling stories about Afghanistan – around, for instance, the low chances of success in the conflict, the corruption of the Afghan government, the uncertain relationship to any reduction in international terrorism, the lack of adequate supplies to the troops – frequently produce a partial displacement and even a direct questioning of the established terms.[15]

Connecting with a selection of these narratives, sometimes by intention and sometimes by happenstance, readerships and audiences find themselves being positioned, positioning themselves and then repositioning in relation to different vectors of knowledge and feeling. Reinforcement of previous views, new doubts and the emergence of fresh perceptions are all likely to be part of this process. When the Afghanistan conflict becomes the topic of different kinds of written and dramatic fiction, a development already beginning, these inter-narrative connections and tensions – what we could call the inter-narrative profile of the topic – will receive significant addition and a further import of communicative intensity.[16]

## VARIETIES OF REALISM

Narrative is an important dimension of 'realism', one of the most influential and contentious ideas about forms of mediation and a focus for debates, embracing power, form and subjectivity, that are regularly subject to revision in their terms. I suggested above that 'realism' is best seen as a quality attributed to a mediation that is known to be fictional, the 'real-seemingness' being the more worthy of remark, and perhaps of further attention, because of its creative, imaginative production. However, it is hard to follow this usage rigidly, given the wide range of other definitions and applications which are current. For a start, there is a distinctive visual realism, applying to painting and then to photography and then to film and television, in a manner already remarked upon. To say that a painting is 'realist' is not necessarily to praise it; it may be to suggest something about the dullness of its approach, but it is to make a point grounded in appearances. Such a point could not be made by a judgement that a novel was 'realist', although realism has been a long-standing idea in literary criticism. Saying that a novel is realist may certainly involve judgements as to the accuracy of its descriptions of the physical world, the extent to which these descriptions evoke a recognisable sense of spaces, places, people and actions. This gets close to the idea of visual realism, although, at best, it is a highly indirect form of the idea. However, a novel can also be seen as 'realist' for its 'social realism', that is to say its sociological engagement, its sense of how society 'really' works not just in its physical spaces but in its social spaces, and how various structures and flows of power combine to provide contexts for forms of ordinary living. Indeed, this form of 'realism', essentially a quality of narrative ambition, is perhaps the most frequently identified in novels, plays, films and television programmes, documentaries as well as dramas. Another variant might be 'psychological realism', the extent to which a fiction depicts a plausible sense of inner life, of the subjectivity of its characters, their contradictions, their desires, fears and motives. Demonstrably, it is possible to have one in a greater degree than the other, and to have both in a novel without any marked attempt at 'visual realism'. Conversely, a painting can suggest a great deal about social conditions and personal circumstances, but it would be very hard for it to display sociological or psychological realisms akin to those of a novel or drama. Often, uses of 'realism' combine, sometimes in stealthy ways, very different ideas of the realist relationship. As many commentators have pointed out, the nature of this relationship, the dominant sense of what is and what is not 'realist', changes across its various dimensions as the dominant social sense of the 'real' itself, and then of how it should be represented, changes. (An early and very clear review of these issues is given in Lovell, 1980.)

While there is a strong tradition of seeing realisms (I use the plural from now on) in fiction and drama as a good thing, a commitment to seeing the world as it is, possibly as a basis for making critical observations about it, there are also well-developed lines of critical dissatisfaction with realist approaches. Realisms may be judged unadventurous, aesthetically and symbolically, against the possibilities of fantasy, allegory, myth, surrealism or variously 'heightened' forms of portrayal in which distortion and displacement from the real are a key part of the design. A significant strand of theatre, film and television studies has regarded realisms as politically complicit as well as aesthetically conservative (an influential account, particularly in film and television studies, is MacCabe, 1974). By offering confirmation of the 'way the world is' in their depictive strategies, they are seen to reinforce conventional perspectives upon it, rather than taking the opportunity to open up a space for sustained questioning and an indication of how things might be otherwise. In Bertolt Brecht's dramatic theory, this was an issue about the terms of audience engagement, about ways in which the audience might be kept alert to the wider contexts of what is shown happening and to possible alternatives (see, for instance, the discussion in Thompson and Sacks, 2006). A variety of 'anti-realist' devices have been proposed to offset or to completely replace realist portrayal. These often involve disruption of the narrative in different ways (e.g. breaks in the action, direct address to the audience/readership, sharp disjunctions within the performance of character) and also attempts at reflexivity in which the artefactual and inherently interpretative character of the portrayal itself is offered for critical examination. Such approaches have had their impact on discussion within the media. They have also been variously taken up in production, albeit mostly at the margins and within those projects where commercial risk is more limited and the anticipated audience or readership is seen to have a cultural orientation that will respond positively to specific kinds of complexity and 'challenge'.

Criticism of realisms has been a part of the discussion of non-fiction media too, including film and television documentary. Whilst this charge can be appropriate in certain cases, it is important to note how 'realism' here is likely to mean something rather different from 'realism' in relation to a feature film or drama series. I have argued elsewhere (Corner, 2008, and see also Chapter 8), that dominant realisms in news and documentary output are often best regarded as a form of 'discursive realism'. They are accounts in which kinds of evidence, testimony, and interlinked and perhaps contesting judgements are offered (with differing degrees of confidence) to state what is 'really happening', the way things 'really are'. Such an essentially *propositional* realism may well be supported by sequences of filmed events in which the mode of shooting and editing produces perceptual continuities resembling those of the direct experience of physical reality (in that respect following some of the conventions established in realist fictional film-making).[17] However, the difference, and then the connection, between the two modes of relation to the real which are active here require analytic recognition. Only in respect of a fully dramatised documentary would the most frequently aired arguments about the limitations of 'realism' have a similar relevance to that they carry when used of fiction. Moreover, the fact that news and documentary materials are, in part, constructed from recording taken from the real, rather than imitations of it, seems likely to reduce the descriptive and analytic force of realism as a critical idea in this application, even allowing for the intervention of extensive artifice at the levels of shooting strategies and editing.

Given these problems with definition and criteria, there are considerable challenges for any kind of journalistic or documentary work that might wish to eschew realisms, since most conceivable approaches would seem to undercut the basic generic assumptions which underpin work in this area, however varied the ways in which particular film-makers have chosen to position themselves in relation to these assumptions (Winston, 1995 is a fine historical and critical review). Certainly, it is possible to make an anti-documentary film or programme, a work that subverts the very idea of documentary, but an anti-realist documentary would have to negotiate a formidable array of aesthetic and discursive contradictions (discussed further in Chapter 8). Not surprisingly, most critical innovation around realism in documentary has worked with a sense of getting a *partial* distance from conventional design, and introducing elements of reflexivity to offset those passages in which a tendency to reinforce prior assumptions, or simply to 'confirm the world' rather than 'disturb' it in the mode of portrayal, offers a potential block to the encouragement of critical viewing.

Discussion of this issue has mostly acknowledged the wide-ranging appeal of realist models, particularly for popular audiences. Their very attractiveness has, it is clear, been viewed as part of the danger they pose, cognitively and affectively. It is notable that the two forms of international television, apart from news services, around which the most intensive critical debate has gathered over the last thirty years or so, soap opera and reality television, both use strong 'realist' structures of different kinds, drawing variously on rhetorics of realist fiction and of documentary naturalism. Both (sometimes playfully) imply ideas about what 'ordinary life is like' that have come in for criticism and rejection both inside and outside the academy. In the case of reality television (the generic uncertainties of which are discussed further in Chapter 6), a model taken initially from work in documentary was given additional narrative appeal by the use of a broader range of options for shaping action and interaction. This involved, among other things, 'casting' specifically for heightened narrative possibility rather than for serious thematic development, using strong directorial encouragement and cues to produce intensified moments of confrontation and, in some cases, devising firm parameters and regimes of behaviour (concerning space, time and action) within which 'spontaneity' could be observed. Although there are regular stories in the newspapers predicting the 'decline of reality television', suggesting a fashion that is now well past its peak, the international evidence is that this area of programming is resourceful in almost continually revising itself, including from hybridic combinations with other successful types of show such as talk shows, travel and cookery series, history programming and, for some time now, varieties of quiz and game formats. For historical and critical commentaries on developments here see, for instance, the critical writing in Holmes and Jermyn (2003), Biressi and Nunn (2004) and Murray and Ouellette (2009).

Underpinning but often only implicit in many criticisms of narrative practice, including criticism of the use of varieties of realism, is the idea that not only do the dominant forms lead to distortions in knowledge and feeling, as discussed, but that these dominant forms tend to articulate a very limited number of social and political perspectives. This connects with the earlier discussion of structures of power (in Chapter 1), and with the problems of achieving an adequate plurality of circulated accounts and values even within societies where the form taken by the dominance of elites allows, at least notionally, some space for this. The issue of the influence of a limited number of perspectives upon narrative production and that of the diverse possibilities for, and the alternatives to, conventional narrative form are essentially separate ones. However, they have not surprisingly shown a tendency to become merged in many debates about the nature and significance of mediated storytelling.

## FORM AND THE GENERIC IDEA

Within most conceptual and analytic work on media form, the notion of 'genre', the order to which something belongs, has become an important descriptive category, one carrying normative implications (within a large literature of commentary and debate, Neale, 1990 and Altman, 1999 provide valuable accounts). Genre defines, even if only provisionally, different kinds of mediated artefact and although it also relates to questions of 'content' it is primarily a categorisation of form. Deciding what 'kind' of thing a given item of mediation belongs to informs a sense of what kind of formal 'rules' it might follow in its construction, what kinds of satisfaction it might give and what kind of criteria might be most appropriate to judgements of its quality. The idea of something being good or bad 'of its kind' is an important constituent of judgement in a number of areas, but it has a particular resonance in the assessment of cultural production, where it is frequently invoked to prevent the framework for judgements developed in one sphere of practice being used unmodified to make judgements of other areas. Too firm a sense of the separate identity of different genres within the generic range would produce a situation in which most forms of cultural comparison, of assessment of relative value, would be seen as inadmissible. This would contradict the established practice of, precisely, making comparisons across often very different cultural artefacts, sometimes within the same media, sometimes not.

However, too 'soft' a sense of generic identity produces a situation in which the distinctive cultural conditions of established and emerging strands of media work, in relation to the broader clusters to which they relate, easily disappear underneath generalised terms of evaluation. These terms may simply connect the specific item to the broadest criteria without any intervening sense of the social and aesthetic history of forms and of differences of function. Within cultural criticism, this has not surprisingly sometimes led to the terms of assumed 'superior' categories (perhaps in 'superior' media) being used across a wide range to enforce judgements of inferiority. It is within these circumstances that a call to 'pay attention to genre' has been regularly made by scholars seeking to check a tendency towards judgements that work against the 'popular', and often against the new.

Writers on genre have often noted the play-off between production genres and consumption genres, where there is considerable overlap although also differences of emphasis. Production genres (and sub-genres – in a proliferating market, diversity requires identification underneath the main classifications) are the categories which, with variable degrees of stability, are used within the cultural industries themselves and then sometimes taken forward in marketing and distribution. Production genres are culturally realised but often economically informed. They are essentially about the reproduction-with-differences of what appears to have worked well in the cultural marketplace but also about the taking of innovative risks in relation to the 'familiar', whether for a broad or narrow target grouping (Bruun, 2010 uses the idea of 'generic schema' to explore the categories at work in production settings). Just how much and in what ways media productions are 'generic' in a manner that is constraining of imagination and originality rather than enabling of them remains an important issue. Within cultural analysis on popular forms it is a point around which regular dispute has been generated (among the many accounts, see Hesmondhalgh, 2007a).

A recognition of the generic is also used by readerships and audiences in their consumption and is formed partly from publicity materials (thus connecting with production) but extensively from the experience of watching different types of material, talking about it with family and friends, and seeking means to classify, however loosely, the distinctive expectations to have of it. A sense of genre becomes a guide to selection from the range of available options.

There is a third source of generic classification too, that from professional critics. Within all the cultural spheres, including popular media, critics have often had an influence upon the labelling and then the evaluation of perceived categories of work that has been relatively independent both of production and consumption contexts initially, but has then had an impact on the perspectives at work in these contexts too (for example, Ellis, 2005 examines developments in British 'reality television' with attention to the impact of press coverage).

One of the issues frequently brought up in discussion of genre is the lack of clear definitions and boundaries in many generic clusters and the rate of change of the conventions followed. Widespread use of the term 'inter-generic' or reference to 'hybridity' has often been seen to be necessary to describe adequately the accelerated shifts and proliferating developments of formal usage that many areas of mediation have undergone (Van Bauwel and Carpentier, 2010 employ the term 'trans-genre' to indicate the degree of fluidity they perceive to be at work). This usage does not entirely resolve the problem, however, since it is in part based on assumptions about an underlying degree of stability to which the 'inter' relations and the 'hybrid' growths relate. A better way forward for cultural analysis is perhaps offered by a more direct recognition of the interplay between innovation and continuity in all media recipes, together with a more complex sense of formation and reformation in recipe design and the wider economic and cultural determinants of what gets made, and how.

I noted above that too heavy an application of the idea of genre can lead to a situation in which everything is judged within in its 'own terms' and cross-comparative assessment of cultural value is thereby severely limited, whereas too little recognition of generic factors fails to note how mediation occurs within (changing) subsets of conventions, guiding production and inviting specific modes of response. The term itself still carries something of the aura of a self-conscious critical and discriminatory discourse, rather than everyday consuming practice, and it is strongly weighted towards forms of fiction. The further out from fiction the application of genre extends, encompassing modes of television

journalism and entertainment where stylistic organisation is often concealed by forms of representational and performative naturalism, as
discussed above, the less frequent the pattern of usage becomes outside
of critical and academic circles. What does this mean for popular practices of generic recognition and the use of such recognition within the
routines of viewing, listening and reading?

This question relates to the more general issue, raised earlier, of how
matters of form, not just of genre, are perceived outside of the sphere of
criticism and scholarship. Form is an active constituent in the production of meaning and of pleasure, but its interplay with audience or
reader subjectivity, including the selective taking up by them of the 'subject positions' which textual organisation and performance cue them
towards, is variously placed within consciousness.[18] The placing may
shift considerably even within a viewing or reading of the same item let
alone across a range of items differently located within generic space.
One of the variables here may be a disengagement from the item, following boredom with its progress or some other perception of its deficits.
Slipping 'out' of communicative connections with it in this way may
involve conscious recognition of form, and then a heightened recognition of genre, as part of the self-consciousness of 'not liking it' and of
identifying the reasons for this. Similarly, heightened engagement and
pleasure may also produce sharper recognition of formal achievement.
For non-fiction forms, phases in which there is a relative 'transparency'
to real world referents accorded to the material may be interspersed with
phases in a which a strong and contested sense of 'mediation' and even
of 'manipulation' prevails (discussed in Richardson and Corner, 1986).
Finding out more about how audiences and readerships work upon
media materials, at the localised level of 'following' them and moving
around in the terms of their engagement while doing so, will continue to
be methodologically challenging. However, it is a necessary route to our
further understanding of how forms, and ideas of genre, work at the
level of apprehension.

The generic assumptions that work to guide and frame the public
experience of media are not always confirmed or reinforced. Sometimes
they are tested and even exposed to dispute by generic innovation.
Research into the kinds of generic map used by audiences, like that carried out in the last decade by Annette Hill (2005 and 2007), provides a
valuable route into further knowledge of the play of media forms within
the terms of everyday routines and perceptions. As with the exploration
of forms of narrative, both textual and reception studies of comparable
thematic material as it is articulated across very different genres continue

to hold promise. Meanwhile, greater understanding of how professional groups conceive of what they are making in a given medium, its positioning across the array of possibilities as social relationship, craft endeavour, commercial product and, perhaps, as mode of art, can only enhance our sense of mediation as a practical achievement as well as a cultural process (here, Born, 2004 is a richly suggestive contribution).

## THEORISING FORM–SOCIETY RELATIONS

The study of media form has inevitably pulled conceptualisation and analysis down towards the specifics of medium, generic and textual detail. This has generated a highly differentiated vocabulary for discussing form, one in which examples, for instance, of radio, photography, film, television, newspaper writing and, now, website design and textuality have been analytically rather isolated.

While possibilities for further cross-media and cross-generic study therefore remain one of the most promising areas for future development (see above), the dangers of working 'down' to examples from too high a level of generalisation are also apparent. Semiotics, in its many variants and revisions (Cobley, 2009 provides a critical survey and Bignall, 2002 a lucid overview of media applications) is perhaps the most obvious instance of this. Richly suggestive in its broad address to the socio-discursive character of signification and illuminating in opening up what were often marginalised questions about visual communication and image/text combinations, semiotics has not provided the breakthrough in the analysis of mediated meanings that it once appeared to promise. One of the reasons for this is the shift the 'science of signs' had to make from its initial, structuralist rigidities towards a stronger sense of variation, contingency and uncertainty. In that sense, it was caught up in the larger post-structuralist movement towards engaging with localised conditions of practice and with significatory indeterminacy that affected most of the ways in which 'texts' were thought about in humanities and social science enquiry from the early 1980s. This movement impacted upon disciplinary traditions in different ways and with varying scales and rates of change, but it made it much more difficult to continue to work with systems of textual analysis posited around high levels of systemic predictability in the generation of verbal and visual meanings, including implied meanings. Such a textual approach was related, in many instances, to ideas of political and social order working with a corresponding degree of systemic fixity. The 'strength' of semiotics, beyond the example of the often idiosyncratic application of it in Barthes' influential writings (particularly Barthes, 1975 and Barthes, 1977), lay precisely in its comprehensively 'scientific' codification of what had previously often been a rather loose, impressionistic dimension of study in the humanities and often reductive, limited engagements with questions of meaning in the social sciences. Convergence with the relative, the conditional, the provisional and the sociological could only be carried so far before semiotics as a distinctive analytic project, rather than a way of freshening up established lines of thinking about the sociality of signs, became a challenge to sustain. It is noticeable that semiotics does not occupy the centrality in discussion of media form that it did in the 1970s. Many of its key ideas have been absorbed more generally into analytic work on media, but this absorption has also involved a degree of dissipation, despite continuing strands of often impressive work self-identified under the label.[19]

For a while, another conceptual area with a claim towards a more general application was critical linguistics, although this claim was expressed less emphatically than in the bold manifestos regarding semiotics, notwithstanding the interconnections between the two perspectives. It was made across a number of different emerging positions in the social study of language (key texts would be Hodge and Kress, 1979, and Hodge and Kress, 1988, pointing in rather different if related analytic directions, and later the widely influential Fairclough, 1995).

In what ways might the close study of written and spoken language in context, drawing on the approaches and vocabularies of linguistics, take further an understanding of media form as political and social performance? In pursuing its analytic goals, critical linguistics hit the familiar problem of attempting to connect a close scrutiny of media form with ideas about social organisation and process, including those concerning power. Detailed formal analysis of writing and speech could offer 'clues' about broader organisation, but just how far did these clues take us towards valuable new knowledge? Did they not have to meet at some point analytic understanding coming the 'other way', that is to say coming 'down' to questions of form from a primary engagement with questions of political and social order? Semiotics often used structuralist-marxist accounts to supply its sociological understanding of this order, and many versions of critical linguistics were also highly dependent on assumptions about the reproduction of 'dominant ideology' (discussed in Chapter 5) as a key part of the connection between the realm of objective structures and institutions, on the one hand, and the realm of meanings and values, on the other. Insofar as 'ideology' itself became subject to doubts about its adequacy as a concept for the analysis of power, so an important strand of critical linguistics became open to question, too.[20] More generally, on what empirical and theoretical basis was the wider contextual understanding active in the linguistic accounts produced? How far did the mode of its combination or connection with the localised formal analysis allow for a relationship other than that of confirmation to emerge? To what degree, if any, was there an opportunity for critical interplay to occur between the two levels? Clearly, development in only one direction raises important questions about prior assumptions and foreclosed analytic frames.

These issues have complicated the sense that critical linguistics offers an independent new route into the plotting of formal-social-political relations (see Jones, 2007 for a critical review). They have also strengthened the recent re-engagement with a more sociological agenda, encouraging linguistically oriented studies in which production and audience contexts have their place alongside close attention to media forms themselves (see, for instance, the use made of guidelines for screenwriting in Richardson, 2010, on the dialogue of television drama). Meanwhile, however, research in media linguistics working with a more restricted, textualist, focus (one that need not exclude a 'critical' attitude) continues to produce impressively detailed accounts of media language use that are accessible and relevant to media studies generally (an excellent example here would be Montgomery, 2007).

An attention to media phenomenology, to the nature of mediation as an *experience* of consciousness in relation to sensory input, has gradually strengthened in media research on form. Much work in this vein has engaged in one way or another with the idea of 'witness', not only in the sense of an effect upon perception produced by formal organisation (the sense in which I discussed it earlier), but in its broader cognitive and affective implications. In recent studies John Ellis (for instance, 2009) has developed this notion as a central theme in his thinking about audiovisual culture, and Lilie Chouliaraki (2006 and 2008) has been influential in applying, not the specific idea of 'witness' itself, but the related notion of spectatorship to the 'spectacle of distant suffering', a theme previously explored in the work of Luc Boltanski (1999), among others. How far and in what way does the distinctive experience of apparently seeing things 'directly' through forms of photography or television/video reportage impact upon our ideas about the world, and about others in it? How do we relate such 'secondary' experiences to the other data out of which we construct, sustain and routinely revise our sense of 'self in the world'? Both Ellis and Chouliaraki, from different theoretical contexts, examine the ways in which prevalent forms of mediated witnessing/spectatorship might operate within current ethical, political and social frameworks.

For Ellis, the emphasis is on the interplay of distance and closeness that the 'witnessing' experience involves. This is seen to produce a situation of 'emotional ambiguity' (2009: 75). The position of witness is a 'mobile one, involving twists and turns of emotional empathy rather than one fixed position of identification or rejection' (2009: 76). He notes: 'we can feel, but always already within a structure that gives *both more and less* than we would gain from a real encounter' (2009: 71). This sense both of the 'excess' of the mediated over the real and also its relative 'deficit' is perceptive and important, connecting, among other things, with the whole history of the debate about realisms and their consequences. Ellis is concerned to stress how any witnessing of traumatic events through the media occurs, not as some intensive isolated experience, but within the context of the routine forms of witnessing that are part of our daily experience of audio-visual culture and are variously complicated by the interplay between our sense of the real and of the textual in relation to what is viewed.

Chouliaraki (2008) places the focus primarily on the mediation of suffering rather than on the everyday forms of spectatorship and therefore her account is much more inclined than Ellis's to pull this mode out of its broader setting of media–self relations. She looks at the way in which the roles of voyeur, philanthropist and protester might variously be adopted by viewers, depending on the form of moral reaction generated to who and what is depicted. How do mediations contribute productively to moral education and moral agency? Or how do the forms of aesthetic construction involved work to 'screen us' from such agency and place us in the managed realm of the hyper-real, effectively denying our active engagement? Although recognising the operation of political and cultural power across the kinds of representation she examines, and identifying many examples of negative ethical outcomes, Chouliaraki finally argues against pessimistic accounts (such as those of Baudrillard, 1988 and 1995) that show little or no recognition of a positive dynamics at work. Instead, she makes the case that many prevalent forms of audio-visual mediation can offer positive ethical positions for viewers to occupy, providing the possibilities for enhanced critical awareness and favourable conditions for social action.

In both cases, it is likely (and admitted by Ellis) that only through work that goes 'behind' textuality, into the political and social circumstances bearing upon production, and also 'in front' of it, through the

continuing address to media audiences, will significant progress be made
on these questions. The ethical impact of our mediated seeing of various
'others', and the extension or holding back of forms of empathy,
together with the consequences this carries for social action, are becoming questions of growing importance within the context of convergent
television/new media settings.[21]

Formal analysis is becoming a more prominent dimension of media
research across a proliferating range of approaches and levels. As a
result, greater emphasis is being placed on the concepts and methods
used to advance it. Current and imminent digital developments will
introduce quite novel ways of relating form to subjectivity, connecting in
some respects with the kind of changes brought about by video gaming
(discussed in Dovey and Kennedy, 2006) as well as having continuities
with more established patterns of use. The forms of mediated pleasure
and of mediated knowledge in circulation across the options will display
aesthetic innovation, partly as a matter of internal creative dynamics and
partly in response to shifts in wider economic, social and cultural settings. Many formal practices will provoke anxiety and criticism as well as
approval, since they will, rightly, be thought to be involved in the construction of the different prisms, socially shaped and socially shaping, by
which aspects of the real enter into public and subjective space through
the artefacts of mediation. These artefacts will have highly self-conscious
but also unwitting components active in their organisation, and although
at times they will appear revealingly controlled when subjected to analysis, at other times it will be their apparent messiness and lack of
coherence which will be found most culturally symptomatic.

The further exploration of the issues that I have outlined, variously
ones of organisation, articulation and apprehension, embracing a range
of aesthetic and discursive practices, will require approaches that are
able to combine humanities with social science concepts and methods
within very different agendas of enquiry. Work at a more general level,
such as Jacques Ranciere's broad-ranging examination of contemporary
aesthetics and spectatorship in relation to the notion of emancipation
(Ranciere, 2009) can inform analysis of a more specific kind, embedding
data and questions within frameworks of power and processes of subjectivity. Form is a central if often taken-for-granted component of our
media satisfactions and of the benefits derived from their activities. Issues
of form are also a part of the continuing anxieties about at least some of
what the media produce and circulate and they inform the widespread
feeling that structures and practices could be different and better. Across

all these matters, the scope for an improved understanding is great and so is the opportunity, also signalled at the conclusion of my previous chapter, for making that understanding carry a resonance beyond the boundaries of academic knowledge.

## NOTES

1  'Reading' is a term that is also used more diagnostically to indicate an analytic approach which seeks to discover that which is 'indicated' by the text but not 'expressed' by it. This is a usage from literary studies widely taken up in cultural studies within different theoretical frameworks. For a formative discussion, see the two volumes of Hoggart (1970).

2  When applied to many texts, including those of the media, 'criticism' can become a term indicating not just close, analytic attention, but also the identification of deficits relating to social and political values. This usage is more closely aligned with ideas of 'critical sociology' and of 'critical social theory' (Dant, 2003 provides a historical review) than with the conventional application of the term in the arts.

3  Ironically, this transition came about at a time when, with digital changes in view, some commentators were talking about entering an era of 'post-photography', where the decline of the photographic, rather than its expansion, was judged to be the dominant cultural trajectory. See the contributions to Wells (2003) and the discussion in Chapter 9.

4  Theatre is a special case here, drawing on the qualities of literary writing at the level of script production (such that plays in the classical canon are also 'texts' to be read) but also offering a performance to see and hear. The way in which theatrical values have been active in critical discussion of film and television, and have variously informed production in these media, is an important part of generic development.

5  The use of terms like 'high end' in respect, for instance, of documentaries or drama series, is one indication of these internal differentiations, traditionally more marked in cinema (which has long had 'art cinema', or more pejoratively, 'arthouse cinema' as a category) than in television.

6  This practice is more pronounced in 'conceptual' works, where the idea of a detailed statement of aims and interpretative guidelines, rather than a requirement for viewers simply to figure out meanings (or not) for themselves, seems to have become established at the formative level of art school conventions.

7  The issue of differential accessibility to the satisfactions offered by cultural forms, including media forms, is taken up further in Chapter 3.

8  In July 2010, the radical redesign of the BBC website was the subject of intensive discussion and complaint in relation to different users' requirements and conflicting ideas about clarity and usability.

9    What is found 'attractive' is, of course, both historically and culturally specific and subject to quite radical shifts.

10    A good example is provided by an exhibition at the Tate Gallery, Liverpool, which is current as I write (July 2010). Reneka Dijkstra's 2009 audio-visual exhibit 'The Weeping Woman' is a twelve-minute film of children's responses to looking at Picasso's 'Weeping Woman', 1937. From the clues of this Cubist image they develop a range of stories both about the woman and her circumstances, variously drawing on a sense of the realistic and the fanciful. Another example might be some of the commentaries in Barthes' famous short book on photography, *Camera Lucida* (1984). Here, the 'naïve' interest in imagining the stories related to the images, rather than solely being concerned with their formal properties, is part of the wide appeal (rich in its open subjectivity) and the continuing suggestiveness of Barthes' critical approach.

11    Among the accounts from within the profession of journalism, Marr (2004) is outstanding.

12    Getting adequate 'closure' on complex, multi-stranded narratives in film and television has sometimes provided scriptwriters with a challenge to their ingenuity and audiences with a challenge to their powers of comprehension.

13    The use of specially designed 'test' items could certainly prove illuminating. However, the costs involved in constructing items that reproduce the production qualities of professional output often place limits on what can be done within an academic programme of inquiry.

14    See the perceptive discussion in Fisk (2010).

15    The narrative profile of 'Afghanistan' across its different formal and thematic elements would make an instructive study. So would what is now the increasingly more complex, and conflicted, narrative profile of climate change as it appears in different types of media account.

16    In summer 2010, the London Tricycle Theatre's series of plays about the long history of fighting in Afghanistan, *The Great Game: Afghanistan*, is one example.

17    The idea of 'documentary naturalism', mentioned earlier, covers these representational practices usefully, although the interconnections with the different forms of dramatic realism in fiction are obvious and variable in strength.

18    The extent to which the idea of 'subject position', as a function of discursive and aesthetic form, includes any space for individual agency in hearers, readerships and audiences is much discussed, replicating aspects of the more general argument about the relationships between social systems and subjects as outlined notably by Foucault. See for instance Corey and Peterson (2003).

19    Among these, 'social semiotics' is an active identifier for certain work in critical linguistics, briefly discussed below, with an international journal carrying that title. See also Kress (2010) for an account of 'multimodality' by a longstanding and distinguished researcher within this tradition.

20  The question of 'ideology', as well as being raised in Chapter 1, is discussed again in Chapter 3. See also the close examination of approaches to its definition and analysis in Chapter 5.

21  To take the example of climate change again, the play-off between abstract and particular and between distance and closeness in portrayals here is likely to become more volatile and to involve the contemplation of various 'others' in worsened conditions of living and kinds of personal distress.

# 3

## *Subjectivity*

The idea of subjectivity, indicating the 'space of the self' both at conscious and unconscious levels and the various factors contributing to the self's constitution and agency within the world, has become steadily more important in a range of social science and humanities investigations, including in areas where it has only quite recently had any significant conceptual presence. This has happened because awareness has grown of the complexity of the intersecting vectors that construct subjectivity, and the complexity, too, of its modes of operation and involvement in different types of social action and interaction.

It is not surprising that 'selfhood', including self-awareness and self-development, has become a focus for enquiry and debate in many modernised societies, ones in which high degrees of individualism are placed, sometimes in relations of tension, alongside changing kinds of commitment to collective organisation and social values. 'Subjectivity' has become, to use the familiar term again, something of an intriguing 'black box' for many different kinds of enquiry, a zone of interiority that has continued to provide a stiff challenge to the concepts and methods by which researchers have variously attempted to explore it. Some research has worked with what can now be seen as reductive notions of the subjective, 'squeezing' it by the application of sociological frameworks in ways that seem to minimise the problems of the 'black box' effect by thickening up accounts of the surrounding objective contexts.[1] In general, as I noted above, this approach is now being replaced by widespread recognition of the need for direct and more comprehensive types of attention to interiority.

Nor is it surprising that media and cultural research has been at the forefront of attempts to engage with issues of subjectivity, placing them more centrally within its accounts. As a major producer of the symbolic environment in which many people grow up and live their lives, the media have always been seen as a formative factor in consciousness and the various makings of 'what people are' and 'who they think they are'. Indeed, there is a tradition of assuming so direct an impact in this regard that part of the intellectual dynamics behind the recent strengthening of interest in 'subjectivity' has been a form of reaction. It has been part of a recognised need to assume less and investigate more, to place the relations between 'media' and 'selfhood' within a denser sense of plurality, of the interactive, of the contradictory and of movement (subjectivity as, essentially, *process*).[2]

The subjective is centrally implicated in any engagement with the production and circulation of knowledge and, perhaps even more obviously, with any exploration of pleasure. It is a site of imagination, of desire and of fear as well as of practical rationality. It is part of the grounding of political and social order (here, the work of Michel Foucault, including those writings collected in Foucault (2002), provides a continuingly controversial set of commentaries about the relationships involved). In particular, it is the space where the dominant structural co-ordinates of class, ethnic identity and gender produce differences in self-perception and perception of others, often in the process reproducing inequalities. In this chapter, I want to discuss some of the ways in which media and media research bear on the various dimensions of subjectivity, connecting my discussion where appropriate with the previous discussions of power and of media form.

I shall first of all look at the general positioning of the media in relation to questions of subjectivity in order to establish a framework within which more specific topics can be coherently addressed. Following this, I will identify a number of distinct if connected issues concerning mediation and subjective space, drawing on a range of writing and examples. Two explorations of a more detailed kind, essentially 'case studies' in subjectivity, follow. The first looks at the question of 'cultural taste' as a long-standing issue in discussion of how the media work to reflect and construct 'sensibility', the individualised as well as socialised forms of relationship with the expressive and aesthetic world, in ways that carry both cognitive and affective implications. The second examines the idea of the 'political self' or the 'civic self' as this has become recognised as a highly media-dependent aspect of consciousness and action. In both cases, the way in which the current situation is characterised by change as well as by continuities with the past will be given attention.

Questions of subjectivity have recently been the topic of intensive theorisation across both the arts and the social sciences but they have also been the focus of very different kinds of empirical investigation. Since most matters concerning the subjective are, by definition, matters which at their core are beyond direct empirical engagement even though a variety of practices (including most obviously speech) can be taken as indicative, the practicalities of enquiry here pose a distinctive set of problems. With this in mind, the connections between theory and substantive investigation will be returned to at several points.

One prominent form in which questions of subjectivity are raised in social studies, including studies of the media, is as questions of 'identity'. In relation to the formation of class, gender, race, political affiliation, region, nationality and a number of other differentiations and groupings, questions about *how* identities are produced, both as a positioning by others and as self-awareness and self-definition, are central. In a contribution to his important edited collection on social theory and identity, Craig Calhoun (1994) notes some of the broader changes that have positioned identity as a crucial term:

> The discourse of the self is distinctively modern, and modernity distinctively linked to the discourse of self, not just because of the cognitive and moral weight attached to selves and self-identity. Modern concerns with identity stem also from the ways in which modernity has made identity distinctively problematic. It is not simply – or even clearly – the case, that it matters more to us than to our forebears to be who we are. Rather, it is much harder for us to establish who we are and maintain this own identity satisfactorily in our lives and in the recognition of others. (Calhoun, 1994: 10)

The emphasis on 'establishing' and 'maintaining' is well placed in bringing out that sense of process referred to earlier. In the preface to his volume, Calhoun also points to the various reductions and displacements which social theories have frequently brought to bear on the idea of identity, mostly in the interests of maintaining satisfactory degrees of stability and coherence in their own, preferred versions of the 'individual' as an economic and political agent.

In a classic and influential work on the topic of identity formation, Anthony Giddens (1991) has emphasised the importance of the new forms of self-awareness, of reflexivity, produced within the conditions of political modernity, particularly within its changed, often highly commercialised, spaces and contexts for experiencing the social. Giddens' focus is on the radical transformations of modernity not just at the level of institutions and social structures, but in their consequences for everyday consciousness:

> In the post-traditional order of modernity, and against the back-
> drop of new forms of mediated experience, self-identity becomes a
> reflexively organised endeavour. The reflexive project of the self,
> which consists in the sustaining of coherent, yet continuously
> revised, biographical narratives, takes place in the context of multi-
> ple choice as filtered through abstract systems. In modern social
> life, the notion of lifestyle takes on a particular significance ... Of
> course, there are standardising influences too – most notably in the
> form of commodification, since capitalistic production and distribu-
> tion form core components of modernity's institutions. (Giddens,
> 1991: 5)

He points to the way in which new forms of public mediation create circumstances in which 'the influence of distant happenings on proximate
events, and on intimacies of the self, becomes more and more commonplace' (1991: 4). These mediations contribute to complex, interwoven
settings in which the relation of 'self' to 'others' now occurs both as
recognition and, increasingly, as *performance*, using diverse and even
contradictory reference points as a guide, both those close and those
distant. Giddens sees possibilities of individual empowerment here, but
also dangers in the new forms of self-consciousness and regimes of
self-development encouraged within unstable and 'dis-embedded' post-
traditional conditions.

Subjectivity is a broader notion than identity and I do not want to
reduce my discussion here simply to issues regarding the latter, important though these are. However, the formation, and re-formation, of
'who we are', both in relation to our own perceptions, the perceptions of
others and to the larger structures within which we live, clearly provides
the basis for all engagement with the 'realities' of the world and judgement upon them. Within this process, producing not only continuities of
the self, sometimes fragile in their unity, but also changing and composite 'selves' in which the play of contradictory elements occurs, the media
perform a major role.

## MEDIATION WITHIN SUBJECTIVITY; SUBJECTIVITY WITHIN MEDIATION

First, it is of interest to note how the relationship between media and the
individual is posed in a different way from that between the media and
society. Emphasis varies in how far the media are conceived as somehow

external to society, acting as a force upon it, or located inside it, inter-linked in its very construction with other institutions and agencies. The 'externalist' perspective achieves a certain clarity only at the cost of rad-ically misrepresenting the way in which media activities are now fully integrated into, indeed are often defining of, what is now meant by the 'social' (on this point, see Couldry, 2009). The 'internalist' perspective frequently presents the problem of differentiating mediation from other socially generative factors in order to make any claims that, even provi-sionally and cautiously, are about the media's particular contribution.

Subjectivity can be seen as essentially introducing a third term here, giving a notional, interactive triangulation of media–society–subjectivity. Within this, even in the most simplistic of assessments, subjectivity is not simply a function either of society or of the media. It has levels of agency that are formative of sociality and it is formed by the social in ways that exceed the activities of the institutionalised media. Media processes bear upon the social in ways that are carried through into consequences for subjectivity but they also bear upon subjectivity directly in ways that have consequences for the social. Activities both at the social and the subjective level carry consequences for the operations of the media, even if in many research accounts the media are often seen to be 'dominant' in the relations that involve them, either in their own terms or in the terms of the elites whose power they are seen to reflect (as my discussion in Chapter 1 suggested).

What are the implications for the production and circulation of knowledge and of feeling in those societies in which media institutions and media forms of various kinds have become routine parts of public and private life? Different ways of asking and then attempting to answer this question have constituted the mainstream of international media research since its inception. A key category here is that of 'conscious-ness', even though the consequences of the media may be expected to extend beyond (or below) the level of the conscious. As a resource of consciousness (to put the emphasis in a way that accounts framed by ideas of domination might contest as too passive) the media are perva-sive in modern societies. This pervasiveness embraces information and understanding but also feeling, since the media will exert a structuring impact on the terms of the individualised emotional economy in relation to its wider social organisation, cueing both that which is judged to be deserving of feeling, and the directions and intensities which feeling might display. I want to develop this discussion further by using a number of subheadings to make connections with different aspects of mediation-subjectivity relations.

## EXPOSURE, ENGAGEMENT, INVOLVEMENT

Under this first subheading, I want to consider how we might conceptually configure the relation of individuals to media, a question that, as observed above, has provoked extensive dispute. The relationship has most often been seen in ways that emphasise 'vulnerability', rather than the advantages and attractions both for individuality and sociality that might follow, but the precise nature of perceived vulnerability and the processes through which it might occur and be exploited have been subject to wide differences of account.

I use the three terms exposure, engagement and involvement, to indicate, if only loosely, three levels of intensity of personal contact with media, easily collapsed into each other but only at the cost, I believe, of a reduced sense of process and interaction.

*Exposure* indicates the very broad and differentiated pattern of contact with the media that people in many societies now have on a daily basis. This exposure is not just a matter of reading newspapers, listening to radio, watching television and using the web. It also involves more casual 'glancing' contact, in the form, for instance, of advertisings on hoardings, buses and taxis, electronic signs, music in shops and other spaces. Any sociological survey of media would quickly show just how wide, various and continuous the profile of daily exposure to the media now is within many societies.

By *engagement*, I mean the selective and more oriented kinds of attention that some exposure is given. This attention involves a degree of cognitive focus that simply will not, and cannot, be given in many of the circumstantial settings in which media products and performances are encountered during everyday routine. It may be accidentally initiated but it is principally purposive, a motivated selection from the range of possible connections with mediation. It will vary in intensity, in some cases being casual and intermittent (as, for instance, in attention to personal media systems) and it may be only partial in its application to a given media item.

By *involvement*, I refer to the forms of processing that occur within the more intensive forms of engagement, connecting with the mediation in a way that involves more sustained cognitive and affective work, the placing of what is read, seen or heard within an existing scheme of knowledge and feeling and the modification, however marginal or simply confirmatory, of the frameworks through which it is 'received'. There will be wide variations in the scale and nature of this processing. News heard over the radio of a disaster in a place where one has friends will obviously be different from looking reflectively from the windows of a stopped train at a hoarding carrying a familiar but still connotatively active advertisement.

'Involvement' may seem a questionable term to use in this context. Moreover, receptive (and then constructive) behaviour of one kind or another is going on throughout all our connections with the media, including the various levels of what I have termed 'engagement'. Nevertheless, I want to use the idea of involvement, with its suggestion of more focused and sustained practices of receptivity, to help explore the problematic but crucial set of processes linking media artefacts to the subjective domain. These are processes which continue to provide a fruitful, indeed necessary, line of exploration for media studies generally.

One reason for being suspicious of placing too much emphasis on ideas of 'reception' in theorising around these relationships is that they may be seen to pose the media–individual relationship in largely passive terms, whereby the individual receives (or fails to receive) something contained in the media product. Although 'reception' is essentially a term from literary and cultural studies perspectives on how texts work, this assumption of passivity can skew the whole account in the direction of unwarranted assumptions about 'influence', a term largely from social science approaches which has its own, even stronger, record of indicating a passivity of relations. Moreover, some uses of the term 'reception' within audience studies have been prone to reductive ideas of isolated, intensive moments (conveniently like those produced in respondent group viewing or reading sessions), abstracting these from the broader, varied contexts and occasions of media encounter. One of the most vigorous, theoretically elaborate (and rather repetitive) conceptual debates in international media research has been around this question of the nature of reception as an interactive process taking place in significantly varying contexts. For a critically retrospective account by a British pioneer of TV audience studies, see Morley (2006), while a very broad survey including literary and film studies is given by Staiger (2005). To what level and in what ways is reception interactive? Champions of the idea of the 'active audience' have, partly in reaction to established ideas of 'influence', of 'reception' and even of 'decoding',[3] often argued for the essentially constructive nature of individual relations with media output, stressing not only the extent to which people 'make their own meanings' from what they read, see and hear but, what is almost a necessary corollary of this, that there is a wide variety of meanings 'taken' from the same media item (Fiske, 1987 provided a very influential account of this position while still retaining the idea that items also cue the reader into specific evaluative and ideological alignments). The 'active audience' emphasis has, in turn, caused a further phase of reaction among some cultural theorists and media sociologists, who have seen important ideas about the defining symbolic power of the media and their relative stability as semantic systems to be unacceptably thinned out if not altogether dismissed by the wish to privilege audience activity within a productive notion of 'interpretation' (see for instance the provocative theoretical account of Fetveit, 2001 and the criticisms advanced by Miller and Philo, 1996). This debate is essentially one about the media and subjectivity, even though its political and social framing is often of the most generalised kind.

It seems clear that levels both of passivity and of activity can be subject to overstatement in assessing what is going on during engagement and involvement with media items. An analysis of subjectivity that takes proper account of media form will be able to recognise that although there is much latitude for interpretative variation in relating to a media item, this latitude is framed by the social stability of many of the conventions of meaning and significance through which the media operate (Corner, 1991 attempts to argue this by using the idea of 'levels' of interpretation). Moreover, it is a mistake – one still made – to see interpretative variations as the result of the application of sharply individualised rather than socially induced frameworks of understanding, since how we 'read' media products is in large part how our social development and position encourage us to read them.

## THE ANTINOMIES OF SUBJECTIVITY AND 'INFLUENCE'

Studies of media influence have varied greatly, not only in their ideas about what 'influence' is and how it works, but also in their conceptualisation of the 'self' that is, or might be, influenced. They have drawn on a range of sociological and psychological accounts in designing their studies and interpreting their findings. Two important variables that I want to consider here are the extent to which the media are seen as involved in the primary construction of subjectivity, rather than being regarded as an occasional source of impact upon it, and the extent to which the routine construction and distribution of knowledge by the media is seen as, in itself, an 'influence' factor, quite apart from any arguments about persuasive force or forms of ideological reproduction at either the conscious or subconscious levels.

I remarked earlier that to see the 'individual' as a largely independent agent, whose consciousness and emotional profile constitute something to which the media relate as external sources of possible 'impact', is now widely regarded as a mistaken view. In the early stages of 'mass communication' research, it was perhaps an understandable position to take, since the scale of operation of the media industries had yet to reach anything like the level it would attain later. Within current contexts, however, recognition of the role played by the media in the formation of social consciousness, of reality perceptions, right from the early stages of childhood through to old age, is a necessary basis for attempting any assessment of impact and consequences in relation to particular cases. Not surprisingly, separating out the distinctive lines of causality at work in any selected instance (e.g. a popular television series' impact on attitudes towards the police) is made even more problematic when the continuingly formative role played by the media in routine, individual engagement with the world is taken into account.

This relates to my second variable, concerning mediated knowledge as a mode of 'influence'. I noted in Chapter 1 that many researchers would raise objections to the idea of seeing the widespread use of the media as a source of knowledge to be an example of 'influence' or of 'power'. Something more to do with persuasive strategies and perhaps with more direct lines of measurable change in attitude is what is being looked for as an effect of engagement with media. However, I think this is to work with too narrow an idea of the media's involvement in subjectivity, one in which unhelpful assumptions about what is being investigated follow from the foreclosure of the initial definition.

It seem an essential preliminary to any more focused inquiries to recognise that a routine dimension of influence is the media's continuous, wide and deep involvement in most aspects of our personal understanding. This sensitises us to the fact that forms of knowledge and of knowing (including what we might finally want to judge as misinformation and mis-knowing) will be a key element of influential processes at all levels. They are obviously implicated in the formation of the 'civic self', the self positioned as 'citizen' within a given political system (discussed below), but they are also part of the processes by which media systems constitute more generally our anxieties and our desires as men and women, adults and children. The evergreen question of the ways in which depictions of violence bear on perceptions of violence in real life (including their role in the formation of a threatened self and perhaps a violent self) is essentially to do with forms of knowledge, and so is the continuingly controversial way in which advertising, with various degrees of playfulness, offers the promise of an improved self or even a transformed self. Raising questions about what we learn from the media and how we variously learn it, accept it, incorporate it, use it, question it or reject it, all this points us towards issues of meaning as a principal constituent of subjectivity.

If we accept as one dimension of media influence the steady flow of knowledge of all kinds from the media and the selective and varied absorption of these flows into individual consciousness and social space, then the core idea of 'influence' becomes far less dramatic (or indeed, melodramatic). We are able to recognise that the media routinely provide ingredients for our symbolic encounters with the world in a very wide range of ways. The questions that follow, about specific connections between particular materials, contexts and groups of media users, about the scale, direction and social consequences of certain lines of influence under examination, are then likely to be posed within a more complex and subtle sense of the broader contours. We are also in a better position to recognise the ways in which the media can be agencies of democratic improvement and cultural enhancement as well as of political management and populist exploitation, a recognition that has sometimes been marginalised if not excluded altogether from research perspectives.

## SUBJECTIVITY AND MEDIUM

In Chapter 2 I discussed in some detail those characteristics of different forms of mediation that gave each one a distinctive semiotic profile in ways carrying consequences for the kinds of sociality and of politicality that could be articulated. Here, I want briefly to look again at medium-specific factors, this time focusing on the ways in which these relate to subjective space and subjective process.

### *Newspapers and magazines*

Management of the terms of engagement with printed media is obviously much more in the hands (quite literally) of the reader than is the case with broadcast forms. A reader is involved in a process of selection which is about perusal of a whole body of text, the sequence of reading the items within it, the depth and intensity of the reading, possible repeat readings, discontinued readings and so on. The reading act itself entails considerable imaginative activity, the words often describing and evoking physical circumstances, events and quoted or reported speech, but sometimes articulating more abstract, propositional accounts. Photographs work variously to cue and direct the production of meanings, both in the reconstruction of the realities reported and in generating the moods and tonings appropriate to considering them. Barthes' (1977) classic observations about the double function of photographic 'anchorage' and 'relay', grounding the text in shown realities yet also serving to give emphasis to details in the account, 'routing' readers through their interpretative work, are relevant here.

Such a form of media involvement strongly privileges the self-consciousness of the reader and the pleasures of contemplation, allowing for 'idle' whimsy as well as for critical reflection. There are no voices heard and no actions seen. The temporality of the encounter may vary from hurried to relaxed, and may shift radically within the same reading session. It is not surprising, with this in mind, that the silent pleasures of spending time with the newspaper and magazine, including the tactile ones of manipulating a communicative object (the ontological allure of the non-electronic and the non-digital persists, if in reduced strength) remain in many cultures a valued, regular experience.

## Radio

Radio also positions subjectivity in distinctive ways. I observed in Chapter 2, how it is the unseen voice, often speaking informally, that gives to the radio what is often a remarkable degree of intimate, humanitarian warmth, a sense of social connection made stronger by the removal of the 'distraction' of visual witness. In the home, in the car, the voices of radio 'come out of the air' in a way that is radical in its unfixed and geographically distant externality, at the same time as it may also seem 'inside the head' in its proximity and intimacy, its depth of resonance. The idea of radio as a kind of 'companion' is grounded in this subjective profile. The fact that, unlike newspapers, radio items are time-based artefacts which impose a degree of regulation on the performance of listening, adds further to the sense of radio as a strongly active 'presence' in the communicative relations it establishes, replacing the self-isolation of reading with the partial but often intense sociality of speech.

## Television

By offering the spectacle of a moving world of people and events, television engages subjectivity in ways that generate a marked sense of exteriority. In my earlier discussion, I observed how, according to different generic formats, this mixed a sense of the world being brought into the home with a sense of the viewer being taken out into the world. Television's kinetic imperatives make it a 'lively' medium, one in which the pace and intensities of programme design have increased in recent years. The home provides a mundane, 'realist' frame for engaging with television, a frame carrying implications for the character of the spectatorial experience and for the basic terms of subjective engagement.[4] Although the profile and patterns of viewing culture have been changing in many countries, what remains notable about medium–subject relations in television is the level of their incorporation within everyday domestic routine, often for several hours a day. For some groups, radio may equal if not surpass this, but usually only for daytime periods rather than evenings. It is now evident that web use, even excluding its use in watching television material, is now overtaking both, with its distinctive combinations of 'task performance' and 'leisure' functions.

The diverse forms of sociality offered by television have been the subject of much research and discussion and they have regularly been revised in relation to wider shifts in social convention as well as new options for programme design and construction. The 'para-social' dimension to television (to draw on the term used of radio by Horton and Wohl, 1956), particularly its capacity to provide strongly personalised performances, perhaps attaining to the (fetishised) level of the 'television personality' or 'celebrity', is greatly dependent on its placement of talk in relation to faces, bodies and actions within seen spaces. This involves a dispersal of the condensed intimacy provided by the disembodied radio voice, replacing it with a sociality in which the viewer is caught up in and involved with, to different degrees of intensity, the demonstrative and the performative and arranged acts of overhearing and onlooking (staple forms, for instance, of the varieties of reality television). I remarked how a comforting 'domestication' of the world is one effect of this regime, but at points the self may be pulled out, sometimes disturbingly, into the unfamiliar. For instance, Hill (2010) provides a suggestive account of the way in which programmes grounded in the paranormal or in magic exert their pull on subjectivity and, more routinely, there is the example of news footage that serves to de-domesticate the world, albeit briefly, as discussed at the end of Chapter 2. In many of these relations, contemplative or reflexive space is generally limited, often severely, by television's tight, rhythmic and sometimes seemingly relentless economy of time, across its popular programming at least.[5]

## *Internet/web*

What are still, with increasing inappropriateness, called 'new media' provide a great variety of possible forms of engagement and involvement, ranging from ones in which the primary relationships are close to those of newspaper reading or of television viewing, through to levels of strongly purposive 'navigation' and interactivity. I discussed briefly in Chapter 2 how a richly combinatory aesthetic and the awareness of live participation produce a subjective 'offer' of a potent and distinctive kind. Both the cognitive and affective character of web use is being modified as a result of the rapid increase in modes of mobile engagement, producing what can seem at times to be an obsessive drive towards connectivity and varieties of device–self involvement. The older model of a person sitting alone in front of a screen is being replaced by a variety of user contexts, having consequences for the multi-modal nature, durational values and phenomenological experience of 'being online' as well as the character of the notional division between 'public' and 'private' space (for a general review, see Baron, 2008). It is the move towards 'active engagement' that has been a feature of so much comment about online mediation, whether this activity is seen negatively or even pathologically, as for instance in discussion of particular forms of gaming, social networking behaviours and the visiting of pornographic sites, or more positively, in terms of an extension of sociality and, through this, of opportunities for self-fulfilment. Certainly, the medium–subject relationship becomes significantly transformed through many if not all of the routine uses to which online resources are put. The idea of 'logging on' as a kind of move out from immediate isolation into a sphere of diverse and ongoing communal possibilities, whether or not these are always consciously recognised as such, has been widely remarked upon. The available varieties of 'self-in-virtual society' have brought with them unprecedented opportunities for 'playing' with identity and of experiencing the self in ways not so easily available, if at all, through the use of media which more firmly work to position those engaging with them (see for instance, Murdock *et al.*, 2010).

## MEDIA AND SUBJECTIVITY: CONTESTED RELATIONS

Having outlined and investigated some of the issues surrounding the subjective as an aspect of mediation process, I want to examine two broad areas in which questions about the media's impact upon subjectivity and about the subjective dimension of our involvement with media have been a matter of wide-ranging debate. Elsewhere in this book the connections between power systems, formal design and aspects of subjectivity have regularly been in focus at the level of ideas and examples. This includes the discussion at the end of Chapter 1 of football and politics as areas in which types of media power variously play out, and the exploration of how we respond to the mediated witnessing of distant events, used to conclude Chapter 2. These further examples are chosen for a more expansive treatment, focusing on distinctive issues of subjective relations.

## Culture and taste

The differentiated pattern of displayed cultural 'taste' in society, particularly insofar at it maps on to differences of class, gender and age group, has long been a point both of policy concern (including in educational policy) and of widespread public and academic discussion. 'Taste' might seem a questionable word here, with its unavoidable connection back to ideas of direct sensory experience, to food and drink and, perhaps, to matters of whim and fancy. Nevertheless, preferences in the area of the arts and entertainment have frequently been seen as the exercising of an individuated set of 'tastes' which are shared with some but not with others. To call this 'cultural taste' is to inflect the meaning given to 'culture' strongly in the direction of 'the arts', the form of relationship with expressive and aesthetic artefacts, rather than the more anthropological sense of ways of living and social values. However, as so often in cultural debate, the two dominant meanings of the idea of 'culture' cannot be easily separated, and often slide awkwardly and sometimes confusingly across each other.

From one broad perspective, the pursuit of taste expansion and improvement is an important cultural goal of democratic societies, an aspect of self-development and emancipation in relation to which the media, with their often commercially organised offer of diversions and pleasures, are regularly seen to act as a countering force. In that sense, the media are judged to form popular taste in unacceptably limited ways, holding back richer and more fulfilling, if also more demanding, cultural satisfactions in favour of the continued profitability of their own fare. From another broad perspective, the values and cultural character of popular media output connect with, and are an attempt to meet, the 'true' cultural preferences and appetites of the majority of people. Viewed from this position, the commercial media are placed as genuinely democratic providers of cultural products because their entire cost structures are based largely on 'giving people what they want' (requiring regular experimentation with new ways of meeting this goal, as well as the repeating of successful recipes).

At the centre of this issue is the play-off between what we might call the taste-reflecting and the taste-forming dimensions of media systems. Judgements about relationships and weightings here can be seen as one manifestation of the broader uncertainties and anxieties about how cultural preferences are developed and about how questions of value in relation to cultural products (the 'good' and the 'bad') might relate to questions about the values established within different sections of society and within the larger patterns of economic and social inequality. Picking up on the point made above about the two meanings of 'culture', we might pose this last issue, if rather crudely, as one about how culture as forms of art and entertainment relates to culture as ways of living.

The French sociologist Pierre Bourdieu has, without doubt, made the most significant contribution, empirical and theoretical, to clarifying the terms in which this issue should be discussed. His work here (most notably Bourdieu, 1984, but also 1993) emphasises the extent to which cultural taste, and the acquisition of those competences which constitute 'cultural capital', are socially formed as 'learned behaviours' within a matrix that includes institutional settings (including, importantly, those of education) and socialisation within the family. Bourdieu's main interest is in the production of 'refined taste', that familiarity with the 'serious arts' which acts as a key marker of social class in many societies, a source of embarrassment and tension for many of those who do not have it, and a continuingly problematic goal for a variety of educational initiatives aimed at the 'disadvantaged' (however suspect that term has become, when used of other than economic inequality). However, his argument carries implications for the production and display of all modes of cultural taste and for their perception (widespread, even if not explicit) within a hierarchic order of cultural quality. This hierarchy is ostensibly to do with the properties of cultural artefacts but it is also, more awkwardly, to do with the nature of people's engagement with works and then the nature ('sensibility') of people themselves. There are many points in his writing where Bourdieu articulates his core argument on these matters, but his 1968 paper 'Outline of a Sociological Theory of Art Perception' (Bourdieu 1968/1993) is one of his earliest and clearest statements of the way in which the ability to appreciate serious art is passed off as a gift of nature, an innate quality of the self, of refined subjectivity, when it is in fact an acquisition, the consequence of social privilege:

> It follows that the most experienced connoisseurs are the natural
> champions of charismatic ideology, which attributes to the work of
> art a magical power of conversion capable of awakening the poten-
> tialities latent in a few of the elect ... ignoring the social and
> cultural conditions underlying such an experience, and at the same
> time treating as a birthright the virtuosity acquired through long
> familiarisation or through the exercises of a methodical training.
> (Bourdieu, 1968/1993: 234)

Lacking this acquired competence in the 'art code', most working-class
people, writes Bourdieu, inevitably respond with indifference if not
incomprehension when confronted with many works validated as being
of cultural excellence. Operating within a very different disposition
towards cultural artefacts, they take a more direct and functionalist
interest in a work's expressive realisms (the extent to which it unam-
biguously shows the world or says things about it), and the pleasures that
immediately follow from engagement with it. It is important to note here
how Bourdieu's primary concern is with the production of taste hierar-
chies through the mystified processes of social and economic inequality,
reproducing positional advantages and disadvantages. Although it regularly, and illuminatingly, discusses established ideas of cultural quality,
his work does not itself offer sustained address to the question of the
'intrinsic' qualities of different cultural works and the different modalities
of aesthetic experience.[6] Writing in a later study about popular taste and
the way in which it contrasts with the kinds of detachment, distance and
focus on formal relations that characterise apprehension within the 'art
code', Bourdieu expands on the point about immediacy and realism:

> In the theatre as in the cinema, the popular audience delights in
> plots that proceed logically and chronologically towards a happy
> end, and 'identifies' better with simply drawn situations and char-
> acters than with ambiguous and symbolic figures ... . (Bourdieu
> 1984: 32)

He goes on to note the desire for 'investment, a sort of deliberate
"naivety", ingenuousness, good natured credulity ("we're here to enjoy
ourselves") which generally rejects all kinds of formal complexity and
experiment' (Bourdieu, 1984: 33).

As a number of commentators on Bourdieu have noted, although he
brings television into his account of the operation of popular taste, his
characterisations take us back into a world just before the full impact of

the modern popular cultural industries in television, films and music worked through into everyday social life, bringing shifts in content and styles and more deeply interconnecting aspects of the 'high' with those of the 'popular', blurring generic borderlines in the process. Both his arguments and his empirical evidence remain of great importance in addressing questions of popular taste, but the situation has undoubtedly become more internally differentiated, the pattern more varied and fluid, since his investigations were carried out (see Frow, 1987 for a thoughtful discussion of some limitations both of conceptual framework and of data).

From the citations above, it can be seen that the emphasis is on the lack of acquired aesthetic-cultural competence in many people from the 'lower' classes, the absence of that steady familiarisation that guarantees confident access to the procedures and pleasures of art. What might this imply about the social routes through which popular taste is formed and popular subjectivity constructed?

There is a tendency in Bourdieu's writing to suggest that the working class are not only free of that specific form of tutoring which produces the cultural capital with which to enter the spaces of cultural 'excellence', but that they operate with an altogether more authentic and direct mode of 'taste'. His focus on the elaborative and often self-conscious 'distinction' of those who have acquired the high aesthetic disposition produces, by contrast, a sense of popular taste that is so otherwise it can appear to be refreshingly and commendably 'honest', if also naïve in a way which cannot help but be suggestive of deficit. Since he is, *par excellence*, the sociologist of the impact of socially systemic factors across all areas of cultural perception, engagement and expression, this is certainly not part of Bourdieu's official thesis. However, we are returned to the question formulated earlier, that of the extent to which popular taste is reflected in the content and styles of media products and the extent to which it is, by contrast a case of 'supply-led demand'. In the latter situation, preferences and pleasures might be established as components of popular subjectivity in ways not entirely dissimilar in some of their basic characteristics (e.g. repetition producing familiarity, an awareness of generic conventions and of the different expectations to have about work across the generic range of different media) from those routes that lead towards competence within the 'art code'. This is so, even allowing for differences in the level of self-conscious, technical-aesthetic 'understanding' involved in becoming 'competent'.

A degree of uncertainty or equivocation around these and related points has appeared in the writing of other major commentators on popular taste and media output. Not surprisingly, it has been a particular feature of those who, unlike Bourdieu in the works cited, take as one of their principal themes not the ways in which the taste for high culture elides the conditions of its own production, but the limitations and deficits of mediated popular culture and the need to work towards its improvement.

One such writer is Raymond Williams, formative in the development of British Cultural Studies. Less inclined than Bourdieu to openly question the terms of appreciation of 'High Culture', although his attitude towards the relation between culture and class is always a critical one, Williams gives a regular focus in his writing to the conditions for the production and circulation of popular culture.

In a classic early essay, 'Culture is Ordinary' (Williams, 1989/1958), he puts forward an important proposition about cultural value:

> The ... false equation is this – that the observable badness of so much widely distributed popular culture is a true guide to the state of mind and feeling, the essential quality of living of its consumers. (Williams 1989: 12)

Now this is an interesting comment in its implications for the relation between media and subjectivity. It sees 'badness' as a clear ('observable') feature of much of the work that is in circulation, but it does not wish to use this as any kind of indication of the consciousness and values of those people who regularly consume it. Again, to use my earlier terms, it wishes to note a disjunction between 'culture as expressive artefacts' and 'culture as way of life'. The potential problem with such a position is that although it works satisfactorily for what Williams wants to say in this part of his argument, it implicitly runs against his more general claims about the need for media output to be improved. These claims are grounded in the idea that such improvement is a political and cultural requirement *because* of the implications for popular value and popular understanding that media output carries. This is very different from arguing that popular consciousness is totally dominated by media output, but it is a position about the *connections* between artefacts and popular consciousness that cannot afford to introduce too much by way of disjunction without losing its cogency.

It is not, I think, coincidental that Stuart Hall, the single most important figure in the development of British cultural theory, shows a remarkably similar difficulty in getting consistency on this point. In his richly suggestive essay 'Notes on Deconstructing the Popular' (Hall,

1981) he makes a number of critical comments about the deficits of dominant forms of popular culture. For instance, talking of the language of the popular newspaper *The Daily Mirror*, he notes that 'It wouldn't get very far unless it were capable of reshaping popular elements into a species of canned and neutralized semiotic populism' (Hall, 1981: 233). This seems quite confident in the adverse judgement. The newspaper is involved in a process of transformation by which 'genuinely' popular elements are turned into that which is politically safe and standardised, reduced from its original qualities. However, a page earlier, Hall has wanted to claim that:

> Since ordinary people are not cultural dopes, they are perfectly capable of recognising the way the realities of working class life are re-organised, reconstructed and reshaped by the way they are represented. (Hall 1981: 232)

So 'ordinary people' do in fact recognise that the representation of ordinary life in the media is frequently subject to politically oriented distortion. This position leaves open, and un-addressed, the question of why such representations are not therefore the subject of more widespread rejection and protest, why they are so evidently 'successful' in gaining widespread attention and approval. What kind of argument about the media's cultural power can be mounted in a situation where a dominant tendency towards the misrepresentation of the popular runs alongside a dominant tendency towards the recognition of this by ordinary people?

There are certainly a number of possible answers to this question, and I would not want to suggest a terminal contradiction here. It is worth noting, too, that Hall's example is essentially about the 'truth' and 'falsity' of popular journalistic representation, rather than the aesthetically richer appeals to subjectivity made by other popular generic forms, so the focus is different from that indicated both in Bourdieu and in Williams. However, the passages from Williams and Hall seem to indicate a wish (in the terms of their broader project, an understandable one) to support the idea of people being 'better' than the kinds of media they are currently getting, and therefore of 'deserving better'. This sense of an audience/public routinely underestimated by the media industries is important, although if articulated strongly it runs the risk of reducing precisely that sense of potential threat (of domination and debilitation) that the media may be seen to pose and which constitutes the most frequently adduced reason for making their reform a matter of urgent attention.

It is worth noting that yet another pioneer of British Cultural Studies, indeed the founder of its first phase, Richard Hoggart, referred to the 'corrupt brightness' of so much popular culture of the 1950s (1958: 340). Like Williams and Hall, Hoggart also wanted to stop short of seeing the values of media artefacts simply reflected in (or simply reflecting) the subjectivity, the cultural priorities and ethical consciousness, of people themselves. He was, nevertheless, more inclined to a pessimistic reading of the consequences of their circulation, a position perhaps partly following from the ethical rather than directly political character of his critique (see Corner, forthcoming, for further discussion of this point).

It might be claimed that these references indicate a rather dated debate, and certainly the changing flows of cultural production and consumption (see Chapter 6) need continually to be brought into the picture. However, this is essentially a set of issues, points of unresolved evaluative engagement, that have not been transcended and which need connection back to their classic, formative articulations as well as to their contemporary instances. Of these latter, work around music has been particularly strong. Here, Chan and Goldthorpe (2007) on questions of social stratification in musical choice offer a provocative sociological account, while Hesmondhalgh (2007b) explores evaluative criteria in a way which is alert to those more complex questions of aesthetics and politics that underpin cultural choices and cultural satisfactions.

## *Formation, reflection, change*

We are returned, again, to the conundrum of taste formation. Regarding popular cultural products as completely determining of popular taste is a dubious position to take, if only because it leaves out of account the other factors at work in the shaping of individual subjectivity. These factors importantly include the patterns of work and of everyday domestic life within whose terms cultural products are encountered with different degrees of purposiveness and in whose settings they are consumed. Bourdieu himself gave emphasis to the 'conditions of necessity', a function of economic and social class and also, crucially, of gender, which variously constrain the times and spaces within which modes of cultural engagement can be pursued. As well as constructing these daily parameters, such conditions also provide orientations and tendencies of mood depending on the nature of the work performed during the day and the character of ongoing domestic activity. The need to relax after a hard day's manual work, the ideas of 'cultural recreation' that might follow from a shift in a factory rather than, say, a day teaching in a school, would be variables producing distinctive predispositions connecting the material world to the cultural world. The class-differentiated and gender-differentiated spaces of work and of home thus need to be brought into any investigation of media-subjective relations, alongside the more directly cultural factors such as education and the range of familial and peer influences that vary within as well as across the social classes. Television studies is one area where this has been vigorously carried through, sometimes leading to heated disputes about generic worth. Soap opera, forms of daytime programming and reality television have been a regular focus (Press, 1991 is an influential and quite early study here).

The contrary view, that mediated popular culture fully reflects pre-formed taste, is equally unacceptable, since the socially developed liking for popular cultural products can only be formed (and perhaps regularly refreshed) in relation to what is being offered in the cultural market-place. It is certainly possible to be dissatisfied with this provision, or critical of it (in the way that Hall's cited comments suggest) but while people can imagine different kinds of work from that currently available, they cannot really develop preferences for kinds of material that are not in circulation.

A point upon which all the writers above seem to place less emphasis than is desirable is the extent to which, while the significance of class-differentiated cultural taste continues to be an issue, there is considerable variation of taste *within* class groupings. Rather than any schematic 'block alignments' between taste groups and cultural products, there is an interplay of formed predispositions with the satisfactions, sometimes familiar, sometimes novel, provided by particular kinds of product within a spectrum of options. The range may be limited and the predis-positions (importantly open to revision as well as to reinforcement) defined extensively in terms of demographic variables, significantly those of class, gender and age, but when arguing about the profile of popular taste, there is still a pressing sociological requirement to map its complex contours in more detail as a necessary part of understanding its forma-tion, maintenance and shifts. This will inevitably involve a variety of factors external to the media as well as the practices of the media them-selves as key agents of socialisation and central providers of popular cultural work both to broad and tightly targeted markets.

What about the idea of 'taste change' as an educational or social policy goal? This might involve the notion of the 'improvement' of a group's tastes towards the appreciation of 'higher' forms, perhaps better seen more as an expansion than a replacement. As we have noted, Bourdieu's disinclination to validate the intrinsic qualities of the 'high' (concentrating instead on its function as cultural capital, reproducing the naturalised inequalities of the economic order) would make him an unlikely supporter of 'improvement' ideas, although many writers on cultural differences, including Williams and Hoggart, have variously included such notions in their overall view of cultural emancipation. 'Improvement', perhaps with less risk of appearing 'elitist' or undemocratic, could also take the shape of action designed to work for change in popular mediated culture. It is interesting that in his later work (e.g. Bourdieu, 1999) Bourdieu himself becomes a sharper critic of certain popular forms, particularly the forms of factual television, as well as a continuing unmasker of the mystifications surrounding the 'high'. However, the possibilities for improvement here are judged within a strongly pessimistic sense of how the medium works, at an essential level, to encourage certain modes of subjectivity and discourage others.[7]

Certainly, any attempts in the direction of 'improving' popular cultural production (it is not hard to imagine the controversial nature of almost any criteria applied to this end) would have to assume that such changes as were introduced would meet with success in gaining an appropriate audience or readership within a reasonable period. The fear that they might not do so would present a major obstacle to initiatives of this kind being introduced by commercial media organisations.

Quite often, a reluctance to probe too far into differences of cultural preference have followed either from a sense of 'natural' variation ('we are all different, thank goodness') or from a nervousness about subjecting the 'popular' to an attention which might turn out to carry negative implications, with the familiar risk of sliding, albeit without intention to do so, from judgement of artefacts to judgement of people. This nervousness has seemed to increase over the last two decades of media research, partly replacing the stronger sense of the problems of mediated 'mass culture' that preceded it and which, by contrast, often worked with unhelpfully fixed assumptions about deficit and decline.

There are good reasons for approaching matters of cultural preference with a flexible sense of qualitative criteria, open to revision and expansion. However, questions about qualities and values (As perceived by whom? According to what demonstrated criteria?) have to be kept sharply in view for the significance of cultural 'choices' to be fully recognised. Here, the framing causes of difference and the wider consequences of it (the implications for what is engaged with and what is not in the continual replenishment of the self) have to be seen as primarily structural in character, whatever role individual agency and subjectivity play at lower levels (see the further discussion of these issues in Chapter 6).

Contrary to this, it is sometimes suggested, particularly by those in the media industries, that cultural choice is now exercised across such a wide range of options, mainstream and niche, and in relation to such a changing, differentiated demographic pattern, that cultural selection is now essentially a matter for personal and social network decisions rather than a 'political' issue or a matter for policy formulation. Notwithstanding the need, observed earlier, to recognise radical cultural shifts and new modalities both of the 'popular' and the 'high', there are strong research indicators that such a view is at best mistaken and at worst an attempt to divert attention from continuing questions of inequality (see, for instance, Frow, 1995 for a broader discussion of the issues in an economic context and Bennett *et al.*, 1999 and Bennett *et al.*, 2009 for relevant evidence from surveys). Matters of cultural variation, including what are widely perceived to be variations of 'taste', remain as important for media research as for social planning and for educational and arts provision.

## *The civic self and politicality*

The second area in which I want to pursue the often stealthy but profound interplay of media and subjectivity is that of civic consciousness, its constituent factors of political cognition and sentiment and its consequences in shaping modes of engagement which, in turn, then work back formatively upon consciousness. This relates directly to the discussion of the structure and processes of power in Chapter 2 and the examination there of the broad arguments about how the media work as agencies of 'political communication'. Not surprisingly, the issues raised have received high priority within international media research but, like some of the other areas indicated earlier, they have frequently been investigated by the use of rather narrow ideas concerning subjective spaces and processes.

Within both democratic theory and institutional protocols, the idea of the citizen, an individual self-consciously located in political space and forming judgements informing participatory action, is a key underpinning of legitimate structure and process (Marshall, 1950 is a classic reference point, and see Bellemy, 2008 for a recent review). The participatory actions importantly include voting within representative systems, but variously embrace a range of other practices (often regarded as 'civic duties'). The perceived failure of many actual citizens in what are at least notionally democratic systems to 'come up to' desirable standards of engagement has been a frequent point of issue in discussion, often from very different political positions, of the shortcomings of democracy-in-practice. Sometimes, the media have been seen to contribute strongly to this deficit by way of diverting citizens from serious attention to matters of civic significance, providing news too superficial to act as an adequate basis for political participation, alienating citizens by the presentation of politics as a kind of 'game' or by dutiful (and boring) reproduction of the views of only a limited number of elite persons. I have discussed these kinds of critique in relation to different dimensions of media activity at points throughout this book. A number of writers (see, for instance, Schudson, 1998 and 2007 and the discussions both in Coleman and Blumler, 2009 and Dahlgren, 2009) have wondered whether the implicit norms of active citizenship, as indicated mainly in specialist texts but with a shaping influence on a much wider range of assumptions, are not unrealistically demanding. They have assessed this role in terms of the allocation of time and effort needed to 'perform citizenship' in everyday life, particularly given the uncertainty about just what degree of difference such a performance is likely to bring to the immediate terms of living. The range of other things to do, both out of necessity and out of enthusiasm, combined with a certain cynicism about the final outcomes of taking the civic role seriously, can be seen to encourage a justified minimalism in the formation and sustaining of the political self. This is with the exception of a minority of 'activists' who have developed the capacity, related perhaps to their stronger sense of goals and of the possibilities of change, to get satisfaction and fulfilment from higher levels of participation. Within such a 'reduced' version of practical citizenship, there would always have to be allowance made for special circumstances, most dramatically those in which political crises, including wars and economic collapse, politically mobilise large parts of the population previously disengaged and seemingly passive in orientation.

Political consciousness is not, of course, entirely the product of mediation. Even in societies in which politics is thoroughly permeated by mediation, a political connection is maintained materially as well as discursively. However, assessment in this area needs care because it is evident that the way in which we view even those things happening most closely to us politically (e.g. tax and pension arrangements, transport systems, healthcare) as well as those things which may be, or at least seem to be, at greater distance (e.g. climate change, foreign policy) are necessarily construed within a framework of understanding and evaluation provided in large part by resources of knowledge gained from the

different supply lines of the media.[8] Such resources may be subject both
to scepticism and to comparison, both across the range of available
mediated accounts and between these accounts and alternative, including more direct, channels of information. However, the placing of clear
divisions between 'mediated knowledge of politics' and 'personal' or
'direct' knowledge of politics would certainly be a mistake, given the
situation in which many civic cultures now operate.

## Civic space and civic culture

One of the most influential and perceptive writers on the question of
how civic dispositions are produced culturally, within the framing terms
of media output, is Peter Dahlgren. Over a number of years, Dahlgren
has developed an analysis of civic culture that places the role and practices of the citizen within a much broader, complex and changing
context of popular culture and everyday life. This avoids that narrowly
normative and 'formal' idea of the self-conscious citizen which I suggested has often informed mainstream political studies' accounts of civic
consciousness and action. A catalytic component in Dahlgren's account
is provided by the new communicative possibilities of the internet:

> The use of the net helps create new conditions for democratic
> engagement, and citizenship as social agency has found new forms
> of expression in this milieu. The sense of empowerment that *can*
> follow from net activism supports newer forms of citizen identity.
> These are emerging in tandem with newer ways of enacting demo-
> cratic politics. Not least, these civic cultures are increasingly global
> in character. At the same time, the loose character of membership
> suggests that civic identity itself is not necessarily anchored in
> organisations *per se* ... Knowledge and competencies are being
> shared and spread through activist networks. (Dahlgren 2009: 199)

At the heart of Dahlgren's arguments is his idea of a 'circuit' involving
six dimensions of civic culture. These are: knowledge, values, trust,
spaces, practices and identities. It is across their interconnected operation that Dahlgren explores present possibilities for civic self-awareness
and action. A marked feature of his account, one he shares with some
other recent writers on 'cultural citizenship' (e.g. Hartley, 1999; Hermes,
2006; Miller, 2007), is his recognition that civic identity will always be in
concurrent combination with other, potentially conflicting, aspects of
identity (most notably, in many societies, the role of 'consumer') and that

it will fluctuate in its salience not only across the population as a whole but within the consciousness of individuals in the course of their various private and occupational activities. He extends his sense of the civically and politically significant to include a range of activities which might in other accounts be regarded as too low in intensity or in clear political orientation to be included in an inventory of civic practice. Some of these activities he sees as constituting spheres of the 'pre-political' and of the 'proto-political' (2009: 100), spheres in which he perceives a kind of informal 'training' in citizenship occurring which in many cases (though not all; note the italicised 'can' in the quotation above) will eventually lead to more directly political forms of engagement, involvement and participation.

Fundamental to Dahlgren's account is his emphasis on questions of identity, on the formation of political subjectivity within particular objective and discursive conditions across a wide range of differentiating factors. How do people variously come (or not come) to regard themselves as citizens, people with a defined stake in the political system? What kinds of affective solidarity with others, at the level of a subgroup (according to circumstances, perhaps that of neighbourhood, region, gender, ethnic group or class) if not more widely, are required for this? How far is the perception of being able, however marginally, to 'make a difference' by your actions a pre-requisite of becoming an active civic agent? In relation to this agenda of questions, Dahlgren also raises the important issue of skills. How do people acquire the various competences that they need to act effectively as citizens when many societies operate with large inequalities of access to education and cultural resources? Is the very notion of a 'civic' identity available to all (within certain legal conditions) something of a pleasing political fiction within the real circumstances of economic and social existence?

Dahlgren shows himself to be worried by some of the structural factors and continuing cultural dynamics (including those of consumerism) that work against the development of the kinds of identities and practices that constitute an active, popular civic culture. However, he is finally a hopeful analyst, wanting to give emphasis to the potential for positive developments in the context of a research literature that has shown a strong inclination to negative, if not entirely pessimistic, assessments regarding the future of civic and public space. Dahlgren grounds this hopefulness in his sense of the radical changes being brought about in the organisation of modern societies, and particularly in their systems of mediation. Paramount here, as the citation above suggests, is the way in which uses of the web have not only added new and diverse knowledge sources to the established 'mainstream' supply but have generated, in the opportunities for 'social networking' that they offer, new modes of interpersonal and social exchange, new ways of working together with other people and being drawn into forms of collaboration and community.

In many respects, this 'good story' about the broadly civic impact of the web is a familiar one in recent writing. Another influential instance can be taken from the work of the Dutch researcher Joke Hermes. For instance:

> New ICTs are not necessarily producing 'new' citizens but they do provide for new citizen practices. Rather disconcertingly, these new practices are not easy to square with older notions and ideals of 'being informed'. Moreover, the Net sits more easily with incidental than with structural citizen practices. The transition from audience member to belonging to a public is not a permanent elevation but a temporary one. However, the enthusiasm and energy that is invested in Internet discussion and in blogs underscores the deep need for community and the exchange of ideas and interpretation that people do have. (Hermes, 2006: 306–7)

Two questions need to be asked of such perspectives. First of all, there is the problem (of which Dahlgren shows himself to be aware) of stretching out the idea of the 'civic' so far as to risking distorting the extent to which only a very few of the activities so described are meaningfully connected with the core political system. I have observed that there is a clear benefit in working with definitions that go beyond the narrow compass of established political science usage. But there is also a danger in becoming so inclusive in the classification of activities as 'civic' that the sense of a continuing and possibly severe problem with democratic political engagement becomes minimised or even disappears. Dahlgren's use of the terms 'pre-political' and 'proto-political' indicates his awareness of the need for lines of connection between the diversity of 'participatory' activities and engagement with core political issues. Not everyone involved in that wider range of activities he describes, many if not all enabled by new communications technologies, will travel down these lines, but any idea of significant democratic process, of critical attention and contestation outside the sphere of the political class itself and its associated elites, depends on there being a 'sufficient' number who do. Dahlgren notes the 'delimiting sociological parameters' on this movement 'inwards' towards the core modes of engagement but also wants to recognise, in a phrase of explicit hopefulness against negative indicators, that though 'the numbers remain relatively small, the political efficacy may indeed be proportionally much larger' (Dahlgren, 2009: 199/200). Whatever the truth of this claim, the point about numbers needs to be recognised as of continuing importance. It is one that can easily become lost in the celebration of new diversities and interactions.

Hermes' cautious play-off between the idea of 'new citizens' and 'new citizen practices', together with her suggestive idea of an 'incidental' and perhaps 'temporary' character to the 'public' roles that the practices support, indicates her own awareness of continuing tensions here, albeit perceived within a positive sense of the widespread 'deep need' for kinds of participatory engagement, even if these are essentially pre-civic in character.

A second question that needs to be posed against the sorts of account that Dahlgren and Hermes offer is one that Dahlgren has raised himself, if sometimes in rather muted ways, throughout his writing, and one that I have brought into the present volume at several stages. We can call this the question of ideology, of the extent to which a society is permeated with the values of its economic and political elite as these are installed in its established institutions and legitimised processes and routinely reproduced through mainstream mass media, among other agencies. How does Dahlgren's and Hermes' civic hopefulness relate to such an overarching idea of civic control? *Some* space for criticism, opposition and alternatives is likely to be identified, whatever the degree to which the formation and capacities of consciousness are judged to be determined by the dominant structures of power, and therefore, as so often in media research, it is precisely questions of 'extent' as noted above that are paramount.

As an example of a prominent media researcher with a bleaker perspective on the current conditions for citizenship within mediation we can take Toby Miller, whose work has engaged with issues concerning cultural politics and the media for several years. Miller, like Dahlgren and Hermes, also sees the need to place questions of civic identity within a much broader range of cultural practices. In Miller (2007) he examines television food programmes and weather forecasts as forms of implicit political socialisation. Where he departs from their kind of perspective is in the weighting he gives to the 'bad story' about contemporary cultural contexts and media performance, a story that is essentially one about ideological management. This does not entirely exclude recognition of elements of the 'good story', as it emerges from a proliferating range of cultural practices and the social applications of new media, but it prevents them from becoming dominant features of the account. Like Dahlgren, but with much stronger and sustained emphasis, Miller sees the imperatives of 'consumerism' within the context of a neo-liberal political economy as the defining feature of the present situation, particularly in the United States. Consumers are 'allowed' a certain space for choice, for the self-conscious exercise of 'consumer power', but this space and power are tightly managed according to principles and values the formation of which occurs well beyond the reach of any popular deliberation. Rather than that welcoming of expanded civic space and enhanced opportunities for self-knowledge which comes through, if cautiously, in the other two writers, Miller observes the way in which the contemporary individual-in-society is widely constructed in abstract as a 'consumer' and then defined within this category as a 'classless, raceless, sexless, unprincipled, magical agent of social value in a multitude of discourses and institutions, animated by the drive to realize self desires' (2007: 31).

Such an emphasis on a climate of conditioning generated through what Miller describes as the 'metaphysical' categories of market relations, a process grounded in if extending beyond, the operations of the media and one which seeks to transform whatever 'genuine' civic dynamics there might be into forms of the individualised drive towards consumption, is in some contrast with the sense of emerging possibilities in the assessments of Dahlgren and Hermes. Even after the financial crash of 2008–9 and the continuing dangers posed to the environment by many established practices of economic growth, it would seem very likely that 'consumer' identities will variously overlay and underlay 'civic' consciousness and action for some time to come, complicating the development of the latter if not actually, as Miller suggests (although he does not presume the total efficiency of the dominant constructions he identifies), threatening to block it. So the question about the relative shaping power of 'top down' flows of meaning and value upon forms of 'bottom up' consciousness and action comes once more into focus. This is a question posed in many different ways, ranging from the findings of the studies that I have referred to in this book through to the generalised and sometimes finally enigmatic pronouncements of the theorists to whom I have referred, including Michel Foucault and Jürgen Habermas. It comes along with attendant questions about the resources of the unconscious brought into play in both directions, 'up' and 'down'.[9]

A distinguishing feature of Miller's account, and in large part the grounding of its pessimism, is its reluctance to lose a primary focus on the main structures of the political economy and its core institutions, whatever innovative forms of social communication and modes of self-awareness may be springing up around these. The way in which this kind of centre/periphery perspective is defined, articulated, and contested is sure to be a primary factor in the continuing debate about indications of civic decline and the possibilities for civic renewal.[10]

Questions about the primary construction of selfhood within the terms of a densely mediated society, as well as about the constraints and encouragements to which the self is variously subjected throughout an individual lifetime, are now seen to be essential to further progress in media and cultural enquiry (for a suggestive commentary, see Pickering, 2008 on the category of 'experience'). The relationships of involvement linking subjective space and the media can be viewed with a negative inclination, as for instance in the perception of consumerism as a kind of 'deformation' and 'diversion' of civic impulses. Ideas of 'consumerism' in relation both to the positive and negative interpretations of its consequences, are a major theme underlying much political and cultural debate, even when not made explicit (Miller, 2001 remains an excellent review of key strands of thinking). The situation can also be seen as frequently more positive, as in some accounts of new media and of the audiences for mainstream production, relations being actively entered into, more critically inflected than is often recognised and personally and socially enabling in many different ways.[11] Hill (2007) on varieties of factual television and the viewing experience is a well-documented illustration here. Whatever route is taken, the kinds of pleasures we take from the media and the kinds of knowing (and mis-knowing) they encourage in us are aspects of a more continuous, expansive and deeper relationship between ourselves, media activities and the structures of society than many earlier researchers into 'impact' and 'influence' presumed.

Opening up the spaces of subjectivity carries implications not only for more general ideas about the range of media–social–individual relations, but also for the specific vectors of formation and re-formation by which the media relate to structures of social class and of gender. This connects back to questions about power and about form. In her influential work on visual media, Laura Mulvey (see Mulvey, 1989) has argued the significance and complexity of gendered images and gendered seeing, while Judith Butler (for example Butler, 1990) provides a broad theoretical context for analysing, and questioning, the construction of gendered identity. More recently, in *Frames of War*, Butler (2009) has made media representations of conflict the focus of an enquiry into key aspects of contemporary feeling and terms of living. In the work of both writers, philosophical and sociological concerns intersect with an interest in exploring psycho-dynamics, attempting to track inwards to the 'core' of the feelings that are in play as they draw from, and then project back upon, experience of the immediate and mediated world. It is not that 'externalities' are exchanged for 'inner depths' in the best work on subjectivity, but that the mutually modifying relations between the two are more precisely registered.

In pursuing further enquiry, the involvement of subjectivity in the practice of research will require more open acknowledgement than it has generally received, even though approaches here are changing.[12] The subjectivities not only of those researched but of the researchers themselves need to be brought explicitly into the design. They are co-ordinates whose role in determining positions and judgements at a number of stages of academic investigation is too important to be ignored. Their incorporation into research practice and publication can be managed in a way that does not threaten the displacement of the main line of enquiry, providing research with an improved (because more honest) sense of the contingencies of relationship and value that underpin it, and thereby better conditions for the production of the understanding that it seeks.

## NOTES

1   Among the approaches which have tended to 'compress' the subjective are varieties of rational-choice theory as well as a range of perspectives using strongly historical and economic models. On the former, see for instance the changing emphases in the work of Jon Elster (Elster, 2007).

2   The recent launch of the journal *Subjectivities* (by Palgrave Macmillan) and the contents of its first issues are testimony to this development.

3   'Decoding' is the semiotically inflected term used most influentially in David Morley's study of audiences for a news magazine (Morley, 1980), developing a line of thinking from Stuart Hall (1981/1973). Although introduced to provide flexibility in thinking about interpretive process, it is clear that the idea of 'code' and of 'decoding' can also carry some mechanistic and potentially simplistic implications. On this, see Corner (1981).

4   I noted in Chapter 2 how Ellis (1982) poses the cinema/television differences clearly and provocatively. See also Lury (2005).

5   The 'rhythms' of television as they are generically differentiated and subject to changes, including those encouraged by technology, are discussed by a number of researchers. Again, Lury (2005) provides good examples.

6   This relative lack of interest in qualitative variables in the relationship between the aesthetic and the subjective complicates if not actually

precludes any idea that it would be a good thing were 'high art' to be more widely appreciated, a point I touch on later.

7 This view of television's 'essential' paucity contrasts with the dominant view among British cultural critics that the medium not only produces some excellent work but has the potential to produce more. The difference is, in large part, a reflection of the cultural positioning and performance of television within different national contexts.

8 The subjective geography within whose terms political issues are variously seen as 'close' or as 'distant' is of significance for any understanding of contemporary political culture and the ways in which the media help to generate it.

9 While in areas like film studies and literary studies, psychoanalysis has been a regular component of critical discussion (see, for instance, Kaplan, 1990), approaches in media studies, wishing to work within a more sociological and less individualistic critical perspective, have tended to be wary of drawing upon it directly. However, a stronger concern with subconscious processes and their linkage with the terms of conscious living needs to be an element of future research initiatives, the response to the challenge of inquiry it poses taking a variety of routes. Some possibilities are put forward in Bainbridge *et al.* (2007).

10 Daniel Dayan's recent discussion (Dayan, 2009) of the various relations possible between mainstream media and new media, producing changed configurations of public knowledge and of resources of social power, is particularly relevant here.

11 In relation to the commentary of these last few pages, I refer readers to my examination of the notion of ideology in Chapter 5 as well as to my discussion of issues of forms of power and domination in Chapter 1.

12 Among recent studies to include a strong element of researcher subjectivity, see Stephen Coleman's exploration of popular experiences of voting (Coleman, forthcoming).

# PART TWO

## INTRODUCTION

As I noted in the main introduction, Part II consists of six articles or chapters that I have written over the last ten years in which issues around power, form and subjectivity are variously taken forward in relation to specific analytic ideas or selected examples. In each case I have added a prefatory note that, among other things, indicates the connections between this work and the more wide-ranging themes and arguments contained in the chapters of Part I.

The work is organised under two headings: 'Terms of analysis' and 'Visuality and documentation'. The first heading is for work that explores contested terms for assessing media activities. Here, the ideas of propaganda, ideology, the public and the popular that are interwoven throughout Part I and serve to interconnect the three central terms of its chapters, get a closely focused examination. The second grouping examines aspects of the continuing use of recorded sound and vision to 'document' reality at the level both of particular and of general truths. There is a sustained emphasis on form here, with examples, but there is also a connection with dimensions of media power and with the variable terms of the invitation to readerships and audiences to make meanings, take pleasure and acquire knowledge. Documentary work has been a long-standing interest of mine, partly because of its distinctive ways of bringing together issues of power, form and subjectivity. The items presented here all attempt to go well beyond what is of interest only to the specialist subfield of 'documentary studies' in order to make arguments of a more general significance about the varied and changing character of media practice.

In preparing the work for this book I have made corrections to the originals, where substantive or presentational lapses suggested it, and I have carried out editing, including both cuts and expansions, to ensure that the non-specialist reader is clearly addressed throughout. However, I have decided against thorough revision of the pieces in such a way as to produce a text that is partly new in its arguments but which retains large sections that variously shadow or replicate earlier material. It seems to me that work of this kind is best offered either essentially as it was first published, with appended comments, or thoroughly reworked into what then becomes an entirely new text. I wanted to indicate something of the variety and specificity of the analytic routes that I have taken in pursuing the principal themes outlined in Part I, and the way in which I have presented and organised the chapters seemed the best way to do this.

# PART TWO(1):
# TERMS OF ANALYSIS

# 4

# *Mediated politics, promotional culture and the idea of 'propaganda'*

## PRELIMINARY NOTE

*As earlier chapters have indicated, 'propaganda' is a term used regularly in political and public discussion of the media, but one that has a less marked and more intermittent usage as a term of theory and analysis in media research. One notable exception to this is in that work using the 'propaganda model' as outlined by Edward Herman and Noam Chomsky over twenty years ago (Herman and Chomsky, 1988), in which the general relations between the political system and the media system are defined in terms of the pervasiveness of propagandistic tendencies. An immediate obstacle to analytic use is the range of contrasting descriptive definitions and normative applications of the term, posing a considerable hazard to clear and coherent enquiry and often leading to assertive question-begging in the context of dispute and debate. The question of just how much propaganda has to be at work in the system for the 'propaganda model' to be 'proved' has been a further obstacle to clarity in empirical work using the model. On a relatively loose definition of propaganda, all media systems will show many examples of different kinds of promotionalism, sometimes involving the activities of government and corporate PR agencies 'placing' their accounts in ostensibly journalistic material. To see this as confirming the 'model' would simply be impressionistic, without firm criteria for scale and intensity. Corner (2003) develops a more comprehensive discussion of the model's limitations as a framework for research and argument, and I have looked further at the question of deceit in politics, in Corner (2010a).*

*Journalism is often a key feature of debates about propaganda since the work of journalists is rightly seen as constituting the most vital agency of public knowledge and therefore a very likely route, alongside more open and direct ones, for political and corporate promotionalism. The extent to which journalists' accounts, with differing degrees of intent, act as relay and amplification for elite promotional strategies (including strategies of deception) will vary from zero to very high levels indeed. Of course, one still active strand of journalism sets itself precisely against the strategies of elites to deceive and to 'cover up', causing continuing embarrassment, retractions, denials and also resignations by its activities. Assessing the overall prevalence of the 'propagandistic' in the journalism of a given country would require the definitional consistency mentioned earlier as well as an appropriate qualitative and quantitative research design.*

*However, arguments about journalism as propaganda carry a force of* critical re-naming *which calling government pamphlets propaganda, or advertising campaigns propaganda, does not. It is because journalism publicly presents itself as having very different aims and ethics from those of covert persuasion that the term carries impact in this context (as an exposing of real communicative identity), even in cases where it may finally be unjustified by the evidence.*

I want to question just how useful the concept of 'propaganda' is in the study of contemporary politics and media–political relations. Discussion of the Iraq war has shown an increased focus on 'propaganda techniques' and their influence, certainly in Britain and the United States, yet there remain continuing difficulties in deploying this term successfully as a tool of analysis and critique. There are also indications that use of it serves to divert attention away from some pressing questions about the pragmatics of modern political communication and about the ethics and expectations that can effectively be applied to political discourse and to political journalism. Here, the extensive development of political publicity in the context of societies where promotional activity is a defining characteristic not only of commercial but of public life has produced conditions very different from the ones in which ideas of propaganda gained their suggestiveness and force. By bringing critical attention to bear on the idea of propaganda itself, I think a number of issues about the character of contemporary politics as a discursive practice, some of them with an ancient lineage and some very modern, are revealed in sharper focus.

It is useful to note straight away that, despite its complex and shifting history as a descriptor, some aspects of which I shall refer to shortly, the term 'propaganda' carries a strong negative inflection in everyday use and in academic study. It is seen as a mode of 'bad communication', whatever qualifications and complexities are introduced into this judgement. It is for what it tells us, and more pointedly what it doesn't, about 'bad communication' and the possibilities and conditions for 'good communication', that I shall primarily be holding it to account here. Whatever my assessment on these matters, the general diagnosis that varieties of bad communication (i.e. communication that falls short not simply of the 'ideal' but of the standards of principle and practice that we can justly expect from those concerned – itself a matter of debate) are widely prevalent in modern politics is not something with which I would wish to disagree. I want my discussion to aid in getting greater clarity about what is at issue in pursuing this diagnosis.

My intention is first of all to look briefly at the history of propaganda as a word applied to the political realm, making some connections here with classical precepts and dispute concerning norms for political speaking. I then want to look at the framing conditions under which politics is conducted as, in part, a business of publicity and mediation, in the broader social and cultural settings of a routine promotionalism. This will allow a fuller engagement with how notions of propaganda and the propagandistic are positioned within the complex and controversial field of mediated political culture. Some direct attention to propaganda's discursive and symbolic character, as the deployment of what is often a strongly connotative discourse with a strategic instrumentalism and a widely assumed potential for 'effectiveness', will also be useful. From these analytic contexts, we can seek to identify what the particular set of assumptions, emphases and lacunae upon which the term is premised might suggest about the further development of critical understanding.


## SLIPPERY SEMANTICS

Nearly all writers on the idea of propaganda note the definitional difficulties caused by the fact that the term has a history of being used in neutrally descriptive, affirmative and negative ways. They also reflect on, and selectively support, a wide range of judgements both as to its scope as a classifier and about those other notions (e.g. 'communication', 'persuasion') against which it can, if sometimes only tortuously, be defined. Many commentaries cite the religious origins of marked usage in the 1622 *Sacra Congregatio de Propaganda Fide*, the Roman Catholic commission established by a Papal Bull. Here, the metaphorical sense of propagation, of sowing, is dominant and has a strongly positive inflection – the carrying forth of the word of God. However, since this Vatican initiative was from the start deployed strategically, in support of the Counter-Reformation and against Protestant interests, the term also necessarily developed a negative dynamics.[1] This became not so much a contingent negativity ('their propaganda, which is bad, against ours, which is good') as a categoric one, if only by implication, classifying as aberrant a kind of practice. This negativity has not, however, eliminated continuing positive use of the term, even in the twentieth century, when the dominant meaning (certainly in English) has been further reinforced in its negative inflection. Following the seventeenth-century model, positive usage has continued most strongly in contexts where highly defined doctrinal truths have been advanced. There is the classic instance of the Russian revolution, in which propaganda is openly claimed as a necessary category of practice in building and retaining popular support. It provides a point of elite dispute as to 'correct' strategies in relation to changing contexts and communicative options right through subsequent Soviet history. There is also the much-cited example of Nazi Germany, with Dr Goebbels becoming Reich Minister for Enlightenment and Propaganda in 1933 and, aware, among other precedents, of Soviet revolutionary achievements in this area, fully embracing the expanded ideas of publicity activities which this position involved. To take one current example, at the time of writing, the Communist Party of Great Britain's website (cpgb.org.uk) refers to 'propaganda' as an aim several times, noting that 'the party conducts agitation and propaganda on the basis of its central organ'. Thus, continuity with established religious and political traditions of affirmative usage is maintained, despite the risk this carries of apparent self-condemnation. Significantly, at one point on the website, the qualifying term 'principled propaganda' is used, indicating some awareness of this risk. It would, I think, be interesting to know how many national organisations world-wide, and of what kind, are still confident in using the term as a self-description of their publicity strategies.

However, as indicated, a negative dimension is built into most modern definitions, even though this dimension is sometimes tempered and even contradicted by recognition of necessity. Harold Lasswell, writing in 1934, noted that:

> Propaganda is surely here to stay; the modern world is peculiarly dependent upon it for the coordination of atomized components in times of crisis and for the conduct of large-scale 'normal' operations. It is equally certain that propaganda will in time be viewed with fewer misgivings. (Laswell, 1934, reprinted in Jackall (ed.) 1995: 22)

One can reflect on how wrong this last prediction turned out to be, certainly in terms of communicative practice openly carrying the label, either through self-definition or critical ascription. Like many early commentators, despite his awareness of the negative associations of the term, Lasswell works with an unhelpfully inclusive definition: 'Propaganda in the broadest sense is the technique of influencing human action by the manipulation of representations.' As so often in this period of concern about the growth of 'mass society' and the sources of 'influence' upon it, great emphasis is placed upon the idea of 'manipulation'. To achieve its force as a qualifier, this requires the possibility of 'un-manipulated' representation, and perhaps even a sense of such representation as an achieved norm, in ways that most current media and cultural theory would find problematic without much tighter specification, and possibly not even then. It is important to note, however, that 'manipulation' is not regarded as *unacceptable*, but mooted as an inevitable option in certain circumstances, following from the modern requirement for social co-ordination. This nervous relationship between propaganda, political order, public opinion and the psychology of mass society is a key matrix for the development of the idea in the earlier part of the twentieth century and it gives to the notion a strongly modernist resonance and anxiety. It becomes an idea in which a perceived need for benign mass persuasion is awkwardly joined by recognition of the threat posed by kinds of malign or 'enemy' propaganda and therefore the need to be vigilant towards it as a general form of discourse. We can say that it thus carries with it in many of these influential usages a sense of 'conflicted ethics', an unresolved tension making it an unstable term in contexts of analysis and certainly in contexts of dispute and polemic.

This dual character to the idea is usefully reviewed by Garth Jowett and Victoria O'Donnell in their synoptic study (Jowett and O'Donnell, 1992). Their own formulation, while cautious of the problems of previous attempts at definition, is one that pushes towards the negative meaning:

> Propaganda is the deliberate and systematic attempt to shape perceptions, manipulate cognitions, and direct behaviour to achieve a response that furthers the desired intent of the propagandist. (Jowett and O'Donnell, 1992: 4)

Here, it is cognitions rather than representations that are manipulated, providing a sharper and more direct sense of propaganda's psychological goals. More importantly still, propaganda is driven by self-interest; any expressed concern for the well-being of its addressees is secondary where not entirely fraudulent.

This definition, the authors claim, serves to distinguish propaganda from a 'free and open exchange of ideas' (1992: 8). Indeed, it is hard to see how it allows any space at all for a neutral meaning, let alone a positive one. In this regard, it contrasts sharply with the views of those academic commentators who have seen the retention and strengthening of a neutral meaning as desirable for the continued usefulness of the concept. Notable here is the leading British historian of propaganda, Philip Taylor, who has written extensively and influentially about the concept and various manifestations of the practice. In a 1992 lecture on the topic he invited his audience to:

> [A]ccept my suggestion that propaganda is a practical process of persuasion and, as a practical process, it is an inherently neutral concept. It must be defined by reference to intent. We should discard any notion of propaganda being 'good' or 'bad' and use these terms merely to describe effective or ineffective propaganda. (Taylor, 1992: 4)

Later, he observed: 'If I can do anything sensible with this lecture, I should therefore like to de-stigmatise the word itself and to re-establish 'propaganda', in a sense, to its pre-1914 meaning' (1992: 12). He finished provocatively by claiming that: 'What we really need is more propaganda not less. We need more attempts to influence our opinions and to arouse our active participation in social and political processes' (1992: 13).

Such an attempt to provide the term with a value-free, descriptive meaning not only faces the challenge of cancelling the intensive history of negative association but it also risks extending the category too far for its analytic good. Propaganda becomes a word of broad, indeed rather gestural, description rather than a term of analysis and critique. There are some advantages here, certainly, but such a shift also overlaps messily with other categories for describing communicative practice.

We can see this problem emerging quite clearly in a recent overview of the area by Nicholas O'Shaughnessy (2004).The author notes on his first page that 'This book differs from other books on propaganda in the elasticity it attributes to the term', an elasticity which extends to the category of 'virtuous propaganda' (the examples of anti-smoking and anti-drug publicity are given). However, a constant tug towards the negative, as inherent in the practice not merely contingent on the purpose, is displayed throughout, even in the subtitle of the book itself, 'Weapons of Mass Seduction'.

The punning reference to weapons brings me to a final point for this section. This is to note the extent to which debate about propaganda, and examples of it (real and hypothetical) relate to the conditions of war and relations between enemies rather than to internal conditions of political order. Some instances refer to both situations, most obviously in the case of material designed to reinforce pro-war attitudes, or at least good levels of morale, on the home-front. However, many notable examples of propaganda cited in the histories and overviews are of wartime use against an enemy, raising rather different questions of communicative ethics than those that might apply in other circumstances. This has not always been recognised in discussion of the term and its applications.

## PROPAGANDA AND THE ETHICS OF POLITICAL DISCOURSE

We can see how the term propaganda increases in its breadth of usage as a consequence of political modernism, including changing practices of government and administration. The more that public opinion figures as a factor in the conduct of political business, including the contest for party support and the management of foreign policy and warfare, the more widespread becomes the need to persuade, to gain acceptance if not agreement. Strategies of publicity and promotion are part of the attempt to retain informational control in conditions of greater political visibility for political managers, where even the negative informational regulator of censorship and methods of direct coercion may have been reduced in their scope and effectiveness. However, before looking in more detail at the conditions of modern political practice and the kinds of discursive convention they have generated, it is worth referring back to some of the earliest writing on the precepts that should guide political communication.

In his recent survey of the changing relationship between political communication and democracy, Gary Rawnsley notes the extent to which Plato and Aristotle, as well as other Greek thinkers, were concerned with the damage that certain kinds of oratory and rhetoric might do to the Athenian political system (Rawnsley, 2005).[2] The stated risk was of the displacement of reasoned argument in favour of oratorical appeal, although Rawnsley observes how social exclusion on grounds of unfitness to speak and, indeed unfitness to hear, was an underlying and constant core concern. He notes, apropos *On Rhetoric*:

> For Aristotle, communicating with the multitude is an important political act; and although he agrees with earlier Greek theorists that citizens must be expected to participate in public affairs, his exclusive definition of citizen remained consistent with Athenian practice. (Rawnsley, 2005: 30)

This combination, in a sense a mixture of democratic and elite theory, complicates our sense of the ethics of political communication at work in these classical texts. Aristotle's *On Rhetoric* is offered as an analytic guide to successful persuasion, of course, and Rawnsley notes the way in which passages like the following presage later propaganda strategies:

> [t]he rule of good taste is, that your style be lowered or raised according to the subject. On which account we must escape obser- vation in doing this, and not appear to speak in a studied manner, but naturally, for the one is of a tendency to persuade, the other is the very reverse; because people put themselves on their guard, as though against one who had a design upon them, just as they would against adulterated wine. (2005: 31)[3]

This is a way of speaking that will mislead the addressee into assuming that no designs are being made upon them when, in fact, the opposite is the case. It is a strategy of deceit for eliciting the wrong cognitive orien- tation from the listener.

However one judges the intentions behind the detailed account of communicative practice in *On Rhetoric*, as both advocacy of an approach and critical analysis of current conventions and practice, it clearly indicates the difficulties encountered in separating political speech from persuasive strategy, even at this early stage in the development of deliberative models.

In a close and perceptive study of modes of argumentation in propa- ganda, Douglas Walton cites Gustave Le Bon to illustrate a cynical, negative and much more recent approach to the gullibility of the 'masses' to such strategies (Walton, 1997). He notes Le Bon's beliefs that 'crowds' think in images and stories and are largely impervious to claims made on reasoning, making it an error to address them in reasoned terms. He quotes from Le Bon's 1896 study:

> We have shown that crowds do not reason, that they accept or reject ideas as a whole, that they tolerate neither discussion nor contradiction ... We have also seen that they only entertain violent and extreme sentiments, that in their case sympathy quickly aroused becomes adoration, and antipathy almost as soon as it is aroused is transformed into hatred. (Walton, 1997: 387, citing Le Bon, 1896)

Walton links this perception to his own interest in tracing varieties of *argumentum ad populum* in propagandist discourse, contrasting it with the protocols for the use of public reason in public dialogue put forward by John Rawls, among others (a relevant text here would be Rawls, 1996).

What we have here, as indeed much earlier in the Greek case, is a tension between the pragmatic (the real conditions for practice, often cynically described) and the normative (what is desirable, if only implicitly indicated). This tension can display itself in the form of a sharp, polemical contrast or it can appear as an ironic or satiric perspective in commentary attempting to make connections with both points of reference.

Among the most severe and influential critics of current communicational practice is Jürgen Habermas, whose own theories of communicative action and ideas of discourse ethics can be seen to exceed the commentaries of John Rawls in respect of the procedural strictness with which rationality and transparency of motive are to be placed at the centre of discursive exchange.[4] One of the requirements made upon discourse by Habermas is that 'participants must mean what they say', a rule that might immediately render much of contemporary professional political communication suspect. Habermas also regards as unacceptable all factors that work against the judgement of offered propositions being made solely according to rational criteria. He therefore places tight conditions both on the production of political discourse and on the terms of its reception. Within this context, all forms of promotional tactic, not just the strategies of deception seen as characteristic of propaganda, would seem to constitute a breach of rules. Whatever their severity, Habermas's criteria continue to be an important point of reference in thinking about the conditions of, and possibilities for, public discourse.

## PROPAGANDA IN PRAGMATIC CONTEXT

I suggested earlier that the growth of a culture of political publicity within the context of a more widespread promotionalism in public and commercial life complicates our sense of what propaganda is and the kind of ethical criteria appropriate to judging it. The increasing sensitivity of governments to public opinion (both a primary site for the publicity efforts of 'public relations' but also a point of reference to be taken into account in policy formation) and the increasing visibility of the political realm, through an intensified and continuous pattern of political news-making, have changed the nature of media–public relations. Much work in political communications has focused on these changes. In a suggestive survey of the conditions of what he terms the 'New Public', Leon Mayhew (1997) outlines the defining circumstances:

> In the New Public, communication is dominated by professional
> specialists. The techniques employed by these specialists are histor-
> ically rooted in commercial promotion, but beginning in the 1950s,
> rationalized techniques of persuasion born of advertising, market
> research, and public relations were systematically applied to politi-
> cal communication. (Mayhew, 1997: 4)

The communicative activities of the political sphere in these circumstances involve, among other things, the initiating of positive publicity
against that of (elite) competitors and the countering of negative publicity arising from accusations made by competitors and/or media
reporting.

This increased level of political publicity becomes the subject of comment itself during phases of notable scandal or perceived excess (as in
the running story of 'spin' and 'spin doctors' as new and threatening elements of political communication, a story to be found widely in coverage
of the British Labour government from 1997). However, there is also a
tendency for its routine character to be naturalised within the larger pattern of promotional behaviour as this pattern, in its many varieties,
extends further into everyday life.[5]

As we have seen, at the core of the idea of propaganda (and also of
the notion of 'spin') is a sense of deceitfulness and, although many commentators are keen to stress how propaganda cannot simply be equated
with lying, there is no doubt that the knowing circulation of untruths has
been a major element in cited examples of propaganda strategies, whatever else went into their devising and execution.

Hannah Arendt provides us with a provocative reflection on 'Lying in
Politics', an essay occasioned by the publication of the 'Pentagon
Papers', a vast body of official documents on the history and conduct of
the Vietnam war, which itself provided a monumental example of
bureaucratic deceit (Arendt, 1973). Building on her earlier writings, she
moves quickly to condemn the 'non-truthfulness' evident in the papers
but also wishes to set this within a broader, and in my terms, pragmatic,
sense of political deceit:

> Truthfulness has never been counted among the political virtues
> and lies have always been regarded as justifiable tools in political
> dealings. Whosoever reflects on these matters can only be sur-
> prised by how little attention has been paid, in our traditions of
> philosophical and political thought, to their significance. (Arendt,
> 1973: 10)

Arendt uses this sense of established practice (and its neglect by analysts) to qualify her judgement of those involved in producing the documents that provide the focus of her comments:

> Hence, when we talk of lying, and especially about lying among acting men, let us remember that the lie did not creep into politics by some accident of human sinfulness. Moral outrage, for this reason alone, is not likely to make it disappear. (Arendt, 1973: 11)

However, she wishes to distinguish between the 'ordinary lying' which has been endemic to politics since its beginning, and which is partly a function of its strongly dynamic orientation to the future and to matters of potential rather than to matters of fact, and what she calls 'organised lying'.[6] It is the latter, institutionally managed and professionally executed, form that she regards as introducing a new level of problem. For while ordinary lying by politicians sort mostly to 'conceal' (including by denial) certain facts within contingent circumstances, allowing them at least to be selectively known and perhaps fully 'revealed' at a later date, 'organised lying' seeks destruction rather than concealment. Its tendency is towards a major and permanent adjustment or displacement of reality and it is a tendency judged by Arendt to be on the increase.

## PROPAGANDA AS COMMUNICATIVE PRACTICE

In looking at the very broad range of practices, performances and texts that have been described, discussed and (frequently) condemned as propaganda, it is useful to identify some of the key components:

1. Lying. This is the deliberate construction and circulation of false information. Notwithstanding the problems, noted above, of assuming that this is an essential element of propaganda, it features in a high proportion of cited examples.
2. The withholding of information. This can be part of a more systematic policy of censorship when it is exercised by public authorities, and it clearly overlaps with lying where denial is involved, as it frequently is in politics. In general terms, it provides a context for propagandist strategies, rather than a component of them. Used more specifically, it is part of strategic selectivity.

3. Strategic selectivity. This is the omission from an account of important information that works against the viewpoint being promoted. It can also involve the inclusion of material of questionable relevance that lends support to the position being advanced (a practice whose analytic identification inevitably involves greater difficulties of judgement).

4. Exaggeration. This involves a distortive presentation either of positive or negative facts in a way that fits the case being propagandised. What does and does not count as 'distortion' will, of course, be open to dispute against other accounts.

5. Explicit or covert affective appeals to desire or to fear, exerting persuasive force outside the terms of any logical argument.

6. Use of a rhetoric of visual display and/or linguistic structure which seek to manage phatic contexts (e.g. of trust, of intimacy) and to organise the flow of meaning and of value in ways not arising out of the rational content of the communication.

It will be noted that some of the above practices are primarily matters of communicative organisation and some are primarily matters of performance, including textual performance. Quite clearly, points 3, 4, 5 and 6 are routine practices of publicity applied in a wide range of contemporary settings including commercial advertising, corporate and public sector publicity (including university brochures) and varieties of personal statement (e.g. CV summaries, interview performances). They are also central elements of political publicity. Practices 1 and 2 also have an extensive history of application, however in many cases (e.g. advertising, employee contracts) they are subject to legal sanctions in relation to the type and scale of the practice allowable.

Given that examples of propaganda may involve use of all six practices, do any of those listed above, either together or in combination, constitute a sufficient case for description of what is produced as 'propaganda'? It cannot usefully be argued that any of the practices is sufficient to use the description, since this would extend the idea of propaganda to cover virtually all forms of publicity and promotional discourse. As I noted earlier, some might welcome such a sweepingly inclusive definition, but extensive overlapping with other routine categories brings problems of analytic and argumentative usage. In fact, only practice 1, lying, has enough discriminating potential to allow the category of propaganda to be sustained as a clear subgroup of such discourse. And since lying itself is not necessarily propagandistic, practice 1 might be seen only (but still controversially) as a core factor, requiring combination with practice 3 to provide the sufficient conditions for such a category.

It might be objected that to assess the definition and application of the term by primary reference to factors of communicative practice is a mistake, and that contextual circumstances need to be brought into this judgement. Of these, two are prominent. First of all, the factor of motive, which a number of commentators bring into their core definition and, secondly, the factor of consequence (e.g. 'harmful') which has been less often brought into definitional discussion, chiefly because the problems it raises of grounding a judgement in adequate evidence are even greater than those raised by using motive.

Of those who refer to motive (for instance, Jowett and O'Donnell), a generalised rather than case-specific negative judgement can follow from the perception that the interests of the source rather than the addressees are primary. But, disregarding the difficulty of making clear assessments of this in some cases, what kind of analytic differentiation is achieved by *grounding* 'propaganda' in the idea of self-interested discourse, when the forms of such discourse have a long, varied history (connecting with the rich and broad histories of social subjectivity and of deception) and are now extensive and legitimated throughout the corporate, public and private spheres?

## PROPAGANDA AS SYMBOLIC PRACTICE

We can extend the terms of an analysis of propaganda as discourse to raise questions about its distinctive symbolic character, that is to say the way in which its extra-rational elements, its forms of emotional appeal, are projected. What can be said about the connotational strategies of propaganda and their production of those deep, affective responses by appeal to what Roland Barthes saw as the politically crucial meaning-systems of 'myth'?[7]

The employment of visual portrayal is often seen as a major factor here, as it is in many of Barthes' own analyses and in the classic literature of propaganda studies, where posters and films figure prominently. Pictorial forms 'condense' the distortive energies of propaganda. They can do this by offering obvious (and satisfying) caricatures of persons and actions, perhaps self-consciously gross in their appeal to prejudice. Other stylings can be more ambiguous; many Soviet posters for example display an iconography at once both physically idealist (bodies, faces, postures etc.) and selectively 'realist' in relation to detail and context (clothing, everyday objects, workplace settings etc.). They can also use photographic portrayals that deploy the evidential realism of the medium to various kinds of rhetorical effect, possibly using fake images, image combinations (including photo-montage) and misleading captions and contexts to this purpose.

We can take two examples. Let us imagine a photograph from a university prospectus. A young man in shirtsleeves and sunglasses sits on an expansive lawn reading a book and taking notes from it into a pad placed on the ground. Handsome old buildings are in view in the background and an abstract modernist sculpture is in front of them. Shafts of sunlight come through the branches of surrounding trees, creating a pleasant pattern of light and shade. Other young people can be seen sitting or lying on the grass in mid-distance, sometimes alone and sometimes gathered in groups apparently engaged in conversation. The caption says 'Between lectures'. Here, a certain ideal and promotional view of the university is offered. The scene depicted may be variously related to the truth (this is the only patch of lawn on the entire campus, the attractive old buildings are in fact those of an insurance company with premises close to the university, the actual incidence of students taking notes from books in situations like this is so tiny as to be insignificant). The mood of the photograph combines with its contents to project a positive sense of the 'typical' in a reader unacquainted with the real circumstances. Does such a reader recognise that the genre of the image is promotional and read it accordingly, with a degree of suspicion, or do they engage with it as fundamentally realist, as imparting reliable information about student life at this institution, extending even to dominant weather conditions? It is likely, I think, that they recognise its publicity goals, given the protocols of reading that are encouraged in those who live in a society permeated with forms of publicity. However, this recognition may not stop them from finding the image attractive and being moved, if only slightly, towards a more positive view of the institution. Is this symbolic interaction a propagandist event? I believe it might well be considered such, even if clearly a 'gentle' example. There has not been a direct appeal to rational processing, there has been some implied distortion of the real conditions and circumstances of the institution itself and of institutional life. An affective impact (perhaps decisive for later action) has been achieved.

The second example is a local poster for an extreme right-wing political party. The image is a drawing of two black teenagers, depicted to distort their faces and bodies. They look at a white girl passing by on the pavement. Their faces show an expression that mixes hatred with lust.

The poster says 'Dirty Streets: Time for a Clean-Up' and encourages voting for an indicated party at the forthcoming local elections. This is a direct and racist appeal to prejudice. It does not entirely assume prior views on the topic, but its communicative style seems premised on the strengthening (into action) of existing negative views. This is in contrast to my first example, which contained no propositional content at all and which was designed primarily to encourage a positive view, whether related to prior disposition or not.

If we wanted to call the second example propaganda but the first one not, we could do this by referring to a number of primary criteria. We could, for instance, make reference to an ethical judgement about communicative ends, incontrovertibly bad in the second example. A rather similar criterion could be offensiveness, sharply present in the second example both in relation to the metaphor of 'dirt' and the mode of depiction of the youths. We might try to differentiate in terms of the degree of certifiable distortion of physical reality, clearer in the second example. My view, however, is that these options do not present us with a clear and satisfactory way of distinguishing between the two in terms of an idea of propaganda as symbolic practice, even though we will have no difficulty distinguishing between them on other grounds.

Of the second example, we might ask the same question we asked of the first: how far are 'readings' of it likely to be made in the knowledge that its primary communicative purpose is persuasion and not 'neutral' information? Some of those who encounter it will see it as an example of racist propaganda. Others will find themselves variously in alignment with the political and social sentiments it expresses, and may even regard the scene it so distortively depicts as having an underlying 'real-ist' credibility. However, that the communication is offering a viewpoint, that it is aligned to a *position*, seems likely to be widely recognised, if only because of the explicit connection with an act of political choice. The social 'truth' it may appear to offer is framed within a discourse of political judgement, even if that judgement is seen by some to be beyond dispute.

The symbolic dimension to propagandistic discourse is often elaborately developed, the strategy of connotation and appeal sometimes relying extensively on cliché conventions, but also capable of invention and wit. What it cannot do, however, is get us very far in defining propaganda as a specific form of 'bad communication'.

## CONCLUSION

I have suggested in this article that the notion of 'propaganda', although it serves to direct us to some of the major, continuing issues in media–political relations, is by itself inadequate to the needs of analysis. Indeed, attempts to work with it as a central term of critique may serve to distract conceptual attention away from areas most in need of scrutiny.

Coming strongly into use in the first part of the twentieth century, propaganda is a term embedded within a modernist perspective on society and on communication. Shifts in the character of public discourse and the huge growth in the scale and variety of mediation as a constituent of political and social life have reduced its theoretical cogency. In particular, the growth of a 'promotional culture', in which forms of strategic publicity permeate public, corporate and even private life has produced a symbolic context now far removed from the particular psycho-discursive and socio-discursive settings in which the term was powerfully employed. The play of power over meaning is now routinely exercised in ways too complex and subtle to be captured by the idea.

The urgent requirement now is for more attention to a critical ethics of public communication, including of public relations and of political claims-making, within an improved understanding of the pragmatic circumstances of practice, including those which encourage constraint, evasion and distortion.[8]

At the same time, we also need to pay more attention to what Arendt called 'organised lying'. If the strategic projection of positive perspectives is an inevitable factor of political debate and of modern government's requirement to conduct 'permanent campaigning' and 'damage limitation' in a context of intensified media visibility, the degree to which calculated deception forms part of this needs close and regular scrutiny. Just what standards should prevail in the conduct of public discourse is an issue that requires a more clear-headed and focused attention than it has received so far. Only in relation to this kind of attention can clearer protocols for political journalism be established. Being called a propagandist may be worse than being called a publicist, but being called a liar establishes the ethical stakes with a useful clarity and resonance. If, as I have suggested, the concept of propaganda is too crude to catch at the more stealthy, partial ways in which discourses of power are at work in culture, it may also, in its very uncertainty of criteria, lack the bold directness to identify the 'organised lie' as the continuing central problem at the heart of 'bad communication' and 'bad politics'. Propaganda is an idea that media–political analysis has now to think beyond.

## NOTES

1   See Jackall (1995) for a range of historical accounts, including introductory comments on the first 'propagandists'.

2   An illuminating and more detailed account of precept and practice in Athenian political discourse is given in Jon Hesk (Hesk, 2000).

3   Citing Aristotle in the 1872 edition.

4   The most influential text is perhaps Habermas (1992), but the emphasis on the discursive conditions for democracy is found extensively in Habermas's writing, receiving a degree of revision and consolidation in Habermas (1997).

5   A good, earlier account is Andrew Wernick (1991).

6   Her earlier writing on this topic provides a theoretical context for the commentary on the Pentagon papers. See Hannah Arendt (1961), reprinted in Arendt (1993).

7   Most celebratedly in Barthes (1957), reprinted in English in Barthes (1973).

8   The scale and nature of the influence exerted by discourses of corporate and political promotionalism, including those discourses that resort to strategic deceit, upon the discourses of journalism, continues to be a focus of international media research. Here, debate about the standards of integrity (both ideal and achieved) of journalism as a form of public knowledge is an important strand of the evaluation and also, for some, a marker against which 'propaganda' can be placed as the 'bad other'. Of course, promotional impact upon journalism can take many forms, ranging from wholesale reproduction of publicity materials (perhaps within an explicitly normative framework) to various kinds of influence introduced more quietly into selection and treatment. Once again, across this spectrum of practice 'propaganda' quickly becomes over-stretched as a label for a type of 'badness'.

# 5

## 'Ideology': a note on conceptual salvage

### PRELIMINARY NOTE

*A number of my comments in the earlier chapters have indicated how issues thrown up by the term 'ideology' remain fundamental, complex and subject to varieties of confusion and contradiction. This is so even though use of the term in media research is now far less marked than two decades ago, when it seemed to fit productively within Marxian perspectives on power, values and consciousness, perspectives that have since been subject to extensive dispute, revision and diverse kinds of theoretical displacement (Carroll, 1998 is a vigorous survey in the context of ideas about 'mass art'). It is worth noting again how the term relates to the idea of 'propaganda', discussed in the preceding chapter. Those who hold to a theory of ideology will generally have less need to use 'propaganda' as a significant term of analysis, since their perspectives already take into account the idea of the structural domination of values and meanings in elite interests. In this context, 'propaganda' as an idea about communicative distortion is to a large extent already 'covered' by the general approach, while the focus which 'propaganda' brings to bear on certain kinds of distortive practice as breaches of communicative integrity may seem too limited in a situation perceived as one in which dominant meanings routinely permeate both social and subjective space and the kinds of communicative practice that can occur within them.*

*Attempts to use 'ideology' as a term of critical analysis have often fallen across or between three inclinations. First of all, there is an inclination to make it more conceptually ambitious and critically inflected than its relatively simple descriptive use in the social sciences (where it is effectively a synonym for 'body of ideas and beliefs'). Secondly, there is the inclination not to allow its critical usage to be about the systematic circulation of 'falsity' as against 'truth', since this line of approach (e.g. 'false consciousness') may quickly seem too neatly dualistic and naïve a way of engaging both with the politics and the social relations of knowledge and of forms of knowing. Thirdly, when taking account of the first two inclinations above, there is a requirement to avoid generalising the term into so pervasive and inevitable a dimension of human social existence that its critical usefulness in focused political argument is diminished.*

*Writing about my arguments in a recent book chapter, John Downey (Downey, 2008) provides a clear and thoughtful counter, putting the case for renewal and 'repair'. Drawing extensively and suggestively on the work of Axel Honneth (including Honneth, 1995) concerning ideas of 'recognition' and 'misrecognition', Downey sees the possibility of new forms of institutional analysis and of intersubjective psychology combining with developments in the tradition of critical theory to make the term newly useful. He reproves me for what he sees as my over-eager move to provide an 'obituary'. I am not entirely convinced by his plan of conceptual restoration, but I take his arguments as a serious and original contribution to the re-thinking of this whole area and a justified correction to my more polemically negative judgements.*

Anyone writing the history of ideas in media research over the last 30 years will note a number of shifts of emphasis. The more they focus on work following the agenda of Cultural Studies, the more they will notice the odd career of the concept of 'ideology'. From being the most important idea in several strands of enquiry, the point around which theory and method gather, it moves quite swiftly to a marginal position, often disappearing altogether. Yet in many studies it is still possible to trace, in the working assumptions about power and in the way a topic is positioned for analysis, the contours of where ideology confidently used to be. One might say that the hole left by the shrinking or disappearance of ideology has not entirely been filled in by newer ideas and terminology. Notwithstanding these indications of conceptual absence, however, the word itself can still be found in the research literature. A fair amount of instances are of what could be called 'pretentious' usage. There is no clear argument taking the term beyond a rough synonym for 'group belief' or 'political perspective', but an attempt to connote some of the term's former theoretical gravitas, as indicating categories of deficient understanding in need of critique and if possible replacement, is nevertheless made.

One immediate explanation for the shift from centre stage to the wings might be found in the larger fate of Marxism as a body of critical thought across the same period. As Marxism became weakened, both by revisions and by critique, as a way of thinking about contemporary economic and social organisation, so the key idea within a dominant strand of Western Marxist thinking was displaced too. In media research, the displacement was either in favour of newer terms of critique, placing a less severely cognitive emphasis on texts and their powers over subjectivity (the chronically imprecise notion of 'discourse' has been found a useful substitute by some) or in favour of a return to the established and more descriptive categories of social science.

In broad terms, it seems to me this explanation is sound. However, it fails fully to address the internal complications that the idea developed. In this brief note of comment I want to re-examine the debate about ideology with a focus on argument in the 1990s, a period when the idea is recognised to be in deep trouble, and only briefly alluding to its earlier history, well documented elsewhere (see, for instance, Larrain 1979).

## REVISING IDEOLOGY

Writing about ideology has frequently had a strongly revisionist character. It has been concerned to revise the concept in such a way as to eliminate what are regarded as unproductive or erroneous modes of usage. Regularly, the concept has been subjected to close scrutiny and attempted rehabilitation in the hope that it can be made fitter for work. Across most, if not all, the phases of revision, we can trace a movement from the epistemic to the discursive, and a movement from an emphasis on ideology as an entity to the ideological as a dimension of a process. There has also been a less marked tendency towards talking of 'ideologies' rather than of 'ideology', a pluralising that carries implications for the way in which the word can be used as a term of critique.

The first stage of revision, forming a backdrop to the more recent debates that are my main concern here, was the shift away from the idea that ideology was, largely if not exclusively, a matter of discrete falsehoods and erroneous belief. This idea was frequently seen to follow from the application of the concept of 'false consciousness' even if the concept did not strictly entail it. Media research has very little work using ideology in this earlier sense because its growth during the late 1960s and 1970s occurred at the same time as the more complicated Althusserian view of ideology was gaining ground both in the Arts and Humanities (Althusser, 1971 is a key text). This view focused on what were seen as the deep and systemic forms of misrecognition at work in everyday consciousness within capitalism, a misrecognition that served dominant economic interests and that both reflected and reproduced inequalities. It was a development of the term beyond much of the earlier Marxist usage. It also went well beyond that merely descriptive, pluralised usage ('body of ideas peculiar to a specific group') which had been common for many years in the social sciences and which still offers a source of conflation and confusion with Marxist versions.[1]

The shift from identifiable 'falsehoods' to more complex and systemic ideas of imaginary relations and patterns of misperception was not by itself a shift away from the terms of a *political* epistemology, although it prepared the ground for later movement. Questions of what was true and what was false were still implicated (sometimes over-assertively in the deployment of the vocabulary of 'ideology' versus 'science'). Within the Althusserian model (see, again, Althusser, 1971) the media were prominently placed – performing the function of an ideological state apparatus. This was part of a critical account in which emphasis on the mystificatory mechanisms of everyday (mis)understanding had to a significant degree displaced the earlier Marxist emphasis on economic determination. What appeared to need the most urgent critical engagement in societies with developed liberal democratic systems were the subjective rather than the objective dimensions of dominance and subordination.[2]

The next shift involved the taking of this more complex idea of ideology and the expansion of it in terms of its discursive features. Perhaps a useful gloss can be got from John Mepham's highly influential essay, 'The Theory of Ideology in Capital', published in 1972:

> The conditions for the production of ideology are the conditions for the production of a language and can only be understood by reference to the structure of forms and social practices which systematically enter into the production of particular concepts and propositions in that language ... we are not aware of these systematically generative interconnections because our awareness is organised through them. (Mepham, 1972: 17)

Ideology has become all-pervasive and regulative of thought to the point where sharp questions about its identification as a specifically political phenomenon, let alone its attempted eradication, are raised. The conditions have been established, though not here proposed, to start letting go of the idea that it is a historically specific 'bad thing' at all (either as a perspective or as a process), and to develop the idea that it is an inevitable level of conditionality on consciousness or some over-arching framing for consciousness. In a review essay, Joe McCarney (1976) noted the problem:

> The concept of ideology itself, once cut off from its material base, begins a new career. It comes to represent a free-floating system of thought, on a par with all the other disembodied systems so dear to idealists. (McCarney, 1976: 31)

McCarney's account of a 'new career' proved accurate. The general trend was towards a philosophical refinement of the concept beyond both a direct application in substantive political argument and employment in practical analysis. Once considered too crude a concept for analytic use, 'ideology' often became too big to move, and increasingly uncertain in evaluative implications (was it 'bad' or not?)

## Retrieval: three accounts from the 1990s

John B. Thompson's (1990) study, *Ideology and Modern Culture*, was a major attempt to revise the term for social analysis. Thompson's perspective and address are essentially those of a sociology wanting to emphasise afresh the importance of the media and of mediation. This sometimes makes for an awkward relationship between the terms of his account and the established literature of media research. After all, media research had been trying to pay attention to the socio-symbolic forms of mediation for a good quarter of a century before Thompson's book appeared, so his sense of new horizons may not have come across quite so strongly to readers within this field. Nevertheless, his approach has a boldness and clarity of exposition that have made it a regular point of reference. His revisionary aims are made quite clear in his introduction. Here, he notes that there have been, in recent writings, two kinds of broad response to the 'ambiguous heritage' (1990: 5) of the concept. One response has been to attempt to 'tame' it, an approach that has resulted in a greater usage of the neutral, non-critical meaning of the term (a meaning convergent with that found in conventional social science enquiry). The second response, Thompson notes, has been to dispense with the idea altogether. At the time he was writing, this would certainly seem to describe correctly what was happening, if on the whole quietly, in a good deal of media research.

Thompson wishes to retain and develop the idea as a 'critical' term and to pursue a more integrated approach to its application. Such an ambition comes out clearly in his comment that it is his intention to 'bring the analysis of ideology into a domain of conceptual and methodological issues which is of more general scope and significance' (1990: 7). This will, among other things, produce a different kind of analysis from that of much previous mass communication enquiry. Many studies, characterised as 'internalist', have 'tended to focus largely or exclusively on the structure and content of media messages and have tried to "read off" the consequences of these messages' (1990: 24). The alternative

model will be one that emphasises interpretation, appropriation, audience activity – in short, the dynamics of the mediation process within
'intersubjective space' (1990: 69).

Once again, there is something odd about this sociological perspective when viewed in the context of the previous decade of media study.
For what Thompson is in fact advocating is very close to that 'turn
to the audience' which slowly worked its way through media research
following the publication of David Morley's *Nationwide* study of viewer
reception ten years earlier (Morley, 1980). It was precisely part of
Morley's project to combine elements from an established sociology
of audiences with elements from a model of ideology as discursive
action. If anything, the problems it encounters and honestly explores in
relation to the question of ideological position and ideological transfer
(see also Morley, 1981) were to contribute unintentionally to a more
general wariness about use of the term both in textual and in reception
studies.

As a conceptual and methodological manifesto, Thompson's account
has most value in its lucid review of the broader intellectual history of
the idea and its problems. His elaboration of a typology of the devices by
which meaning can be strategically articulated to power (e.g. dissimula-
tion, unification, displacement, fragmentation) also has suggestive force
for all analytic thinking on this topic. But it is hard, finally, to see it as
significantly moving things on either at the level of general theory or
local application.

Thompson's book was a contribution to critical social theory. One
year later, Terry Eagleton's *Ideology* (Eagleton, 1991) emerged from the
rather different tradition of critical literary theory. The aim, like
Thompson's, was rehabilitation against the current of criticism and
declining usage. More strongly than Thompson, in a way that perhaps
reflects differences between the intellectual climates of social research
and of literary studies, Eagleton also saw postmodernism and post-
structuralism as working to discredit use of the term. Eagleton is less
concerned to promote its employment in specific kinds of academic
analysis (there is very little, for instance, on the question of its use in literary studies), and more interested in 'giving the term back' to political
debate.

The primary use of 'ideology' is seen to lie in its capacities for political discrimination:

> The force of the term ideology lies in its capacity to discriminate
> between those power struggles which are somehow central to

a whole form of social life and those which are not. (Eagleton, 1991: 8)

The phrasing 'somehow central' strikes a note frequently heard throughout the book – a crucial vagueness compromises the propositional force of what appears to be a tough argument.

Of the many discussions of Eagleton's account, one of the most illuminating (and funny) is that by Mark Edmundson (1994), in an article on the problems of cultural criticism more generally. A passage from it is worth quoting in full:

> Eagleton's criticisms of his Marxist predecessors are vaguely post-structuralist: he thinks he's locating significant epistemological fault lines in their writings. Often these are points where expression and intention – or the figurative and the literal – seem to part company. When it comes to his postmodern contemporaries, however, Eagleton is inclined to excoriate them for leading readers towards relativism. In other words, he uses something like a post-structuralist stance to discredit the canonical Marxist writers and – implicitly – a classic epistemology to undermine the postmodern types. Though Eagleton does find things to applaud about the majority of the figures he considers, the most energetic impulse in the book is, if not dismissive, at least severely critical. (Edmundson, 1994: 223)

Edmundson goes on to express his surprise at the way in which, following this succession of criticisms, Eagleton moves towards terms of reconstruction:

> The conclusion begins by promising to summarise Eagleton's own views on how ideology ought to be understood. To this task he devotes three dramatically vacuous pages. The nadir comes when Eagleton admits that 'it is doubtful that one can ascribe to ideology any *invariable* characteristics at all'. Not much later, England's premier Marxist literary critic signs off. (Edmundson, 1994: 223)

The book is finally characterised as a very odd gesture of defiance, rather than a project of inquiry. This is the only way in which Edmundson can make sense of the idea of 'publishing a book now in which ideology survives as a concept, based on the writer's willingness to trash its every manifestation, but without giving it up' (Edmundson, 1994: 223).

I have drawn on Edmundson's discussion because I think it exposes very neatly some of the problems encountered by Eagleton's approach to 'retrieval'. A key factor here is the degree of criticism which each version of ideology in turn receives (and I think Edmundson is right about the contradictory terms in which this is applied). Another factor seems to lie in the relaxed inclusiveness with which Eagleton treats radically differing perspectives in his occasional summarising comments. The typical move is, having noted the limitations of a particular version of the idea, historical or current, then to note how with qualifications (sometimes heavy), it has a certain usefulness when combined with others. The difficulty if not impossibility of ever using it in analysis or argument in such a combined way does not appear as a problem.

Eagleton also fails to recognise the strength of the arguments, not just the political prejudice, ranged against the concept. He finishes the book by attempting to give the idea a final, irrefutable validation by reference to practical political struggles and the transformation of consciousness. But it is not made at all clear how the concept of ideology itself is instrumental in such transformation, let alone why other accounts and concepts from political sociology or psychology are not up to the job of analysing this process. For the reader in search of consolidation and development, these entertaining freehand observations do not add up to much.

The third contribution I want to consider comes towards the end of the 1990s. Again, it is a book-length treatment, van Dijk's *Ideology* (van Dijk, 1998). Van Dijk launches himself on the road to a comprehensive ('fully fledged') theory of ideology aware of the history of confusion and failure lying behind him. In his introduction, he informs the reader that this history will be used as a departure point for his own arguments and ideas, for the development of his own 'new notion of ideology' (1998: 8). In what does this 'new notion' consist?

Van Dijk calls his approach 'multidisciplinary' – it will bring together ideas from philosophy, political studies, sociology, the cognitive sciences and linguistics. It will employ a triangular conceptualisation of cognition–society–discourse in order to avoid the various kinds of reductionism that he thinks have beset other approaches. The relation to discourse he sees as vital but this relation decidedly does not amount to reducing ideology to discourse. A social, particularly a 'social interests', dimension and a 'mental' dimension need always to be taken into account too. Ideologies (the pluralisation, as always, is significant) are seen to provide the 'basis of the social representations shared by members of a group' (1998: 8). Perhaps most importantly, and fully in line with the plural usage, ideology is not to be regarded as a pejorative term. It describes a commonly found dimension of situated social speech and action (though not *all* speech and action) which may or may not be implicated in the reproduction of dominant power relations. Robustly defiant in face of the idea's long history of variously signalling something amiss, van Dijk feels that this no more takes the critical edge off the use of the term than the non-pejorative use of 'power' precludes analysis of power abuse (1998: 11).

It is interesting that van Dijk starts out by reversing the move made both by Thompson and Eagleton by arguing explicitly *for* the neutrality of the concept, rather than opposing it. In fact, this is a quite a rare move across the whole of the recent literature (although Larrain, 1996 finds both negative and neutral usages independently valuable). In terms of discourse analysis, a good contrast can be made with the strongly pejorative account of Fairclough (1995). We might immediately ask, how does van Dijk's usage differ from a) the 'inflated' model of ideology criticised by McCarney in the 1970s, and b) the neutral use of the term already present in the social science literature?

My view is that van Dijk's usage cannot be completely separated from these two versions – the first by the late 1990s a 'historical' version, the second still current. However, one difference from the 'inflated' model is that although he presents us with a quite pervasive ideology, he does not present us with a unified system or an oppressive system, one that has as its primary effect the closing down of agency.

What about the connection with the existing, neutral use of the idea? Perhaps the key difference here is the emphasis placed on the complexity of the cognition–society–discourse relationship rather than the abstractable content of 'beliefs' and 'opinion'. This is very much more a process rather than an entity model, to use my earlier terms.

Despite his emphasis on the development of a 'general theory', it is hard to see precisely in what such a theory would consist, given the sheer range of variables which van Dijk wishes to consider across both the macro and micro levels of his ideological analysis. His account directs us to the socially contingent nature of discourse and the devices by which that contingency is a constitutive factor in particular communicative acts. This is not, by itself, more than the re-stating of a commonplace. Inclusive and exclusive criteria of social identity, unreflectively held core values, prejudices, partiality of perception based on objective economic position, self-interest and opportunism will be present in many forms of communication ranging from casual conversation to academic books, never mind about political debate and conflict.

In moving further than this, van Dijk confronts two problems, a problem of identification and a problem of linkage. The problem of identification concerns how he intends to distinguish between ideological and non-ideological components of any discourse under scrutiny. Since, in his view, ideology is not necessarily part of domination, it cannot be identified clearly in terms of its thematic character and direction (its 'thought content'). There are then two broad possibilities – that it is identified in terms of its discursive characteristics, which risks making it essentially a formalist category, or that it is identified by the particular mode of its economic or political articulation with interest-group structures and practices. Here, we move on to the second problem (linkage), only to be returned to the first (identification). For the plotting of any such linkage will require drawing on broader, pre-established historical and sociological knowledge. It will then require the applying of this knowledge 'down' upon a given specific discursive instance in order to identify its ideological character. But the precise way in which the broader knowledge will guide the local reading is not at all clear. Taken together, the two problems present yet another version of that established conundrum of interpretative circularity in Humanities and Social Science enquiry – the reading of texts from contexts and contexts from texts. Van Dijk's chapter (Chapter 28) in which a practical analysis is demonstrated, a study of racist commentary, works illuminatingly within this interpretative circle, but it does not show its key concept able to break out of it. It is also interesting, in view of the book's general thesis, that this example is of a negatively assessed social belief, widely seen as dependent among other things on false information. Perhaps examples of 'good' ideology are harder to find after all, or simply less analytically interesting?

The overall character of van Dijk's treatment is that of a scrupulous and intensive survey of the relationships between social conditions, mental frameworks and communicative practice. With its sustained attention to matters both of cognition and of language, it is a genuinely original set of analytic reflections on the sociality of communication. However, it stops short of being a 'theory of ideology' or of being a clear guide to its local analysis. At neither macro nor micro levels can it achieve anything like the prescriptive closure, the degree of propositional precision, to be applicable in these ways. At one level, it elaborately confirms the idea that communication and indeed perception occur within the shaping variables of social structure and social group identity, however much they may attempt to transcend these (or create the impression of having done so). At another level, it charts the complexity of this linkage with a new attention to questions of cognition.

## IDEOLOGY AND MEDIATION

In examining the use of 'ideology' in media research, we need to note not just its broad theoretical profile and the problems this poses, but the way in which it fitted within and shaped the distinctive analytical concerns of the field. For a period of about ten years from the early 1970s and then, with less confidence, for a further few years, the attempt to identify and explore the operations of ideology was a central part of the broader enquiry into discourses of mediation. It raised political questions about textuality and audience subjectivity complementary to those more technical ones posed by semiotics. In effect, two separate structuralist projects were combined to produce a framework for plotting both the political identity of signs and sign relations themselves.

Here, the theoretically dense developments inspired by Althusser often had reference to the highly influential, and much more impressionistic, commentaries of Roland Barthes in *Mythologies* (1973). The notion of 'myth' was effectively another way, one more anthropologically resonant, aesthetically rich and less directly Marxist, of thinking about ideological process.

We can perhaps identify four main foci for media researchers in pursuit of the mechanisms of ideology. There was a focus on narrative structure; on the use of the visual image; on linguistic organisation and on the conventions of dramatic realism. In certain media artefacts, all of these were found combined. In each of them a potent degree of systematic misperception was seen to be encouraged by devices of, for instance, implication, concealment, diversion and closure.

Within the semiotic ideological critique developed by the Birmingham Centre for Contemporary Cultural Studies, and particularly by Stuart Hall, the notion of 'preferred meaning' became widely used (see for instance Hall, 1973). Initially a term about textual power, and then only later applied to audience analysis, this notion indicated how media texts tried to get across a politically strategic meaning without seeming to do so. Two rather different contexts for this process might be the apparent impartiality of television news reporting and the apparent political innocence and 'openness' of popular drama and situation comedy. In both cases, the argument went, attempted closures around dominant values and perceptions were indicated by mechanisms of 'preferral' in the text (e.g. matters of vocal inflection, of editing and combination, of narrative resolution, of thematic turn). 'Preferred meaning' (or 'preferred reading') was a term which critical media studies frequently employed when investigating the issue of ideological transfer.

Its indications of discursive sleight-of-hand and, importantly, of a routine effectiveness, served it well, in the absence of any clearer theorisation. They also served to deflect attention from the messy mix of textual, cognitive and sociological questions which were often being begged (see Williams, 1994).

The idea of ideologically generated 'preferral' was essentially a text-analytic notion. Although Morley (1980) is suggestive in exploring qualitative audience data, it appeared much easier to identify those elements of a media text that might cue socially significant meanings and resonances than to identify the success of this process in what audience members said. The idea of 'preferral' did not really survive a double-shift in critical media studies. This brought a more sustained and empirical focus on audiences at about the same time as the whole idea of ideological reproduction was being revised and then undercut by post-Marxist, including post-modern, currents (Sparks, 1996 gives an excellent account of the relation of cultural theory to politics during this period).

## SOME CONCLUSIONS

I have looked briefly at three quite recent attempts, from different inter-disciplinary positions, to render the notion of ideology fitter for use. Where does this leave us?

First of all, it would seem clear that around the idea of 'ideology' there is no coherent theoretical scheme that can effectively guide the analysis of the ways in which meanings and values relate to material interests. The term can be used plurally as a synonym for 'belief', 'social group norms' and so on, without any evaluative judgements, as in the continuing vein of social science writing that employs it. It can be used negatively in political dispute to indicate thought content or frameworks of understanding found to be unacceptably partial and compromised (e.g. 'bourgeois ideology', 'capitalist ideology', less often 'communist ideology'). It can also be used to describe the varying relation of consciousness and ideas to material conditions, a use that can be critical or neutral and follow either idealist or materialist tendencies (perhaps sometimes a combination of the two).

There is no doubt that in the 1970s the term served productively to open up issues concerning structure and agency. It helped pose questions about the role of the symbolic in sustaining relations of domination. But it was unable to support further development of these questions. In addition to its 'inflation', a growing problem for its use in media research was the way in which it suggested a theoretically precise grasp of mediation processes that was simply not present. Paradoxically, it finally worked to limit further exploration of the very factors − for instance, the linkage of media systems and practices to the resources for popular understanding and action − to which it drew attention.

Does the idea still have potential? Can some combination of eclecticism, revision and innovation make it newly productive? I think not. It would be better to hope that we are coming to the end of attempts at repair. We might then be in better shape to pursue further research and argument about the interconnections of meaning, value, social structure and power.

## NOTES

1   Larrain (1996) looks at variations in Marxist usage in respect both of negative and neutral forms and singular and plural forms, citing the works of Marx, Lenin, Gramsci, Laclau and Hall to make his points, which include those about internal inconsistency. Hall (1983) is a reappraisal of the idea of 'distortion' implicit within many uses of the term. He too notes 'severe fluctuations' in Marx's own employment.
2   A view contested from political economy perspectives. See, for instance, the critical commentary in Murdock and Golding (1977).

# 6

## Public knowledge and popular culture: spaces and tensions

### PRELIMINARY NOTE

*Discussion of the nature and relationship of the 'public' and the 'private' has been a feature of media research for some time, with 'private' both indicating the personal sphere and also, in some usage, the sphere of market-based institutions and activities. I wanted to relate the vulnerable idea of the 'public', as a civic commonality, to ideas of the 'popular' as these have been changed both in their grounding and their articulation by the cultural industries, which produce popular products and contribute to the ways in which 'the popular' is a dimension of everyday living. The 'popular' — its construction, internal variety, the interplay involved between expressive forms and consciousness and its political orientations — has been a necessary and problematic focus in media and cultural research for many years. In cultural sociology, it gradually replaced the earlier and more immediately negative usage of 'mass'. Perhaps the central difficulty for analysts using the term has been that of recognising adequately (and sympathetically) the 'life values' of groups often subject to extensive economic and cultural exploitation and injustice, while also recognising the shaping impact of the cultural industries upon popular tastes and consciousness. This has presented itself as both an ethical and a political problem, producing a degree of ambivalence in much writing on the topic.*

*It seemed to me that in examining the two terms one could see not only the tensions and uncertainties of value internal to each, but also the growing disalignments of their relationship. To play off 'knowledge' against 'culture' raises (or perhaps begs) a few questions that the piece has not space to engage with properly, but it made sense in terms of my reading of the situation in Britain. As Peter Dahlgren pointed out to me some years ago, it can also be useful to think through the principal issues using reversed terms, that is to say 'public culture' and 'popular knowledge'. However, while the latter term has always been relevant and is gaining wider applicability through new cultural technologies, the first one continues to suggest something unattractively 'official', and this sense has, if anything, got stronger.*

*The piece ends pessimistically in its assessment of the political economy underpinning dominant forms of the popular, whatever spaces are (intentionally or otherwise) opened up within or alongside these. Meanwhile, the critical revision and refurbishment of the idea of the 'public' in ways that can significantly inform policy across a range of areas, including informational access, more extensive provision for open dialogue and broadened cultural opportunities, seems likely to face a continuing struggle.*

*My more recent belief concerning the possible impact of the financial crisis of 2008 on general attitudes towards state intervention and 'regulation in the public interest', looks at the time of writing this note to have been too hopeful.*

The relationships between the circuits and agencies of public knowledge and both the economy and the values of popular culture continue to be central to change in the politicality and sociality of media systems. This is so internationally, allowing for wide variations. At the level of broad dispute about media policy and practice and also at the more specialised level of debates within media and cultural studies, the terms of the relationship remain crucial even where (perhaps especially where) they are only implicit or hidden. Around them, there have developed tensions and lines of fracture that have had a shaping influence on much commentary and enquiry. Rather than being a connection between two distinct if loosely defined domains, the form of the linkage is often one of imbrication, the patterns and flows of the one overlaying or underlaying those of the other in a mixture, itself the subject of debate, of determining power and responsive adaptation.

In this commentary I want to examine aspects of the linkage, giving attention to the descriptive and normative categories used to identify it, the realities of structure and process they signal and the ways in which different lines of enquiry into the present and likely future performance of media systems have addressed it. I am aware that the pattern of connections and tensions I am addressing is a familiar theme in the international literature of research, even if contesting frameworks are used to describe and analyse it, and that I am therefore in part 'shadowing' many earlier accounts. My aim here is a combination of the synoptic (trying to review the issue across its many, changing aspects) and developmental (giving certain points a sharper focus).

## BINARY TENSIONS?

To play the two phrases off against each other directly might seem to pose too crude a dichotomy, immediately impairing the kind of analysis that can follow. Certainly, there is a requirement for care in what is implied and assumed by the core terms and just how separation and

opposition are put to work. In fact, two broad lines of relation are implicated, that between knowledge and culture and that between public and
popular.

The relationship between knowledge and culture (in its inclusive,
'ways of life' sense) is recognised to be primary and deep, since knowledge systems and their products are widely perceived to be necessarily
embedded in, and variously the product of, cultural systems, to the
point of presenting difficulties of analytic separation. This is so even
where there is a strong cultural internationality at work and where
the knowledge is 'scientific' rather than 'humanist' in character. The
relation is therefore more often gauged as supportive rather than antag-
onistic, although the ways in which cultural factors can limit and
impede the production, expression and circulation of knowledge has
been a regular theme in many different kinds of enquiry. Cultural
cross-currents are also at work in the allocation of different degrees of
value both to the types of knowledge in circulation and the kinds of
knowing encouraged and practised. What, for whom (with class and
gender often strong variables here) is it necessary or desirable to know,
and for what ends? What are the most useful ('reliable'?) routes of production and distribution for various knowledge requirements? *How*
should things be known? (For instance, what role might the emotions
play in kinds of 'good knowing'?) Here, the public and politically constitutive category of 'news' is pertinent to this discussion. Journalism as
a form of embedded cultural production, one with a professional
requirement to offer a satisfying cultural performance, not merely a
'knowledge input', is routinely the focus of affirmation but also of
anxiety and of critique.

The relationship between ideas of the public and ideas of the popular
is one that has a more marked history of tension. Both terms have independent legacies of varied, contested usage, often ones in which current,
descriptive application (things as they are) is either played off norma-
tively against future potential (things as they might be) or even, in moves
of 'descriptive idealism', strategically fused into a sense of that potential.
It is interesting to note the other terms against which these two are most
often defined. For 'public', this would have to include 'private' and
'market' (against which 'state' still provides a more usual contrasting
descriptor). For 'popular', in the sphere of culture, 'high' and (more negatively) 'elite' are regular contrastive pairings, while in the sphere of
politics a range of less clear indicators, including 'authoritarian' and
(again) 'elitist' occur. In this sphere, the awkwardly proximate notion of
'populism' has continuing presence and force as a term often indicating

a simulation of the 'popular' idea, a deformation of it in the service of established power that needs to be placed at a critical distance in relation to the core values that inform this idea's more radical, demotic heritage (see the perceptive engagement with this issue in McGuigan, 1992).

In her recent, illuminating discussion of concepts of the 'public' in relation to notions of 'audience', Sonia Livingstone (2005) takes up the ideas of 'the public in the private' and 'the private in the public' to engage with the way in which it is the complexity and scale of the embeddings now at work that warrant analytic attention in pursuing issues of publicness further. The sense of a significant reconfiguration of 'boundaries', together with extensive boundary-crossing and boundary-blurring, has been one of the recurring points of reference in work in media and cultural studies over the last decade. This reconfiguration has variously been identified, according to the normative frameworks applied, as indicating a deepening 'problem' or, by contrast, as a route to new forms of 'resolution', a point that will be returned to later.

The relationship of 'public' to 'popular' immediately differs from that to 'private', in that it has not routinely served as a conventional boundary line, a part of the divisive vocabulary of social regulation, but, instead, has often enjoyed a relationship of assumed proximity and, at times, of unity, albeit one created and sustained by strenuous rhetorical work. Against this sense of normative proximity, it has been registrations of specific, real gaps between the two that has been the subject of unease and the focal point for either critique or for renewed rhetorical management. This establishes a very different relationship from that towards the 'opposite'. Historically, the grounds for the construction of the normative community of the 'public' (the preferred designation for modern national and sometimes international, civic collectives) have differed from those at work in constructing and revising the terms of the 'popular'. And as the latter has become ever more identified internationally with the generative conditions of market-based cultural consumption, the difference and 'value gap' have been sustained in new forms. At a point in this development, it is the idea of the 'public' that begins to seem the more uncertain, indeed suspect, term in many of its cultural applications. This occurs not least because of the way that the ideas of market relations embedded in, and underpinning, dominant notions of the 'popular' become naturalised (and often nationalised as well as internationalised) beyond effective questioning.

## CONFIGURATIONS OF VALUE

Given the situation described above, a split in evaluations, not just increased uncertainty, can be seen to have developed around both 'public' and 'popular'. We can talk, with some simplification but a useful sharpness, of the 'good public' and the 'bad public', the 'good popular' and the 'bad popular'.

Ideas of the 'good public' follow from a continuing sense that the notions of cohesion and collective values and purposes that gather around the word offer a necessary marker for future social development. Whether this development is given theoretical elaboration as a condition whose grounding terms, economic and discursive, are still to be achieved (as most notably in the debates about Habermas's notion of the 'public sphere') or viewed more pragmatically, as a desired inflection of policy and practice within the broad arrangements of existing institutionality, the term is positioned as a descriptor deserving of affirmation and commitment. Versions of the 'bad public' may simply follow from observing instances of the discrepancy, some of them spectacular, between apparent endorsement of the term and the actual conditions, of managed inequality, exclusivity and denial of participation, which prevail. Against this, there can be placed alternative versions, as in the idea of 'counter publics' (see for instance Fraser, 1992 and the overview in Downey and Fenton, 2003) strongly contesting installed values and criteria with action perspectives intended to achieve impact in possible future contexts for 'publicness', either unitary or multiple.[1] Alternatively, the 'public' idea may be seen as tainted beyond use as a value-orientation, even in revised form, by the fact of its routine hijacking by political and media elites as a preferred term for the legitimising of their gendered, ethnic and social class controls (including by the use of selectively constructed 'public opinion' data – see for instance Lewis, 2001).[2]

The senses of 'good popular' derive more or less directly from the broad and imprecise idea of affirming the (ordinary) 'people' in relation both to cultural and political goals. This is a powerful dynamic in the context of struggles against manifest elite control and is therefore a prominent theme in political history, including the history of anti-colonialism and of nation-building. The 'popular' is a term that is not compromised by the senses of the official and the approved that have frequently gathered around uses of the 'public', making it stronger for enlisting commitments and signalling liberating, perhaps radicalising, energies.

Historically, the 'popular' can be seen as bad, either politically or culturally, or both, from a perspective which is disturbed by the possibilities for political unrest or for faulty cultural judgment (the misrecognition of 'quality') that might follow from an increase in its prominence. In his indispensable survey of the word in *Keywords*, Raymond Williams cites usage of this kind (Williams, 1976). However, in a way that has had a defining impact within media and cultural studies, it can have 'badness' attributed to it from a radical perspective. Here, the 'badness' follows from the extent to which the popular is seen to be predicated on market infrastructures, and specific cultural products, which shape tastes, values and consciousness across an extensive front. Such a shaping is regarded as variously blocking the possibilities for progressive expression, subjectivity and affiliation that might (or in stronger versions, would) emerge were this regulating matrix of relationships not to be there. As many writers have noted, one important characteristic of the 'bad popular', as judged from a radical position, is its *passiveness*. It is a mode of inhabiting the 'life-world' that is extensively, if not totally, governed by the terms of 'system', to borrow from Habermas (1985). This is in sharp contrast to the sense of active agency at work in accounts of the 'good popular'.

In an essay that remains illuminating in its attempt to work through some of the problems and potential contradictions surrounding notions of 'the popular', Stuart Hall (Hall, 1981) identifies the importance both of the radical tradition and what he calls 'the "market" or commercial idea' (which he notes is the one that 'brings socialists out in spots', 1981: 231). Against these, and other, variants he proposes what he calls a 'dialectic' definition, in which the popular is always placed in relation to the 'dominant', in an historically mutable play-off of tension and struggle.

The advantage of this widely influential view is that it sees the 'popular' as involved in a dynamic that is necessarily political as well as cultural. The 'popular' cannot usefully be thought about (and certainly not celebrated or condemned) on its own, outside of this connection. What Hall offers is not a real alternative to the existing senses of the word, an ambition towards which his essay occasionally hints, but a better way of theorising the power relationships at work in and through them.

A significant aspect of Hall's view of what I have termed the 'bad popular', the popular as shaped within the terms of the market, is that it is not entirely to be regarded as distortive or imposed, but to be seen, instead, as making a selective connection with real elements of popular experience, consciousness and aspiration, and providing them with a partial but valuable articulation. This more nuanced judgement of the commercial popular is a strand to be found in Williams' writing too, although it appears here less boldly than in Hall, partly because Hall engages more directly with specific commercial popular forms, including but going beyond the cultural offer of television.[3] More broadly, it is a feature of many different lines of work contributing to Cultural Studies. In many instances, the precise nature of the relative proportions and relationships of (in my crude terms) the 'good' to the 'bad' is a critical and often troublesome issue, one that sometimes poses a threat to full coherence of analysis. This is particularly so in an area where the interplay between affirmations of popular culture and critiques of its limitations has become so dense and mobile. The evaluative range of the profiles generated around specific cultural instances is extensive, with shifting assessments of the impact of markets a significant variable.[4]

## PUBLIC KNOWLEDGE: FLOWS AND FORMS

The diverse forms of journalism are now established not only as producers and circulators of daily knowledge, but as key cultural brokers for a diverse range of cultural options and products, most of which are positioned within a marketplace subject to intensive advertising and consumer commentary. Two related challenges for journalism within this context have been, first of all, how to retain an acceptable level of readership/audience for 'news' output against the range of non-news competition and, secondly, how to attract and satisfy target audiences/readerships against the range of competing news provision.[5] The growing use of web sources for news, including but not limited to those provided by traditional news suppliers, has introduced an important recent shift in the terms of the challenge here, widely discussed both within the media industry and beyond.

The contexts are both economic and cultural, in what is often a complex interrelationship between the changing terms of viability and profit in different market segments and the kinds of communicative recipes, formats, modes of address, visual design and stylings that can win and sustain attention within shifting patterns of accessibility, orientation and 'taste'. Inevitably, there will be extensive repetition of recipes that seem to work, but also a premium on successful innovation that achieves 'wins' against the competition in established market spaces, and possibly helps develop new spaces too.

In the situation as described, the identity of news as 'public knowledge', an identity always open to critical scrutiny in respect of its demographic construction (By whom? For whom? With who implicitly excluded?) has undergone a loosening. This has occurred first of all in relation to the position of news within the 'mediated day' as this is variously constructed across options and temporal frameworks by readers and viewers, working from their choices of print, broadcast and online sources. It has, secondly, occurred in relation to the generic features of news, where issues around content and form have become subject to increased levels of producer uncertainty and variation as to the nature of their fit within changed market settings and profiles of consumer expectation.

## THE EXAMPLE OF TELEVISION

In Britain, shifts of this kind have recently shown themselves very clearly in television. There has been extensive modification (and sometimes re-modification) of studio settings, to provide more 'contemporary' or, by contrast, reassuringly retro, settings for anchoring the news, for signalling the 'place' of television news knowledge. These shifts in the styling of the *mise en scène* of the news base and literally, given the positioning of news-readers within it, the *embodiment* of news talk, have occurred alongside experiments with different schedule points and durations. More significantly still, as part of the rebranding of news as a televisual experience, the nature of content and treatment has been revised too. For instance, the BBC has noticeably increased the emphasis given to crime and human-interest stories at the head of its bulletins. The importance given to these stories is reflected not only in placing and duration, but also in the expanded array of reportorial modes, including location presentation (often without significant local enquiry), used to report them.

A broader feature of these changes has been the strengthening of the 'fairytale factor' in all news that lends itself to such treatment. By 'fairy-tale factor' I mean not a resort to falsehood (although that has been a long-standing option for some kinds of journalism) but the deployment of an intensified cultural resonance, dramatic play-offs of value, particularly involving desire, fear and uncertainty, which can be generated around an item. This can have darker or lighter tones, but it usually works with a distinctive sense of priorities concerning the ways that the journalistic core of the story can be given optimal connections outwards towards markers (terms, images, precedents, parallels) providing cultural amplification. The effect of these markers is to increase the magnitude and cultural reach of the item, giving enhanced theatrical force, without significantly adding to specific knowledge about it. Nowhere has this tendency, with its fetishisations of place and its recourse to obsessive repetition and emphatic personalisation, been clearer than in the coverage of crime stories. In Britain, the treatment of

the 2007 Madeleine McCann 'missing child' case, both by television and
the press, is an obvious, if extreme, example.

A much broader area of media output, internationally, where these
tensions and shifts both of practice and of evaluation are seen to be at
work is that of 'reality television'. The very wide range of formats that
have been placed within this category, some less easily than others, has
produced a major fracture line in thinking about quality, purpose and
social power in television. Importantly, this has been a debate conducted
within the media industry as well as within public and academic settings.
Some documentary producers, including those committed to observational formats, have widely criticised the new programmes for their
departure both from conventional 'ethics' in their ways of working with
people and from conventional 'public' principles in their sometimes
exclusive commitment to the imperatives of entertainment rather than of
social investigation and exposition. Such critics have perceived an unacceptable compromising of documentary's 'public' standards brought
about by a capitulation to market populism. However, other (often but
not always younger) producers and directors have championed the new
formats for reasons other than their relative profitability. They have
done so first of all for reaching a wider (popular) audience than conventional documentaries usually managed to do and, secondly, for casting a
'social eye', albeit an entertaining one, on dimensions of the everyday,
including dimensions of occupational, family and emotional life previously at the margins of, or completely ignored by, documentary
production in its self-consciously 'public' modes.[6]

The debate about reality television has clearly been one of the most
sustained points of focus concerning media culture over the last ten
years. The volume of recent writing about it exceeds that about established forms of documentary. Not surprisingly, the academic debate has
involved a wider range of reference points than that within the industry,
including issues concerning the media economy, gender and class identity, the aesthetics of performance, audience participation and the
'politics of pleasure'. On the negative side, a very early essay by the US
documentary scholar, Bill Nichols (1994), is hard to beat for the sheer
energy of its rejection of what is seen as a gross deviation from kinds of
public purpose and connection. For example:

> The very intensity of feelings, emotion, sensation, involvement that
> reality TV produces is also discharged harmlessly within its dra-
> matic envelope of banality. The historical referent, the magnitudes
> that exceed the text, the narratives that speak of conduct in the

world, of face-to-face encounters, bodily risk and ethical engagements ground themselves harmlessly in circuits devoted to an
endless flux of the very sensations they run to ground. (Nichols,
1994: 57)

Against this kind of position, variously critical and rueful when not, as
above, plain angry, there have been a number of modulated, or indeed
affirming, positions advanced. These have mostly wanted to highlight
the ways in which the new modes precisely refuse the system of 'public'
social relationships at work in conventional programme forms, opening
up (whether intentionally or not) on more inclusive, productively messy
and interactive modes of display and portrayal. In short, competing versions of the link between popular culture and popular politics within the
broader settings of existing structural power (the theme given emphasis
by Hall) are often what are centrally at issue here.[7] The debate is prone
to muddle, not least about generic criteria, but it is one that is likely to
continue as the developments on which it focuses continue to reshape
factual television.

## CONCLUSION

The modifying pressure which market-related models of the 'popular'
have placed on ideas of the 'public' and on the flows and forms of public
knowledge is clear across a range of instances. It is a dynamic that has
brought with it forms of articulation of 'ordinary life' and orders of significance that can be seen to show an expansion and an enrichment
beyond previously established 'public' frames (Hall's careful insistence on
this point continues to require attention in any analysis). However, it has
also displaced and marginalised significant strands of approach to civic
value and civic culture, and hindered the working through of how different kinds of knowledge might relate to the enabling conditions for
'cultural citizenship' in changing conditions of society and of communicative opportunity.[8]

   How applications and uses of the web will play into this broad situation has clearly become a major area for international assessment,
growing in complexity. The web has emerged as a public space, a
counter-public space, a private space, a popular space, a market space
and (to some degree) a state space, with various and shifting configurations between these aspects as they affect localised profiles. Among the
many commentators here, Peter Dahlgren has offered wary but finally

affirming overviews of its continuing 'civic' potential (see for instance Dahlgren, 2003 and 2009). The ways in which these spaces will move through relations of imbrication, contradiction and dominance, producing shifts both in the character of knowledge agendas and available forms of knowing, will intensify and give further volatility to the terms of the perceived tensions affecting older media.[9]

The play-off between frameworks of 'public' and 'popular' carries implications for structure, process and value. The flows and the spaces of the dominant 'popular', economic and normative, frequently shape the contexts in which versions of the 'public' as a communicational principle with entailments for knowledge production, circulation and exchange are now defined and operated. They regulate the terms of public communication *as an experience* and have a bearing on the particular combinations of the highlighted, the visible, the marginalised and the concealed out of which a social optics is constructed. No effective revision of, or indeed alternative to, ideas of publicness (e.g. in relation to the 'private', to structures of accountability and notions concerning 'citizen–consumer' dualities and the emergence of 'cultural citizenship') can occur without concurrent, if not prior, attention to the conditions of this outer frame. The terms upon which the popular is constructed are not beyond the possibility of crisis (involving, for instance, forms of 'rejection' of what is offered and perhaps even more systemic disjunctions), and they certainly contain internal contradictions. Nevertheless, the dominant modes have shown themselves to be resilient and to be 'managed' across change with aggressive imagination. In this way they contrast markedly with notions of the public, which (outside the academy) have often had the space for critical review and renewal foreclosed upon by a 'pragmatic' scheme of economic and institutional priorities.

In different ways, the next decade of research will have the public/popular interplay, framed by broader economic, political and technological factors, running through its agenda of enquiry. Alongside analytic attention to particular instances, continuing debate about its general profile and implications will therefore be a good idea.

## NOTES

1   The move away from singularity immediately 'relaxes' the issue of a unitary value framework while, at the same time, introducing problems of overall coherence and priority/precedence.

2    Here, I might note my attempt many years ago (Corner, 1991) to suggest that media research into audiences could be characterised broadly as either concerned primarily with the 'public knowledge project' (centred on news and current affairs) or the 'popular culture project' (centred on fiction and entertainment). My descriptive scheme was sometimes taken to promote the elevation of one project and the virtual dismissal of the other. This interpretation, though mistaken, was accompanied by often entirely convincing arguments about the risks of taking established views of the 'public' for granted.

3    Richard Hoggart is another obvious, and interesting, point of comparison. *The Uses of Literacy* (Hoggart, 1957) was written without reference to the cultural dynamics introduced by popular television and popular music in the mid-to late-1950s. Within its eloquent, autobiographical reading of shifts in the 'popular', the culturally commercial (often aligned with 'Americanisation') is judged almost entirely negatively and in a way that connects more directly with older ideas of 'mass culture' than with (then) emerging, ambivalent, ideas of 'popular culture'.

4    The relationship between popular culture and the project of feminism is an important example. This is vigorously reviewed in McRobbie (2004). For an interesting and suggestive discussion of how the mediatisation of sport has impacted upon dominant ideas of the 'popular' and the 'authentic', see Blain (2002).

5    Among the many overviews of the situation, Philip Schlesinger (2006) perceptively examines the different economic and cultural factors at work within the UK, including the challenges of the web. See also Deuze (2005) for an exploration of journalistic values and the 'popular' in relation to ideas of 'tabloidisation', drawing on the working perspectives of Dutch journalists.

6    The annual Sheffield International Documentary Film Festival is a key arena for debate among those in the industry. For a quite early attempt at overviewing the different positions, see Willis (2000).

7    Among the many contributions here, the collections by Holmes and Jermyn (2003) and Murray and Ouellette (2004) engage with the debate about values directly.

8    'Cultural citizenship' is a term around which some usefully expansive questioning and reformulation, connecting elements of 'good public' with those of 'good popular', have been advanced, despite the risks of losing sharpness of political focus. See, for instance, Hermes (2006) and Miller (2007).

9    Laura Stein (2008) helpfully examines public space and speech rights on the web in respect of existing US law.

# PART TWO(2):
# VISUALITY AND DOCUMENTATION

# 7

# Documentary expression and the physicality of the referent: writing, painting and photography

## PRELIMINARY NOTE

*This piece of writing was, in part, an attempt to do some close comparative work across different media, the analytic benefits of which were suggested in Chapter 2. In particular, it seemed to me that 'documentary' studies had, with a few exceptions, displayed less interest in work outside the field of film and television than was desirable. Even photography, for many decades the defining 'documentary' medium, had often dropped out of view, except perhaps for passing references, in debates about documentary forms and functions. This meant that a rich literature of scholarship and commentary (some of which was referred to in Chapter 2) was only thinly referenced, if at all, in much study of the documentary in cinema and broadcasting. While the contemporary economy and imperatives of academic knowledge almost inevitably lead to a measure both of duplication and of mutual ignorance across what are sometimes closely related fields of enquiry, the need for better cross-referencing here seemed obvious.*

*Painting and writing present a rather different challenge, operating outside the context of mechanical 'recording' and often intentionally working their 'realist' ambitions in combination with a commitment to subjective, authorial or painterly, expression.*

*The main thrust of the piece, the way in which the physical world is a primary point of reference for documentary work, however abstract, argumentative or propositional a film or programme may also be, seemed to me to be under-recognised in many debates about documentary forms and functions. In one sense it is obviously there as an element of the referential or iconic dimension of the relationship between documentary texts and the world portrayed, but quite often it does not receive the direct attention that its aesthetic and discursive centrality to documentary practice, and to documentary's appeal as a mode of mediation, deserve.*

*Although the emergence of sub-fields nearly always carries the danger of increased degrees of intellectual hermeticism, I think there is a possibility that 'documentary studies' can be carried forward as a rich and productive area of interdisciplinarity, opening up rather than closing down on the range of theories and approaches it draws upon, and connecting both with humanities and social studies agendas. I have looked at some aspects of the history of this area of study, essentially emerging from Film Studies but now with important contributions from elsewhere, in Corner (2008). Currently, it shows signs of becoming an area attracting strong international interest, as documentary production itself reworks its ideas and representational modes for different kinds of purpose within a changing array of media formats and markets.*

The physicality of documentary expression is an aspect of its construction and its discursive range that takes us to the core of the uniqueness and complexity of the documentary project. By physicality, I mean the way in which documentary works with impressions of a particular, concrete object world and uses these impressions as the material from which to build more generalised accounts. The international tradition of documentary work is methodologically and technologically committed to this physicality because of its grounding in pictures, in a discursive infrastructure of visualisation, whether this is the still photography of a continuingly rich strand of work, or the achievements in film and television to which the documentary label has been widely applied. This has given to much documentary work a distinctive phenomenological character, rooted in obdurate particularity, whatever the degree of generality, descriptive, propositional or more implicitly evocative, which is organised from this basis.

Here, I want to try and get an improved critical understanding of this aspect of documentary practice by looking at some examples from writing, painting and photography. Such a venture may seem odd, but I think that, through it, a richer as well as broader sense of *documentation* can be developed and 'carried back' to the rapidly developing body of work on film and television forms. The idea of documentary writing is an awkward one in a context where the established use of the term documentary applies to work using technologies of recording to portray or 'reproduce' physicality (including the physicality of sound in radio feature work). However, writers working within various generic frameworks (including novelists but certainly biographers, diarists, travel writers and journalists) have often sought a 'documentary effect' in the sense of an immediacy of apprehension of a specific physical world projected as the 'real world', not some 'imagined world'. When they have done this, a strategy of description sufficient to evoke a strong visualisation in the reader has been one part of their approach.

I want first to explore some aspects of this 'proto-pictorial' quality to documentary expression in writing. I shall then consider comparatively another mode of portrayal, painting, to which notions of 'documentary' can be applied only with some awkwardness (despite the directness of visual engagement), but nevertheless often with some illumination too. Finally, I want to consider how the photographic image, around which an extensive literature of comment on documentary functions has developed, works within its distinctive alignments of the pictorial and the physical.

## THREE WRITTEN ACCOUNTS

### Example 1: George Orwell, The Road to Wigan Pier

During 1936, George Orwell spent approximately two months in Wigan, a Lancashire mining town badly hit by unemployment and poverty. His account of what he saw and heard during that period was published in the following year, becoming a classic of documentary writing. However, his diary notes have also been published, and it is possible to compare accounts of events in the diaries with those in the book. This is not just a matter of comparative 'styling', although that is interesting enough, but of more fundamental matters concerning the organisation and discursive management of a factual account.[1] First of all, let us consider an account of an event recorded in the diary entry for 15 February:

> Passing up a horrible squalid side-alley, saw a woman, youngish but very pale and with the usual draggled exhausted look, kneeling by the gutter outside a house and poking a stick up the leaden waste-pipe, which was blocked. I thought how dreadful a destiny it was to be kneeling in the gutter in a back-alley in Wigan, in the bitter cold, prodding a stick up a blocked drain. At that moment she looked up and caught my eye, and her expression was as desolate as I have ever seen; it struck me that she was thinking just the same thing as I was. (Orwell, 1968 (1936): 203)

This passage gives a concise physical description both of the women and the action observed. It then moves from the physical scene to an account of Orwell's own thoughts, which are those of a quite precise, temporary empathy. Orwell's self is extended outwards to the objective scene, in an act of connection aided both by observation and imagination. This act of thought and feeling coincides (in a way which gives a degree of immediacy to the account) with another physical act on the part of the woman, looking up, making eye contact and showing her facial expression. Orwell then notes a further thought that was prompted by this behaviour – that she was having the same thoughts about the dreadfulness of her situation that he had just described. Again, this strongly reinforces the sense of simultaneity indicated earlier. It does so with the effect of shock, a sharp adjustment in the organisation of the relations of objectivity and subjectivity. The observer's judgement on the scene is the same as that of the person within the scene. Orwell's empathetic assessment turns into his recognition that it is in fact *her* assessment too. We can now look at the 'same scene' as it is described in *The Road to Wigan Pier* a year later:

> The train bore me away, through the monstrous scenery of slag heaps, chimneys, piled scrap iron, foul canals, paths of cindery mud criss-crossed by the prints of clogs. This was March, but the weather had been horribly cold and everywhere there were mounds of blackened snow. As we moved slowly through the outskirts of the town we passed row after row of little grey slum houses running at right angles to the embankment. At the back of one of the houses a young woman was kneeling on the stones, poking a stick up the leaden waste pipe which ran from the sink inside and which I suppose was blocked. I had time to see everything about her – her sacking apron, her clumsy clogs, her arms reddened by the cold. She looked up as the train passed, and I was almost near enough to catch her eye. She had a round pale face, the usual exhausted face of the slum girl who is twenty-five and looks forty, thanks to miscarriages and drudgery; and it wore, for the second in which I saw it, the most desolate, hopeless expression I have ever seen. It struck me then that we are mistaken when we say that 'It isn't the same for them as it would be for us' and that people bred in the slums can imagine nothing but the slums. For what I saw in her face was not the ignorant suffering of an animal. She knew well enough what was happening to her – understood as well as I did how dreadful a destiny it was to be kneeling there in the bitter cold, on the slimy stones of a slum backyard, poking a stick up a foul drain pipe. (Orwell, 1962 (1937): 16–17)

Here, there has been a radical change in the physical organisation of the scene. An encounter on foot in the diaries, it is now described as an observation from a train. It is not now an encounter at all (although the proximity 'almost allows' the catching of her eye). The scene is now filled out with descriptive detail, of the context, of the woman and of her actions, beyond the terms of the diary entry. Indeed, the detail is such as to stretch to the limit our sense of what is plausible as observation from a train carriage in motion. Nevertheless, the train frames the incident in a way that gives both an extended distance (spatial and interpersonal) and something of the vivid intensity of the ephemeral. Orwell now expands on his earlier act of empathy, explicitly connecting with his readership ('we are mistaken') and drawing a more general social meaning from the particular, physical circumstance. The woman's own realisation of 'dreadfulness' is still affirmed but she is now a passive figure within Orwell's documentary observation, her predicament turned into a more fully worked reflection on its general significance. There is a sense in which Orwell is more protected, less vulnerable, in this version. Not only is he not seen, not implicated by a mutual awareness, he is also on the move inside a train rather than placed on the streets, where the physical terms of his witness carry a more awkward, disturbing and potentially more compromising force. The object of his observations might be located upon another plane altogether, given his own containment within the enclosed, moving compartment.

## *Example 2: Sebastian Junger's* The Perfect Storm

My second example comes from a highly successful 'documentary' book of the 1990s, also the basis of a feature film. Junger's book displays a number of features of more recent trends in documentary writing. These centre upon the reconstruction of a particular incident in intensive detail, drawing on a range of interview materials, various archival sources, media accounts and relevant scholarly materials. The broad approach can be seen as essentially historiographic, a past event or perhaps circumstance is recounted within a strong narrative design but also with developed contextual detail, often bringing esoteric or 'technical' references into the story. The approach is necessarily different from those accounts, like Orwell's above, grounded in first person experience. In one sense, it is more like the reconstructive, 'drama-documentary' approach in film and television, around which so much controversial commentary has developed (Paget, 1998 is a useful survey). Its commitment to circumstantial detail and background carry it into a level of digressive exposition that most narrative fictions would find an unacceptable constraint on character and plot dynamics. In the scene below, the fishing boat *Andrea Gail* is awash in heavy Atlantic seas, as a freak storm (the 'perfect storm' of the book's title) hits the area in which it has been working:

When the water first hits the trapped men, it's cold but not paralysing, around 52 degrees. A man can survive up to four hours in that temperature if something holds him up. If the boat rolls or flips over, the men in the wheelhouse are the first to drown. Their experience is exactly like Hazard's [a previous capsize described a few pages earlier] except that they don't make it out of the wheel-house to a life-raft; they inhale and that's it. After that the water rises up the companionway, flooding the galley and berths, and then starts up the inverted engine room hatch. It may well be pour-ing in the aft door and the fish hatch now too, if either failed during the sinking. If the boat is hull-up and there are men in the engine room, they are the last to die. They're in absolute darkness, under a landslide of tools and gear, the water rising up the com-panionway and the roar of the waves probably very muted through the hull. If the water takes long enough, they might attempt to escape on a lungful of air – down the companionway, along the hall, through the aft door and out from under the boat, but they don't make it. It's too far, they die trying. Or the water comes up so hard and fast that they can't even think. They're up to their waists and then their chests and then their chins and then there's no air at all. Just what's in the lungs, a minute or two's worth or so.

The instinct not to breathe underwater is so strong that it over-comes the agony of running out of air. No matter how desperate the drowning person is, he doesn't inhale until he's on the verge of losing consciousness. At that point, there's so much carbon dioxide in the blood, and so little oxygen, that chemical sensors in the brain trigger an involuntary breath whether he's underwater or not. That is called the 'break point'; laboratory experiments have shown the break point to come after 87 seconds. It's a sort of neurological optimism. (Junger, 1997: 141)

At this point, the narrative is, as it were, slowing down time in order to organise around the fact of the physical incident a sense of the boat's topography of escape possibilities and the physiology of drowning. The first part of this approach is a very direct attempt to make the reader visualise the objective features of the scene in more detail – its spatial character, the darkness, the sounds – than another kind of account might do. The passage nevertheless retains a close, chronological design *as time runs* out for the trapped crew. Given the lack of a precise record as to what actually happened, the passage sets up alternative possibilities. However, this speculation does not diminish narrative dynamic, carried throughout in the present tense in a way that provides the account with a dramatic immediacy, the sense of co-present witness, more typical of the experience of audio-visual media.

The technical detail concerning the withholding of breath under water relates to an 'inner' story being developed within the passage, a story about the physiology of death by drowning. This is very different from the 'inner' story of thoughts and feelings which documentary writers more often use (as in the Orwell example above) as foil and complement, as necessary duality, to the object worlds and event worlds that primarily engage them. It is, in fact, a continuation of the object world *inside* the body. Its effect is a calculatedly shocking one, contributing a literally 'clinical', detached dimension to an account working also with empathetic features, and reducing the men we have come to know as full characters in the earlier pages to the automatic body functions which occur at 'break point'.[2]

## *Example 3:* The Guardian *reporting of '9/11' on the day following*

This third extract is taken from *The Guardian* newspaper on the day following the attack on the World Trade Centre. Most of the paper that day was given over to various kinds of reporting on the attack, and the front page, in common with other news outlets, carried a full page photograph of the doomed twin towers, with the second aircraft just about to make its strike. The extract is co-authored by three journalists and, following on from earlier stories summarising the events of the day and their immediate implications, it attempts to document the experience of the physical event by drawing on eye-witness accounts, sometimes in direct quotation, sometimes not.

> Geoff deLesseps was on the telephone at 8.45 am, talking to his wife from his office on the 80th floor of the northern tower of the World Trade Centre in lower Manhattan. 'I was meant to be going on a business trip tomorrow and she had this strange feeling about airplanes, I swear to God', said the 37-year old chief executive officer.
>
> Then the first of the kamikaze planes hit the building a few floors above, cutting a cartoon-like outline into the 1,362ft building, once the tallest in the world. The most spectacular terrorist attack on the United States had begun.
>
> Twenty minutes later another plane hit the second tower of the complex. Soon people were hanging on for the their lives – and

falling – 1,000ft above the ground under blue skies and a pale half-moon.

Forty-five minutes later people were still clinging on to windows, clearly visible from the street below, still against the ruptured symbol of US power and influence, debris fluttering like ticker-tape and stricken birds, catching the sunlight as it twisted to the ground. Finally, the unluckiest of the thousands who work each day in the towers lost their grip or jumped from the smoke and flames.

'I'm moving from this city', one man shouted as he ran. A homeless woman, shuffling along West Broadway, muttered: 'They're doing this for what? To save the world from what?' Now both towers were ablaze, columns of smoke billowing into the blue.

Schoolchildren stood in the streets; some of those working close by ran from the scene. Most just stared, in the middle of the broad boulevards, stung.

But as the crowds stood paralysed, one of the towers did the unthinkable; it suddenly disappeared into a cloud of its own making, and, in slow motion, collapsed to the ground with a deadly, horrible thud – punctured by screams on the streets: 'Holy Shit – it's gone!' (Michael Ellison, Ed Vulliamy and Jane Martinson, New York (*Guardian*, 12 September 2001, p.6))

These are only the opening few paragraphs of a much longer piece, but an organisational structure to its documentary account is clear. There is strong chronology, given by the sequence 8.45, 'then', 'twenty minutes later', 'forty five minutes later', 'finally' and 'But as the crowds…'. The irruption of the hugely abnormal event is grounded in a first paragraph about normality and routine, the telephone call recounted concisely but with a detail that works to consolidate its reality as a datum point in an object world, as well as a social world, about to be radically transformed.

The piece is doing its descriptive work in a context where most readers will already be terribly familiar with the event as a visual phenomenon, through the replays of varied television material the previous day and photographs of the kind that feature on the paper's own front page. Nevertheless, the awesome physical character of the event is still a necessary reference point for any experiential account and for any relaying of emotional responses too. So central and overwhelming is this visibility that the piece works almost as an elaborative commentary on the picture that will be in almost every reader's mind. The 'cartoon-like' outline of the damage to the building, the 'blue skies', the 'pale half-moon' intensify our sense of a basic image we already hold. The description extends itself to a restrained metaphoric level, with the 'ruptured symbol' and the analogy with 'ticker-tape' and 'stricken birds'. So powerful is the sheer horrifying aesthetics of the spectacular here that noticing the way in which debris was caught in rays of sunlight does not figure as inappropriate. Into this sequence of visualised events, localised voices of response, frightened or questioning, are placed, a human context for the objective disaster unfolding. The dominant feeling of simply watching, a feeling which connects both witnesses on the grounds with readers of the piece, is brought across powerfully in the last lines of the extract, as one of the towers slowly does the 'unthinkable'.

It is the particularity of disaster, conveyed partly in the local, unfolding moments of its perception, that gives this account, and the much larger article from which it comes, its documentary strength.

What general points can be taken from these examples that might inform our sense not only of what is specific to written documentary accounts but of what is common to what I have termed the physicality of the documentary enterprise?

Primarily, there is the centrality of a visual engagement with the physical world, necessarily achieved here by deft description, rather than a more direct portrayal. This is not a mere referencing of the physical in the interests of resourcing a more general exposition and argument. It is the holding of physical particularity, at least for part of the account, in a quite intense act of contemplation (in some work in film and television, this can be fixated enough to suggest an element of fetishisation in the observational/viewing relations). Around, or upon, this 'proto-pictorial' work of representation a number of possible moves can be made towards exposition and argument, which may or may not include a clear narrative design. The organisation of an image sequence within a framework of speech, possibly including narration, is important here but so also is the way in which the meanings of the images themselves extend beyond their particular referential connections through relations of typicality and the logics of metonymy and metaphor.[3] All three extracts call readers into a vicarious act of witness as well as an engagement with an affective order and a moral world. Only extract 1 provides a first-person sourcing; extracts 2 and 3 document (as in many documentary accounts) from a position of greater distance and anonymity, although the perceptual particularities of observation in 3 imply a particular observer and give the passage an element of first-person voicing. Extract 2 is the severest in its terms of engagement, creating its impact through its grim, dense factuality and its status as a cool hypothesis about what must have happened rather than an account of what *did*. The details generate a visualisation approximating to vicarious witness, but with the added pull on subjectivity that this is a forensically specific *imagining*.

## PAINTING AS PICTORIAL DOCUMENT

I want now to look at how painting figures in the kind of documentary relations I have begun to explore. Perhaps painting is generally regarded as of an even lower status than writing in respect of documentary credibility. There are genres of writing committed to detailed reportage, and writing, like film and television, has the capacity to develop narrative accounts and therefore to portray events in time. Painting, like photography, works essentially through the 'captured moment', whatever narrative implications this can generate by various cues in the framing, composition and local detail. However, painting is not only (like writing) a wholly authored impression of the physical world rather than (like photography) in part an attempt to work with a direct physical record, it is also a form of expression in which *what* is painted has often been regarded as merely the basis for a visionary creativity that extends far beyond this. Within the terms of this creativity, the very idea of documentation, even as an intention, is problematic.

Within the rich strand of commentary on this and related questions in Art History, work on Dutch seventeenth-century interior painting is particularly pertinent. In her influential but controversial 1983 study, 'The Art of Describing', Svetlana Alpers advanced a view of this body of work which emphasised its qualities as a kind of documentary portrayal, a rendering of the properties of the physical world, approximating in some respects to a scientific exercise. This view was advanced against the influential judgement that such paintings were essentially kinds of symbolic 'code', deriving their organisation and detail from implicit moral and aesthetic protocols rather than a sense of direct perception and therefore becoming 'emblematic', illustrative of ideas rather than vision. Writing of her position ten years later, Alpers put it thus:

> If we take the pictorial mode – the reality effect – not as hiding moral instruction, but as offering a perceptual model of knowledge of the world, then pictures are related to the empirical interests of this age of observation. The picture takes its place beside the

many other devices – the eye, the microscopic lens – which squeeze and press nature so that we can experience (or experiment, in the seventeenth-century use of the word) her. (Alpers, 1993: 59)

This scholarly perspective perhaps approximates to a common response to such paintings, from outside the art historical world, that, whilst allowing for the pleasures generated by their creative qualities of pictorial design, they also work as partial precursors of the photographic. However, this view continues to be challenged by those writers who stress either the normative or the symbolic function of the object worlds portrayed. Insofar as it is moral, the portrayal may show how things *ought* to look in some idealised view of the domestic that is self-consciously at odds with existing reality. Insofar as it is aesthetically over-determined, the portrayal might extensively borrow from the history of art as well as from contemporary symbolic systems. The sheer virtuosity of pictorial detail and the sense of verisimilitude may thus disguise, especially in a modern encounter with the painting, the discursive conditions of its production. Such a debate connects with ideas concerning the iconographic and iconological character of paintings, their 'readability' or indeed 'decipherability' only within an informed sense of the cultural and subcultural systems within which they were produced. These ideas, initially advanced by Erwin Panovsky, inform a major strand of subsequent critical commentary.[4]

It is important to note that Alpers did not suggest that the paintings could be used as firm visual evidence of domestic topography and routines. Recognition is clearly made of the play of norms and ideals over and upon what finally appeared on the canvas, as well as of the essentially aesthetic transformations involved. So the paintings are not 'documentary' in the sense that we would often use this word of photography to indicate its capturing of sociological truth through its reproduction of the object world, although their combination of naturalistic portrayal with mundane, routine subject matter may encourage us to invest in them in this way. However they are, she argues, 'documentary' insofar as they work with a strong dynamics of vision, of how the world looks, rather than being the product of ideational (including literary) resources translated to canvas through a process in which the eye hardly figures at all as a means of securing reference.

The idea of the painter 'documenting' a scene in ways that make the claims of record equal to, if not greater than, those of creative imagination, extends well beyond the exquisite detail of seventeenth-century Dutch painting.

We can take the case of J. W. Turner, a painter whose pictorial method involved a considered, and highly original, transformation of the object world almost to the point of abstraction, but whose work often claimed a degree of documentary authenticity as to the core events it depicted. Take for example, his 1834 painting, 'The Burning of the House of Lords and Commons 16th October 1834'. Turner, learning of this real event, joined the crowds 'spectating' at the scene and spent much of the night with his sketchbook. He used both the Thames bank and a boat on the river as viewpoints from which to work, later developing the sketches in his studio, as watercolours and then oils. Turner's final rendering of this dramatic event is grounded in his own experience of the scene and it therefore works with an open subjectivity of approach which contrasts markedly with the apparent objectivity of the Dutch genre paintings discussed above. The 'witness' function is an important part of the identity of Turner's painting but it does not deny his personal imaginative contribution. Of course, in many paintings where the subject is 'real', including portraits and landscapes, the contribution of 'the imaginative', and then within this category the scale of the self-consciously so, is a matter of uncertainty and dispute. The difference between a desire to be faithful to a visual experience in full recognition of its subjectivity and a desire to 'improve', by way of exaggeration and concealment, on what is seen and registered can often be difficult to discern. Hence the debates, sometimes slipping into banality, about the 'true' as opposed to 'portrayed' beauty of many subjects of portraiture and the obvious adjustments of scale and perspective made in the creation of landscape paintings. In both cases, it was often primarily promotional rather than documentary values that were being served by the pictorial design.

The idea of the artist as, among other things, a documentary witness also comes through intriguingly in relation to another of Turner's powerful paintings of elemental turbulence, 'Snow Storm – Steam-Boat off a Harbour's Mouth', 1842. The critic John Ruskin, an admirer of the painting, reports of a letter he received from a friend containing personal witness to Turner's own testimony as to the origins of the work. In response to his comment to Turner about his mother's liking for the picture, the friend notes that:

> [Turner] then said 'I did not paint it to be understood, but I wished to show what such a scene was like; I got the sailors to lash me to the mast to observe it; I was lashed for four hours, and I did not expect to escape, but I found bound to record it if I did. But no

one has any business to like the picture'. (For a full account of
these circumstances and the letter, see www.art-bin.com/art
/oruskin4.html)[5]

There are a number of issues here. First of all, that concerning the documentary veracity of the account itself, and certainly the account of
Turner's words, in a letter itself quoted at second-hand. However,
allowing for this uncertainty, what is presented has several engaging
features. There is, most obviously, the sheer commitment to 'record', to
'show what such a scene was like'. This is a documentary commitment,
at the level both of visual experience and also of physical experience
(the body not just the eye is implicated in the phenomenon). On any
reading, an element of the melodramatised self seems to appear in the
idea that he 'did not expect to escape', as well as in an assessment of
the physical plausibility of his being lashed to the mast for four hours.
We can see this merely as overstatement generated by annoyance at the
initial comment. Whatever credibility we give the details of the account,
it presents us with an interestingly emphatic sense of artistic commitment to the real.

The documentary connections are further reinforced by the idea that
'liking it' is not what is intended and may, indeed, be an unacceptable
response. Such an idea suppresses, sincerely or not, the aesthetic production of the work in favour of its status as 'record', a recurrent feature
of more conventional forms of documentary expression. However, the
extent to which 'record' here incorporates not only what was 'observed'
but what was *experienced* is, as I have suggested above, a significant factor,
complicated further by the extent to which both observation and experience allow for a significant subjective dimension. At one point, this
dimension would give emphasis to the painting's autobiographical character over other kinds of link to the external world.

Painting may use pictorial representation, the documentation of the
object world, as a way into a more expansive and penetrative documentation of the circumstances and conditions which obtain in that world.
However, its concern both with the variables, including subjective, of
visual experience and then with the arts of picture-making itself, introduce 'filters' into the portrayal of object world which serve to privilege
the creative visuality of the portrayal. As a consequence, documentary
connections are attenuated, even though they remain variously, and perhaps confusingly, active. The arrival of photography introduces a wholly
different emphasis, whatever the artifice of its own pictorial practice.

## The photographed world

Although photography develops as an amateur and professional practice
with a strong stand of continuity with painting, in terms of the imaginative 'scenes' it can portray (often copying those of painting) and in the
creative licence the photographer can introduce (Winston, 2000 discusses the freedom for 'adjustment' even accorded to early press
photography), there is a well-remarked 'scientific' strand too. As a copy
produced in part by the physicality of that which is copied (see the discussion in Chapter 2), photography clearly enters a different ontological
and epistemological realm from that occupied by writing and painting, a
fact which has generated a large and rich literature of critical commentary and theoretical reflection (Barthes, 1984 and Sontag, 1979 are
major reference points here). The troubled 'indexicality' of the photograph would transfer itself eventually to the now familiar debates about
film and television documentary which are still the preoccupying focus
of much 'documentary studies'. The extent to which photography, in
terms both of its techniques and its motivations, accurately depicts the
physical world before the camera becomes a recurrent theme, but it is
joined by a further consideration, the extent to which any depiction of
the world of appearances can provide knowledge of the 'reality' that lies
beyond appearance. This was never a problem in documentary writing,
of course, since writers were quite free to combine passages of close
physical description with passages of general analysis and judgement.
Nor was it a general issue raised in relation to painting where the relationship between image and the world beyond appearances is openly
symbolic or allegorical, and possibly biographically subjective. However,
as I suggested above, where the level of detailed naturalism (or, as in
Turner's case, the painter's testimony of purpose and practice) is intense
enough to provoke it, later critics have raised not only the question of
specific verisimilitude in painting but also that of the 'documentary relationship' between the specific image and the realities of the social world.

   Photography has at times taken this latter question to the level of a
'crisis' for two principal reasons. First of all, because of the increasing
circulation of photographic images throughout society as a primary
element of claims-making discourses in public, commercial and private
spheres. The sheer scale of the permeation of society by the 'visual
evidence' of the photograph has attracted critical attention to matters
of status. Secondly, as noted above, the emphatic indexicality of the
photographic claim at the level of physical record has, within some critical responses, served to intensify anxieties about its capacities to offer

knowledge beyond this level. Photography has been viewed, quite often, as a way of disguising core truths by means of a technology of superficial truth-to-appearance. One of the classic comments of this kind is the much-cited remark by Brecht (the first and most influential citation of it is by Walter Benjamin) that a photograph of the Krupp factory reveals almost nothing about what is going on inside it or about the social and economic facts of its existence.[6] Brecht's own interest in the discursive possibilities of photo-montage partly derives from this sense of the discursive and analytic limitations of the conventional photographic image. Susan Sontag, citing Brecht herself, notes how 'understanding anything' from a photograph is a doubtful outcome, while at the same time she is one of the most sensitive writers on the medium's capacity to have an impact (Sontag, 1979: 23).

The problematic character of the photograph as evidence *at any level*, an issue compounded by its seductive obviousness in appearing to perform this function, becomes a key point of debate in the emerging idea of 'documentary photography'. The term 'documentary' is often applied retrospectively to photographs taken before the self-conscious moves to documentary representation (and to the use of this term as a self-defining category of practice) that has characterised a number of movements from the 1920s and 1930s onwards. However, the growth of a 'documentary project' in photography brings with it a critique that is, not surprisingly, very similar to that which develops around documentary film practice, although the two critical literatures have not, in general, developed that level of mutual awareness that would enrich both.[7]

Without the narrative dynamic provided by in-shot movement and shot sequence and supported only by the 'external' discourses of caption and connected reportage rather than the 'internal' discourses of commentary and interview speech, the relationship of the *physical testimony* of the photograph to any level of *social testimony* is even more problematic than that of film and, later, television. No explicit story unfolds through the image, no descriptive and propositional accounts speak to us directly from within the image-world of its contexts, of the feelings and thoughts of those within it and of its wider significance. There is not even the possibility of music to cue mood and deepen affective impact. To see this categorically as a 'lack' however, is to miss the beguiling, indeed sometimes awesome, resonance of the still, silent image in time and in both physical and historical space. The power of photography is partly grounded in the mysteries of its mute, static interpretability. The contemplative opportunity, the space to gaze, which it offers (in this respect, like painting) is joined by the distinctive perceptual and cognitive impact that is provided by its status as a kind of record. As we know, this a point to which Barthes' writing regularly returns, as it does to the dynamic interrelationships between text and image as both forms of 'anchorage' and of 'relay' (Barthes, 1977 is perhaps the classic statement on this theme).

It is clear that the 'documentary problem' of the photograph is not seen only to be a problem of physical–social relations, a problem, so to speak, of the kind of epistemology that the underlying ontology has warrant to provide. As in the discussion of documentary film and television, questions of inherent subjectivity, of a displacing desire to achieve kinds of aesthetic distinction, of power relationships between observer and observed, and of a straightforward subjugation of practice to official, regulatory ends (e.g. early forms of visual surveillance) are brought into the debate. Martha Rosler provides a classic and influential survey of these themes in an essay that has been widely republished (originally Rosler, 1981 but Rosler, 1989 is an expanded and extensively illustrated version). Among other things, this polemically replaces an emphasis on a reformist or even radical imperative in documentary practice with a sharp sense of the exploitation and the 'violence' that it may involve. The literature on this theme is extensive, but a notable recent contribution is Julian Stallabrass's (1997) extensive questioning of how the internationally recognised pictorial impact of Sebastiao Salgado's images of manual labour (those of the open-cast gold miners of Serra Pelada in Brazil being the most widely cited examples) contributes to social knowledge and possible social action. Here, as with other photographic examples, the question of mode of display becomes a variable of more significance than in discussion of film and television work. Location on the white walls of the art gallery will give a stronger sense of the abstracted, dehistoricised physical moment (bodies and loads, cliffs and ladders), beautiful as well as terrible, than will captioned insertion within pages of critical reportage in a magazine or newspaper.

Perhaps an example will help to bring out some of the issues with increased sharpness, as earlier in the article with respect to writing and painting. An image by the German-born British documentary and art photographer, Bill Brandt, is useful for this purpose. It was taken in 1937 and is entitled 'Northumberland Miner at his Evening Meal'. High permission fees prevent its reproduction here, but it is easily available on a number of gallery websites.[8]

The image shows two figures sitting at a table (only their upper bodies are visible) upon which plates, dishes and pots are laid.

Immediately behind them is an ornamental wooden vase-stand with a vase upon it and behind that a wall upon which a painting and a bag (hanging from a hook) are placed. Items of clothing are hanging from the ceiling, their lower parts entering the upper frame of the photograph. The man is eating with knife and fork and gazes at his plate. The woman is to the right of him and her look, seemingly reflective or distracted, is at an angle downwards. The man's face, hands and shirt are thickly covered with coal dust.

In a way that invites some comparison with Dutch interior painting, discussed earlier, the scene sets the two figures within a composition of objects whose number and proximity seem to challenge the eye. At least twelve separate items surround the two bodies, from the table foreground to the back wall and the hanging clothes. Within this framing of a domestic object world, a space seemingly further constrained by the items located within it, it is clearly the face of the miner that immediately holds the attention. The juxtaposition of the action of eating at the table with the coal-begrimed face, hands and shirt condenses both a stylistic impact (quite possibly self-consciously surreal) and a social commentary on the conditions of work within which this has become domestic normality.

The photograph offers itself for interpretation at a number of levels. A viewer familiar with Brandt's work might be prompted to wonder how the 'naturalism' of this scene, in which the two human subjects show no awareness of the camera (a contrasting pictorial convention from that of family photography), squares with Brandt's record as a photographer who extensively 'staged' many of his shots, sometimes using relatives. However, discounting for our purposes this level of challenge to the primary integrity of the image (although, as in documentary film, questions of 'staging' run across a considerable spectrum), there is the question of how we move from the shock of these particulars to any more general, propositional, understanding and response. What kind of implications does the picture carry, perhaps about the exploitative nature of the mining industry or (even, for some viewers) about the limited hygiene awareness of its workers? The emotional tone of the picture is negative, an interpretation partly following from a viewer's likely reading of the man's condition and one internally reinforced by the expression on the woman's face, upon which ideas of hardship and forbearance can easily be read. A cramped and, in its human details, outrageous, physicality is construed into a life – *this* home life and behind it, a working life – and then into lives more generally and the structures that determine their differences. For part of the calculated shock of the photograph follows from an acute recognition of difference by the implied viewer (difference from *me*, difference from normal).

I have wanted to pursue some issues about documentary expression outside of film and television practice and outside the growing body of scholarship that takes this practice as its focus. It has been my intention by so doing to freshen up our sense of how the activity of picturing the object world enters into the documentary project. This activity is a factor both in documentary's referential and its aesthetic strength, providing images of a world with a phenomenological impact of this world's 'thereness'. Framing and composing of worldly elements is undertaken in ways that are often beguiling in their mixture of strangeness and familiarity and in the formal qualities of dense *presence*, the spectacle of exteriority. At the same time, getting from this level of a pictured world through to meanings about its social conditions and circumstances, a movement from depicted physical particularity to the generalities of context, process and implication, is a project in which the pictorial achievement can become a source of limitation, displacement and even replacement. This acutely problematises the more ambitious forms of documentary accounting in ways that are widely and intensively debated in the documentary studies literature.

I have also wanted to put some emphasis, not just on the discursive and ontological implications for documentary accounting which the primacy of the 'object world' entails, but on the special character of 'physicality' within this primacy. Such a character involves the form of our visual relationship with *things*, with (quite literally) the *matter* described in the writing or portrayed in the painting or photographic image. It opens on to questions about shapes and textures, about the way in which perception of the historical world is achieved through an often sensuous and even erotic and fetishised engagement with its localised planes and surfaces. Even in work which seeks to generate high levels of discursive abstraction and perhaps to call attention to the disturbing and the politically and socially unacceptable, this can amount to what I think can be called a 'romancing' of the particularities and densities of the physical world, that is to say a generation of feelings of wonder, mystery and perhaps love. Necessarily, documentary projects will vary greatly in the kind of emphasis they place on physicality and the constituents of the aesthetic which they draw upon to portray it. In a related way, documentarians themselves will also vary in the relationship (personal and then technical) they establish with the physical as a matter of distances and proximities, of perceived linkages and disjunctions, of modes, for instance, of cool witness and of warm participation.

By looking at writing and painting with a documentary intent, where the basic relationship with the object world is necessarily imaginative, a declared product of constructive design, the complex, primary drive towards representing an object world as the basis for knowledge is opened up in ways that can enhance our sense of what is going on in more technologically resourced modes of the referential. Equally, by examining some of the debates arising from the emergence of the photograph as a revolutionary and seemingly definitive documentary medium, we can see instructive connections with, and differences from, the intense academic commentary on seeing and knowing now developed around film, television and, increasingly, modes of online documentary practice.

## NOTES

1   Bernard Crick discusses the contrast between the diary and the later 'reportage' in his excellent biography of Orwell (Crick, 1980). He briefly comments on the passage I discuss below in the context of his broader sense of a socio-psychological awkwardness and a tension in Orwell's approach to acts of 'witness' (1980: 187–8).

2   It is interesting to compare this with the equivalent scene in Wolfgang Peterson's (2000) film version. Junger's dense factual speculations are replaced by dramatic reconstruction with dialogue and a musical score, including the final words of Billy and Bobby as the water level approaches their faces (Bobby says: ' We had to try. Hey, it was a hell of a fight though, huh?'). Although the film contains scenes in a documentary mode, this scene is inevitably generated within the subjectively intense narrative space of fictional cinema, exchanging Junger's forensic distance for closeness and having no direct way of placing what is happening in a broader context of knowledge.

3   The mutual relations between literal and figurative levels at work in images and sequences is, of course, a continuing point of focus for scholarship on film and television documentary, involving a range of metonymic and metaphoric devices, some foregrounded and some more covert in their operations.

4   Erwin Panovsky (1955) is perhaps the most cited text. The precise difference between iconographic and iconological study has been the subject of some confusion as well as debate, particularly in relation to where and how questions of 'subject matter' rather than 'form' enter into the analysis.

5   Accessed November 2006.

6   The key citation is in Benjamin's 1931 text, *A Short History of Photography*. In the reprinted version I am using, Benjamin (1980), the relevant phrasing appears on pages 213–14. A published source for Brecht's comments does not appear to be available in English.

7   Scholars of documentary in Art departments are obviously likely to show more awareness of this than those located in other academic contexts. My judgement, as a teacher of documentary film and television studies for over 30 years, is that many programmes of study, including mine, could benefit from more attention to the history and development of documentary photography, and to its professional and scholarly disputes, than they presently offer.

8   Search engines display a number of options, with varying size and quality but  www.healeyhero.co.uk/rescue/collection/ian/art/a046.jpg  gives a clear image of decent size (accessed December 2010).

# 8

## *Documenting the political: some issues*

### PRELIMINARY NOTE

*Here, I attempt to explore some of the more important dimensions of documentary as a range of forms for, among other things, political investigation and political portrayal, forms which generate a variety of ways of knowing and feeling. Although I examine the manner in which documentary necessarily grounds itself in images of the physical world (the subject of the previous chapter), my primary concern is with the kinds of propositional discourses about politics (implied or explicit) that specific combinations of vision, speech and sounds can serve to generate. This concern connects together questions of power, form and subjectivity in a direct and sustained way.*

*Despite the massive international success of varieties of documentary in which an intended political purpose, designed to be read as such by the viewer, is almost entirely absent, documentary productions for film, television and now the web show a continuing strand of commitment to political exploration and critique. Quite a lot of this work, rather than engage primarily with formal politics, politics as established within core institutions and through officially legitimated processes, connects most strongly with the 'politics of everyday life', examining domestic and occupational contexts in which an 'official politics' is merely implicit. This seems to me a very important strand of production, some of it closely related to developments out of 'reality television', some of it coming more immediately from previous forms of political documentary-making and still other work drawing its inspiration from newer styles of social networking and web presentation. I engage with aspects of this development in Corner (2010b) while here I concentrate on work which is defined by its explicit, self-conscious engagement with core political issues. A better understanding of the range of documentary production that continues to be effectively political in different international contexts, and in relation to changing ideas both of 'the political' and of its connections with aspects of personal and social life, would be a welcome contribution to film and media scholarship (see, for instance, Chanan, 2007).*

Documentary has a long-standing, often highly self-conscious and some-times controversial connection with the portrayal of the 'political'. This extends from direct attention to core political structures and processes, through to indicating the broader manifestations of politicality (that is to say, the various aspects and dimensions of the 'political', ways of being 'political' and of doing 'politics') in everyday life and culture, often involving spaces in which politics has an understated, implicit or even denied presence. In this article I want to explore aspects of documentary 'politicality', pursuing a synoptic agenda and placing recent examples within this, both as illustration and development. After some preliminary comments about the character of documentary as a form of political dis-course, including questions of definition, I will develop my discussion under four subheadings. 'Visualising politics' will allow attention to be given to the way in which 'picturing' activity of different kinds is central. 'Talking the political' will examine the very important function that speech performs in establishing and developing political specificity. I fully recognise that, in practice, 'visualising' and 'talking' are combined and not separate in many of their effects, but I think they can benefit from individual attention here, provided that their combinatory nature is also acknowledged. 'Reason and affect' will look at the terms of the play-off, frequently the subject of dispute, between the cognitive and the emotional offer that documentaries make. 'Addressing audiences' will explore assumptions and strategies concerning addressees and modes of address, together with the character of documentaries as agents of change in perceptions, opinions and actions.

## DIMENSIONS OF POLITICALITY

One dimension of the difference between documentary and news jour-nalism has been an imaginative capacity to extend portrayal beyond the presentation of descriptions and propositions and to work with a discourse whose symbolic range can handle contingency, the incidental and the casual as well as the pursuit of a tight 'informational' agenda. At the same time, a key difference between documentary and publicity, another major communicational mode of modernity, might be seen to be a commitment to 'truths' that lie beyond the parameters of official or corporate partiality.

This line of difference has always been problematic. It has been so first of all because of the framing of many documentary accounts (including the classic 1930s and wartime documentaries of British cinema) within the terms of state-sponsored national publicity, however much space was found (or not) within these terms for an independent and perhaps questioning directorial voice. Moreover, many documentaries in the various strands of 'radical' and 'independent' work have been widely deployed as a way of attacking established accounts (including established histories) and presenting counter-perspectives in the most strategically persuasive way available in order to encourage changed attitudes. The case of independent cinema in the United States is one well-researched instance of this, but internationally there are many examples of 'documentary movements' achieving various levels of success and distinction with projects of strong partisan commitment. To question this approach by reference to ideas of some available political truth transcending the parameters of an evaluative perspective, of 'point of view', would be naive. But it is significant how, at times, a quite intensive debate about the political ethics of documentary persuasion, about the use of evidence and the protocols of argument, has been conducted between individuals and groups who are nevertheless agreed on the need for documentary to be critical, perhaps radical, and grounded in declarations of value. Occasionally, an 'ends/means' split has been discernible, whereby the ends are to publicise 'the truth' and the means are extended to any rhetorical device that might do this job effectively, qualms about the local 'integrity' of the discourse therefore being suspended.

Bill Nichols' perceptive study of the films of the 'Newsreel' group, made or distributed by a US radical collective in the 1960s, brings out some of the tensions and disputes well (Nichols, 1976, and see also the discussion of this group in Renov, 2004) while the whole debate about documentary realism, to which I will return below, is often premised on anxieties about the political and epistemological integrity, and then the political efficacy, of the film-making.

As a final preliminary, it is useful to raise here the question of the level and degree of 'the political' to which I am referring. There is a sense in which all documentaries are political, whether or not they or their audiences are aware of it. This is worth noting as a way of framing the political as a quiet but pervasive dimension of culture *per se*, but it is not useful for my purposes here. For the sake of specificity, I want to focus on films and programmes which engage explicitly for a significant part of their length with matters to do with the control of resources, nationally and perhaps internationally, and the exercising of social power through formal institutions and procedures of regulation. Within political studies, there has recently been recognition of the way in which the term 'politics' has often been used too narrowly, foreshortening a sense of the politicality of many areas of everyday life. I want to connect both with formal and 'colloquial' versions of the political in documentary film, but I judge explicit address to questions of institutional power (both as structure and process) to be a useful marker for this article. If pursued as a general principle and applied too rigidly, this criterion would leave out a number of documentaries that have a significant political dimension.[1] However, it would be my argument that the politicality of these documentaries can be better appreciated alongside a firmer analytic understanding of more direct and explicit attempts at political engagement.

## VISUALISING POLITICS

The visualisation of politics in documentary works across certain basic variations in framing, whatever the finer distinctions. We might distinguish between politics seen as a *sphere*, a designated space, and politics seen as a *level* or *dimension*. Offering representation of spaces, people and actions predefined in terms of their politicality engages with the political most directly and accessibly. It reflects established ideas about the hierarchy of politics, its nature as an arena of contestation and perhaps about its boundaries, although it may do this with the purpose of questioning these ideas rather than simply working within their terms. Politics regarded as a level, a dimension of many aspects of everyday life perhaps conventionally appearing unpolitical, offers the challenge of revealing or illustrating this non-self-evident layer. It offers the possibility of a portrayal that 'politicises' the world by using its representations to show the 'hidden' politicality beyond the terms of the taken-for-granted, although as I shall show later, it may depend extensively on speech in order to carry out its work of revelation.[2]

We can also distinguish between pictures which work essentially as *illustrations* of the political, grounded in the primacy of a discourse of commentary and perhaps of interview speech, and those which are offered as *observation*, in which the 'raw visibility' of the political (as either sphere or level) is offered for the viewers' vicarious witness.[3] How do these various modes, frequently combined in their use within documentaries, work to deliver the political as both an experience of knowing and of feeling?

Michael Moore's *Fahrenheit 9/11* (2004) has received an extensive amount of commentary and will receive more. It nevertheless remains an important, one might say indispensable, example to engage with because of its status as a film both explicitly political and phenomenally successful and one with a wide discursive range. *Fahrenheit 9/11* works at a number of levels to install and develop the political visually, although it is clearly a documentary in which the theme is continuously managed by a dominant directorial voice, deployed either in commentary or in in-shot speech. We can list the more important of these levels and modes as follows:

a. Archive news material of key political figures, sometimes revealing their 'backstage' behaviour (e.g. in sound checks prior to media presentations) and working always to *illustrate*, implicitly or otherwise, the film's developing thesis.[4] President Bush is, of course, the most important personalisation of established politics in the film and, throughout, his visual rendering is crucial (Merck, 2004, illuminatingly refers to the way in which the film is an 'exercise in critical physiognomy', with Bush's features and physical behaviour presented as almost continually revealing). The sequence in which Bush continues to read a story from a reading primer to young children in a Florida classroom, after his aide has informed him (by whispering in his ear) of the 9/11 attacks, attains pivotal status within this logics of portrayal. It pictures the President within a closely personalised framing at a moment retrospectively charged to the limits of signification with disaster and geopolitical shift, and it makes his somatic response available for critical examination.

b. The central political event of the film is 9/11 itself, politics in the form of awesomely destructive activity. Here, Moore moves away from the reportorial directness that characterises most of the elements of his strategic design and uses the expressive, symbolic device of voices and screams over (or, in effect, within) a black screen, giving way to a slow-motion sequence of shredded paper falling from the sky and horrified crowds looking upwards at something that the film does not need to show. By providing nothing to see for a full minute, he positions the viewer within a dynamics of active engagement. Sounds cue imagined pictures of the experience for those trapped within a 'political' gone nightmarishly dark and bad.

c. In many other scenes, Moore variously *observes* the political, identified as a process hidden within the settings of the everyday. For instance, there is the scene of Marine recruiters 'working' the entrance to a shopping mall, attempting to interest teenagers from a poor district in a military career. This has a productively bizarre quality (helped by music on the soundtrack), not least because of the contrast between the immaculately uniformed marines and the dress of those they are there to proposition, but also because of its framing as an event inside the broader political understandings already established by the film, ones which constantly work to inform our interpretation of, and often our amazement at, what we see.

d. Elsewhere, the visual is sometimes a key part of Moore's intervention into the political space of others. This occurs most obviously in his scenes of interview, where testimony and answers are sought about personal, and positionally specific, feelings and understandings. An important figure here is Lila Lipscomb, whose son's death in Iraq leads to a change in her political attitudes, a conversion that the film enlists for its own play-off of truth against officially encouraged misperception. Visualisation makes Lipscomb a powerful presence in the film, both in the interview settings of her home (with the US flag flying from a pole outside, complicating – but not too much – our sense of the key political coordinates in play) and, more dramatically, in her trip to the White House, during which the camera closely attends to her movements and demeanour in a manner at times close to that of the self-conscious portrayal of bodily performance and of performance space (theatrical space) within a fictional diegesis. Visualisation also generates a narrative that moves (through Moore's management of real historical times in relation to times of shooting) from the presentation of a mother whose son is serving in Iraq toward the revelation that her son has been killed. Presenting this 'turn' in the story as, in effect, a politically decisive piece of occurring eventuality, rather than establishing it earlier (Moore, in fact, didn't meet her until *after* the son's death) provides greater narrative scope in developing visually the political meaning of Lipscomb. It also presents her as having a change of viewpoint in a way that we see happening in the film, rather than as something we hear about having happened.

e. At points, intervention in the political sphere becomes more direct, using 'stunts' with a calculated visual appeal and impact in a manner that Moore has made part of his signature style. We see him driving an ice cream truck around the Capitol building and reading sections of the US Patriot Act through a loud-hailer. Following an even more typical strategy of 'false-footing', he stops members of Congress in the street to ask them whether they have sent, or are prepared to send, their sons and daughters to fight in Iraq. The embarrassment and difficulty they show in handling this unexpected and abrupt questioning is seen to be as important and revealing as their answers. Both approaches construct politics as, in part, 'farce', with Moore's own performance generating a mood that transfers itself outwards to aspects of the political world thus targeted.

In all these ways, and in others that I have not included in this brief survey, Moore's film, despite being essentially grounded in the speech of its director/presenter as well as that of those who appear in archive and interview, articulates its political themes visually.

An illuminating contrast can be made with a documentary three-part series made by a British director also released in 2004. Adam Curtis's *The Power of Nightmares* was shown on BBC television in late 2004. Like *Fahrenheit 9/11*, it concerns itself extensively with politics and terrorism. However, rather than being focused on a particular incident, it attempts to explore the context of contrasting ideologies in which ideas of the 'terror threat' have emerged and become, so it argues, a powerful point of reference for the maintaining, and strengthening, of political control in the West. Curtis's film is remarkable for the boldness with which he attacks what he sees as contemporary 'myths' of terror, but it is also original in its use of visual material. Drawing on a tradition of archival and found-footage usage (notable, for instance, in the work of Emile De Antonio),[5] Curtis reaches out widely across the genres, importantly including fiction, to gather images and sequences with which to 'illustrate' his thesis.

To give an example, the pre-credit sequence of his opening programme, *Baby, It's Cold Outside*, lasts 2 minutes 20 seconds and contains over forty separate shots taken of different people, interiors and locations, including pictures of Bush, Bin Laden, Blair and Rumsfeld, doors opening, lights going out, aircraft landing, forests, cities at night, explosions and scenes from feature films, one involving a mysterious, turbaned figure. Some of the shots are briefly held in freeze frame. Across many of them, a brooding organ-based soundtrack runs underneath the commentary. This commentary (which I shall examine further in the following section) is cool, tightly formal in its phrasing and grounded in sharply categorical distinctions. It is thus in strong contrast with the loose, associatively rich and often bizarre sequence of images on the screen, coming at us at a rate of around one every three seconds. These

images are certainly not observational but neither are they directly illustrative in the manner of much of *Fahrenheit 9/11*. What they produce is
a heady brew of connotations (a 'dark' political imaginary) supporting by
their generalised suggestiveness the thesis about an illusion at the heart
of contemporary politics that the commentary tells us will be the primary topic of the series. Given this hectic start, it is not surprising that
in its subsequent exposition, this episode, and the series as a whole,
revert to more literally illustrative strategies, using contemporary footage
underneath descriptions and analyses of developments in both Middle-
Eastern and American politics.

However, such sequences are often not long in duration, giving way
to further exercises in associative editing, involving 'play' of a kind that
formally defines the whole project. One of the advantages of this
approach, apart from the space for ironic contrasts it creates, is that it
permits the voiced-over commentary to pursue a theme of considerable
abstraction (in fact, a polemical exercise in the history of political ideas).
It thus solves the problem of 'what to show' while getting through substantial verbal business. A conventional use of archive footage would,
here, carry the risks of diminished significatory power and therefore of
lowered viewing engagement. A fascination with the open-ended
imagery and an attention to the closely focused exposition work together
in a relationship of mutual reinforcement.

We can make a comparison with the visual strategy of *The Fog of War*
(2003), Errol Morris's film about Robert McNamara, former US
Secretary of Defence. Morris, too, attempts to generate a level of associative meaning from many of his sequences, using fast cutting between
images from diverse sources to achieve this. However, there is a greater
degree of symbolic closure on the material, which draws far less on clips
from fiction and thereby restricts the affective range within which it
works, keeping a closer relationship with its specific politico-historical
theme. Indeed, for much of his film, the core visual engagement is with
material providing a sustained 'look' at particular moments and incidents. This serves as illustration for the development of McNamara's
interview accounts, the core discourse of the film (as indicated, not without a degree of irony, in its subtitle – *Eleven Lessons From the Life of Robert
S. McNamara*). A narrative continuity is sometimes constructed across
several shots, as in the title sequence, portraying scenes on board a US
warship preparing for action, offering access to an unexplained world (a
little dumb-show story from the archived past) whose implications for the
exposition will only be established later (it actually relates to the Gulf of
Tonkin naval encounter of August 1964, part of the lead-up to the

Vietnam War). In one of the first sequences of interview, McNamara's account of the Cuban missile crisis is run across various images of a magnifying glass slowly being moved across aerial photographs. The aesthetic organisation, in its framing, durational values and repetitions, takes the images from simply having a literal connection with the speech to becoming more broadly and symbolically resonant with meanings about the centrality of surveillance to politics and the elaborate, close scrutiny of the 'enemy' which is often the prelude to conflict. Importantly, as in *The Power of Nightmares*, the impact of many sequences is greatly enhanced by a musical score, here specially written by Philip Glass, combining a sombre ground-tone with quiet menace to cue the mood of viewing.

## TALKING THE POLITICAL

Establishing and developing themes by speech is a central feature of documentary design, whatever the range and power of visual display. More than most other topics, the political requires specific identifications to be made, articulations of relationship to be offered and arguments to be put. These can 'follow' or 'lead' visualisation, they can be generated outside the frame of documentary depiction (by commentary or voiced-over testimony) or within it (by on-screen presenter, in-shot interview, or observed speech), but in whatever mode they appear they will be essential to the portrayal. A useful way of developing my analysis here is to take the openings of the documentaries I discussed in the previous section. How is the political theme or topic introduced? How is it installed within the documentary design and with what expectations encouraged in the viewer?

The first episode of *The Power of Nightmares* opens with a firm statement of its perspective and its assessment of a shift in the nature of political claims-making:

> In the past, politicians promised to create a better world. They had different ways of achieving this but their power and authority came from the optimistic vision they offered their people. Those dreams failed and today people have lost faith in ideologies. Increasingly, politicians are seen simply as managers of public life. But now they have discovered a new role which restores their power and authority. Instead of delivering dreams, politicians now promise to protect us … from nightmares.

Spoken over the wide-ranging, at times rather hysterical, sequence of associatively linked images, this neat and confident account gains extra force. As I noted above, two kinds of discursive power are combined and they remain so throughout the entire exposition of the thesis put forward in this programme concerning the development of fear as a means of political management.

*The Fog of War* slides into its topic much less directly. It can afford to do this because its primary speaker is Robert McNamara himself. Politics is talked from 'within' rather than analysed from 'without', McNamara *is* the political subject, in both senses of that term. Morris filters his opening through suggestions of the business of 'mediation', suggestions that then frame the viewer's close engagement with McNamara's interview speech.[6] A pre-title scene shows McNamara in a monochrome archive clip, getting ready to deliver a press briefing during the Vietnam War and checking out the set-up with assembled reporters. It then moves through the title images and music to a scene in which McNamara is being interviewed by Morris and querying sound levels and cutting options before moving to substantive talk. The sequence goes as follows:

[*Archive film, map in front of podium at press briefing, McNamara preparing to offer briefing:*]

McNamara:        Is this chart a reasonable height for you? Or do you want it lowered?
                 Earlier tonight ... Oh, let me first ask you, are you ready? All set?

[*Then follows the title sequence with various shots of activity on a warship, described above, leading to the opening of the film's McNamara interviews.*]
[*McNamara in medium close-up*]

McNamara:        Let me hear your voice level, to make sure it's the same as mine.
Morris:          OK. How's my voice level?
McNamara:        That's fine.
Morris:          Terrific.
McNamara:        Now I remember exactly the sentence I left off on. I remember how it started. It was cut off in the middle but you can fix it up somehow, I don't want to go back and introduce the sentence, because I know exactly what I want to say.

Morris:         Go ahead
McNamara:       Any military commander who's honest with himself
                and those he's speaking to will admit he's made
                mistakes in the application of military power, he's
                killed people … unnecessarily.

The idea that this film will involve, in part, a kind of 'confession' but
that it will also show McNamara as an assertively self-confident and sea-
soned media performer, still concerned with the technicalities of his
portrayal, is thereby established within the opening minute or so.

At many points, *Fahrenheit 9/11* resembles both examples above by
employing a 'montage' approach to pictorial design across which to
project its speech, although the associative range here is thematically
tighter than in *The Power of Nightmares* and looser than in most sections of
*The Fog of War*, referenced as this is not only to specific events but to one
specific political actor. *Fahrenheit*'s pre-title sequence concerns the US
Presidential elections of 2000, with the farce of the Florida recounts and
the 'wrong call' made by the media. Over archive news images, we hear
the following (I have cited here only the first and last section of the full
sequence):

Gore:           God bless you, Florida! Thank you!
Moore:          Did the last four years not really happen?
                Look, there's Ben Affleck. He's often in my dreams.
                And the *Taxi Driver* guy. He was there too.
                And little Stevie Wonder, he seemed so happy…like a
                miracle had taken place.
                Was it a dream?
Crowd:          We want Gore!
Moore:          Or was it real?
                It was election night 2000, and things seemed to be
                going as planned.

[*Moore then develops the account, with clips, of how the election was first 'called' for
Gore by television stations, and how Fox news then called it for Bush, to be followed
by the networks reversing their earlier predictions*].

Moore:          How does someone like Bush get away with
                something like this?

[*Across shot of Bush laughing with colleagues*]

> Well, first, it helps if your brother is the governor of
> the state in question.

Bush [*speaking to his brother in aircraft*]:

|  |  |
|---|---|
|  | You know something? We are gonna win Florida. Mark my words. You can write it down. |
| Moore: | Second, make sure your campaign chairman ... is also the vote-count woman and that her state hires a company ... to knock voters off the rolls who aren't likely to vote for you. You can usually tell them by the colour of their skin. Then make sure your side fights like it's life or death. |
| James Baker: | This talk about legitimacy is overblown. |
| Crowd: | President Bush! President Bush! |
| Moore: | And hope the other side sits by and waits for the phone to ring. And even if numerous independent investigations ... prove that Gore got the most votes ... it won't matter, as long as all your daddy's friends ... on the Supreme Court vote the right way. |
| Gore: | While I strongly disagree with the court's decision, I accept it. |
| Senator Tom : Daschle | What we need now is acceptance. We have a new president-elect. |
| Moore: | It turns out none of this was a dream. It's what really happened. |

[*He finishes with the story of the joint session of the House of Representatives and the failure of the Congressional Black Caucus to have its objections to the result on grounds of procedural misconduct taken forward.*]

Here, Moore's speech is developed as 'chat' with the audience, carrying quiet irony as it follows the twists and turns of events. Its description, initially in hushed tones (acting out the idea of still trying to come to terms with it all) is constructed from discrete comments. These build a little 'reconstruction' of what happened, slipping occasionally into the present tense (as in the recognition of celebrities) and thereby injecting further immediacy into the visualisation, before falling back to develop the story as past event. The level of corruption he perceives in the political process and the comic lack of integrity displayed in the media coverage are not offered as a completed, cool judgement, but rather as a series of still-bewildered moments of perception bordering on disbelief, connecting with a growing, cynical understanding of the way in which the 'game' has been played. The buoyant musical score gives ironic strength to the 'dream' idea, contrasting with the sorry spectacle of what is finally seen to be happening and the mordant power of the analysis.

## REASON AND AFFECT

My third subheading introduces considerations of a more general kind. In fact, 'reason and affect' generates questions that connect directly with 'addressing audiences' and I shall try to follow some themes across these subheads. The extent to which rationality and deliberation are essential values of documentary discourse (Nichols' notion of 'sobriety' is relevant here), ones to be placed in a degree of contrast, and perhaps then of careful combination, with matters of 'emotion' and 'feeling', has been debated across a number of different documentary spaces. We can look, for instance, at the way in which this issue has been raised within television current affairs documentary, where emphasis on rationality of design has often been seen as a marker of journalistic integrity, of 'good reporting', in the context of strengthening imperatives towards providing infotainment (see the discussion of the British situation in Goddard, Corner and Richardson, 2007). The precise terms of the play-off here, in documentary journalism, will be different from that found in discussion within observational film-making, although this too is an area in which ideas of a 'cool' and un-rhetorical depiction, a 'straight as possible' engagement with reality have tended to hold sway.[7] In the first instance the communicative rationality is seen as a product of the design and mode of the reportage and in the second, of the close and possibly sustained witnessing of specific circumstances and events, scrupulously rendered in their 'directness'. In neither case is an emotional response denied, but it is placed primarily as a consequence of what is reported, heard and observed and then thought about, rather than being a function of the film or programme's own discursive work, of orchestration. The nervousness of much documentary journalism and observational work about the use of music on the soundtrack (see Corner, 2002) is one indication of this judgement about how emotions should be 'contained' in documentary, albeit a judgement often radically modified by developments in reality television.[8]

Where political themes are concerned, the emphasis on rationality is likely to be at its strongest, particularly in television productions framed by journalistic protocols. Here, an institutionally framed anxiety about the 'proper' (i.e. balanced, impartial, 'fair') treatment of the political is often high. However, as I noted earlier, many examples of political documentary making internationally are not framed by these concerns and they use the documentary form to advocate specific political positions and strongly criticise others. How are questions of rationality and emotion posed in the broad tradition of the 'radical' documentary? How does argument work alongside more affective devices, including devices of shock?

If we return to my three examples, we can see various deployments of affective discourse, all finally (if, at times, uncertainly) placed as secondary to rational structures. This differs from much promotional film-making and also from many British documentary films of the classic 1930s period (e.g. Basil Wright's *Song of Ceylon*, 1934 and Grierson and Cavalcanti's *Coalface*, 1935, both made for the GPO film unit) where a combination of music and markedly rhetorical speech quickly establishes 'feeling' with a primary force, seeking to make affective relationships a central and open part of the business of engaging with the topic.

*Fahrenheit* deploys a sustained but carefully modulated affective level through Moore's commentary, which as well as presenting facts and arguments also cues the viewer into moods of surprise, indignation and comic disdain. Throughout the film, the viewer, following these cues, is placed in a politically superior position to the unfolding pattern of causality and connection, a position which is both cognitive and affective in character, creating the space for modalities of critical humour to be a dominant, recurring component in 'reading' the account. At other times (for instance, the rendering of the Trade Centre attack; the interviews with the woman who has lost her son), emotion follows from the contemplation of other people's pain and grief.

*Nightmares*, as I indicated earlier, works with a clear separation of communicative design in its visual and speech components. The style and delivery of the commentary is so strong in its indications of the coolly rational (politicality dissected) as to become mannered, while the hectic flow of images with music works to produce emotional volatility and a pervasive sense of the sinister as well as the bizarre.

*The Fog of War* provides another example of tensions across the visual/verbal combination. McNamara's self-accounting is nothing if not an attempt at the 'rational', indeed at 'rationalisation', yet the film is also interested in the idiosyncrasies of his delivery as part of its exploration of the personal as well as historical dimension of the events it covers. This can be seen in the opening sequence. Immediately establishing McNamara as concerned about 'performance' (the remarks about sound levels and editing), this organises the viewer into a viewing and listening relationship with a strong affective dimension. McNamara is, to some degree, positioned as the 'object of emotional curiosity' as he carries out his sustained exercise in reflexivity. The dynamics of personal alignment, of disgust, disapproval or indeed of empathy and understanding, are an important dimension of the audience experience. The politics of *Fog* are to a degree carried in the face of McNamara, a face regularly seen in close-up, the camera registering its movements of expression, its shifts of mood, what it might suggest about an 'inner' McNamara, the microphone picking up the hesitations and the tonal shifts. This compares interestingly with the use of faces and bodies made by Moore in *Fahrenheit*, picked up in Mandy Merck's uses of the phrase 'critical physiognomy'. In both cases, a sense is generated of the camera catching 'truths of the person', positioned for critical contemplation (and for connection to the broader themes) within the film's overall offer. However, in neither case is this feeling given any explicit closure by the speech, even though Moore's commentary performs many closing functions in developing the argument of his film, putting certain matters emphatically 'beyond doubt'.

*Nightmares* does not have the level of concern with particular individuals to carry out strategies of emphatic personalisation through sequences of sustained 'display', as described above. However, working with its wider thematic plan and its imaginative interest in the aesthetics of the unsettling, moments of symbolic 'essentialism' are constructed. Of these, the slow-motion image that closes the first programme, of young Taliban dancing together underneath the soundtrack of the pop classic, 'Baby, It's Cold Outside', was often cited in discussion of the film's ironic eloquence and its staging of radically cross-cultural interconnections. The swirling gracefulness of the exotic image (emphatic 'them-ness') is designed to combine pleasingly, but more to the point instructively, with the Western romantic urbanity of the lyrics ('us-ness').

There is a further dimension of rhetorical design that needs attention here. That is the extent to which a film works with a singular sense of the truth of its own account (explicitly contrasted, perhaps, with the falsity of others) or offers a more openly pluralistic version of circumstances and events. 'Pluralism' in documentary journalism is conventionally the product of varied sourcing, putting into a film a number of what are perhaps explicitly contested viewpoints. Film-makers can give their work the energies of 'open dialogue' by not privileging any one version over others or they can, by various means, give one version dominance as the version approved and advanced by the film. A 'dominant' judgement can be openly offered, as a consequence of the documentary's own investigations and framework of values, or it can be implicitly estab- lished, by the weighting of accounts, their organisation within the logics of sequence and the kinds of visual support they receive. As I suggested above, just how much covert 'management' of the argument, and of what kind, a political documentary should allow itself, has been a long- standing issue among both film-makers and critics. The avoidance of mechanisms of deceit, of those covert forms of support seen as typical of 'propaganda', becomes a principal point of reference for some involved in the debate, whereas others work with a far more extensive sense of discursive options.

Nichols' writings (for example, 1991) point to another way in which a documentary can be 'plural', not by working across a number of distinct perspectives on events so much as by questioning the possibility of arriv- ing at *any* definitive version. This more radical scepticism regarding epistemological premises, involving reference to such factors as multiple causality, the 'pre-narrativisation' of many so-called primary sources, and the contingency of memory, works to problematise the whole busi- ness of knowing as well as (and sometimes rather than) advancing a particular account. It has for obvious reasons not found much favour in broadcasting, where the forms of journalistic positivism seen as essential to the professional quest (the truth may be very hard to find, but it's there somewhere) have not aligned well with the levels of 'uncertainty' it introduces and broadcasters have feared problems of accessibility and acceptability with popular audiences. Its 'postmodern' character has also caused acute problems for some radical political projects, which have seen their first objective to be the displacement of established official falsehoods and their replacement with 'truer' accounts, an objective that too strong a sympathy with epistemological relativism might serve to undercut.

Of the three films I have taken as examples, two have little interest in developing 'pluralism' of either kind. Moore's film is driven strategically by his commitment to a particular set of casual connections which he takes to be unproblematically true, a commitment which, together with his mode of assembly of the evidence, has been the principal reason why his film has received heated discussion in relation to the 'propaganda' label.[9] *Nightmares*, more explicitly and narrowly a 'thesis film' than *Fahrenheit*, voices its interconnecting propositions with a total confidence in their status as revealed analytic knowledge. Only *Fog* introduces a degree of contingency and doubt, at times presenting McNamara as a kind of 'unreliable narrator' whose retrospection is, at points, conflicted. This is very different from presenting him as lying or as untrustworthy and the film is concerned, at many points, to make '*the* truth of events' (as, for instance, it is captured on tape recordings) a primary point of reference, while nevertheless signalling in a variety of ways the complexity both of their objective character and (more easily done) of the subjective judgements that informed their shaping. Unlike both *Fahrenheit* and *Nightmares*, *Fog* operates with no explicit framing discourse of its own. It hands explicitness entirely over to McNamara, a move that made some critics believe it was at risk of appearing too much like an 'apology' for him, at least within more naive readings.[10]

## ADDRESSING AUDIENCES

The question of who a given documentary is for, and what intentions it might have towards its audience(s), is clearly an important one, carrying implications for the entire communicative design. Documentary-makers sometimes have firm ideas about categories of viewer, what they know already and what they are likely to believe about specific issues, but they also often have to operate with a broader sense of possible markets and routes for distribution/exhibition. Work with a radical political edge has often faced the risk, if not always acknowledging it, of 'preaching to the converted' by using modes of address and levels of content which serve mainly to engage people already politically alert to its themes. Such a function is certainly not without its benefits, but it is often out of line with a commitment to extend and deepen political understanding, to act as a means (possibly implicit) of political education or indeed mobilisation.

One of the reasons for *Fahrenheit*'s popular success internationally was Moore's already tested formula for holding diverse audiences with his mode of address and mix of contents. This formula is one in which a particular kind of sociability is offered to viewers, an inclusive sense almost of 'hanging out' with Moore to follow through on explorations having both a serious and a comic dimension. One might describe this mode as that of a *critical geniality*, and it is certainly very different in tone from those sometimes austere exercises in radical exposition which have been a part of political documentary work internationally.

*Fog* provides its viewers with points of personalised engagement, as we have seen, but its approach is altogether more demanding and it is impossible to imagine other than a small proportion of the cinema and DVD audiences for Moore's film choosing to watch it. It is also a much quieter film politically, essentially an exercise in McNamara's defensive reflexivity and Morris's subtle judgements, and unlikely to have an initial appeal for people not already oriented towards the continuing debate about US foreign policy in the period it examines.[11]

*Nightmares*, seeking a national television audience, works with its own, strong version of a 'television of attractions'[12] at the level of visual design, and it keeps its commentary clear and emphatic, if necessarily complex in some of its historical and theoretical content. Despite the visual busyness and originality, its 'watchability' is finally grounded in the ability of a viewer to follow the almost continuous voiced-over speech and remain interested in the propositions and connections it develops. Again, this approach suggests a smaller audience than that for the Moore film, and one, as in *Fog*, predisposed towards political analysis, although the analysis works hard to engage and hold, and the 'hook' of the whole series is a powerful populist-radical one, combining as it does the theme of the War on Terror with ideas of a state conspiracy to deceive.

Just by what strategies of revelation, exposition, argument, testimony or emotional intensity political documentaries attempt to create change in their viewers is, as indicated, a matter not only of different approaches but of dispute (I have noted some outlines of this dispute in Corner, 2008). A regular point at issue here has been the extent and kind of 'realisms' employed, seeking variously to place viewers in a seemingly direct spectatorial or evidential relationship with the historical and political world. Conversely, there is the range of more symbolic, associative discourses that can be put into play. Through their very indirectness and possible ambiguity, these latter can give expanded scope for articulating political ideas. In relation to my comments above about forms of calculated *indeterminacy*, they can also work to break up and problematise the dominant terms upon which political reality is established and routinely perceived. The championing of elements of political modernism (and now, postmodernism) against modes of realism (as, for instance, in Nichols, 1976) has usually gone along with at least a recognition of the popular reach and cognitive power of realist design, grounded in its 'easy' mimeticism and (apparent) directness of sourcing. Such power is, not surprisingly, quite frequently seen as the defining problem for documentary, leading perhaps to the conundrum well expressed by Paula Rabinowitz: 'Does the invocation of reality destabilize realism, or more firmly install it? Why pick up a tool used as much for social control as for radical change?' (Rabinowitz, 1994: 6).[13]

It is important to note that 'realism' cannot productively be applied to documentary analysis without recognising the differences between documentary discourses and those of fiction, where the 'realist' project is essentially about creating a reality-effect from that which is openly offered as the product of artifice (see the discussion of this issue in Chapter 2). To use Brian Winston's (1995) powerful title phrase, documentary 'claims the real' in distinctive ways, some of which relate to the devices of fiction (e.g. shot continuities in displaying the physical world and action within it, narrative structure, development of character interest) but some of which do not. Of those that do not, the inclusion of a strongly descriptive and argumentational strand using direct-address speech by commentary, in-shot presenter or participant, is often defining. This strand can only be considered 'realist' within a different set of criteria from that used to assess pictorial and narrative devices of realism (where ideas of 'illusion' predominate). The way it operates is much closer to the *propositional* discourses of journalism, history and sociology. This difference clearly requires acknowledgement in any assessment of how the offer of political knowledge made by a particular documentary is structured and pitched to the viewer.[14] For instance, each of my three examples above is driven strongly by spoken, propositional accounts. *Nightmares* disrupts realist pictorial expectations routinely but it uses brief sections of archival material for their (realist) 'transparency' to historical events. *Fog* is also pictorially disruptive at many points, while also working in a sustained way with 'realist' combinations of McNamara's voiced account and the archive footage. *Fahrenheit* works mainly with Moore's own style of reportorial realism, rarely settling down into pictorially realist continuities for long, given the amount and range of the material that underpins its commentary. To describe any of these three examples as 'realist' in primary identity might be to push an already overstretched term beyond useful application.

In an illuminating review of some of the broader issues affecting the cognitive profile of documentaries within the 'realist' context, Jane Gaines (1999) uses the idea of 'political mimesis' to describe a line of impact different from that suggested by ideas of the didactic and the pedagogic. She describes this as the way in which many films, through 'aesthetic supplements', are able to make 'visceral appeals that work to rouse audiences' (1999: 99). These appeals might, she suggests, provide a sensuous rather than analytic route to politicisation (or re-politicisation), forming a wish to imitate, sympathetically to 'body back' as she puts it, the struggles and acts of opposition portrayed in the film. Such a theory, essentially one about a documentary's capacity to generate a productive 'political imaginary', one that *excites* change in the viewer, provokes questions about just how far the presumed effect is likely to develop from being an individualised *experience* of emotional alignment to being a *behaviour* (e.g. joining an organisation, changing lifestyle, becoming involved in forms of political activity). Nevertheless, the issues opened up by the idea of 'political mimesis' are ones that deserve attention in any consideration of how documentaries can change political understanding and promote action. Among other things, they point towards forms in which the exposure of wrongs and the advancing of critique are accompanied by indications of active opposition and of alternatives. From my examples, only the 'critical geniality' of *Fahrenheit* gets close to establishing this kind of solidarity of feeling with viewers.[15]

## CONCLUSION

The identification and interrogation of aspects of the political have been marked characteristics of international work in documentary, carried out from within a range of institutional contexts and according to a variety of aesthetic recipes using different kinds of propositional structure. Whatever the diverse, and sometimes anodyne, purposes to which documentary methods are routinely put, a number of films and programmes continue to appear with strong political themes and content. The forms of portrayal they use, the 'political aesthetics' they develop and apply, relate to developments elsewhere in the mediasphere, including the changing discourses of television journalism (with which some documentaries establish convergence and others strongly take issue). Significantly, they also recognise developments in screen fiction, particularly the political fictions that continue to be an important part of international cinema production, including Hollywood. Articulating the political will continue to be a changing project, at the levels of storytelling, visualisation and filmic argument. The volatility of international political culture (significantly, all three of my examples concern matters of 'foreign policy') is likely to offer new opportunities in terms of emerging fracture points in public consciousness, new anxieties around which to construct a claim upon viewing attention, new configurations of argument and 'iconic moments' through which to fashion connections across the flows of power, including those undeclared or denied. Meanwhile, the expansion of audio-visual markets and their internal revision, including by web-based distribution, will make finding audiences a continuing strategic challenge.

I have wanted briefly to explore something of the aesthetic and discursive character, including the tensions, of recent documentary work committed to exploration of the political as both an objective realm (of structures and processes) and a subjective realm (of ideas and feelings). My terms of analysis, drawing on previous studies and only provisional, could be applied to a wider range of productions. Developed and revised, they could help inform assessment of that emerging work which, whatever the continuities, will struggle anew with how 'politicality' can be constituted and be made engaging, using the resources of non-fiction images and sounds.

## A NOTE ON THE ACCESSIBILITY OF EXAMPLES

At the time of preparing the material for this volume, all three of the main examples I have used were available on DVD, with copies of *The Power of Nightmares* easier to obtain through web-based outlets than through mainstream distributors.

## NOTES

1   Of particular significance here are documentaries about family life, and of women's roles within this, that only engage politics implicitly and as it embeds personal relationships, but which nevertheless have the potential for positioning the audience politically in important ways. See, for instance, Sue Holmes and Deborah Jermyn (2008) on issues around the reality show *Wife Swap*.

2   A quite recent example of visual design 'politicising' the world is Hubert Saupers' *Darwin's Nightmare* (2004), about the impact on the culture and economy of Lake Victoria, Tanzania, of a fishing industry centred on the Nile Perch, a predatory fish introduced in order to be sold to European export markets. The recurrent image of giant Russian transport aircraft coming in to land, or taking off, over the lake makes symbolic connection with the 'predatory' in relation to the fish, to Africa–Europe relations and to globalised capitalism.

3   Given the common interest in the picturing of the real, photography shares with documentary film and television some of the key issues surrounding its politics (among the extensive writing here, Sontag (1979) remains suggestive while Hariman and Lucaites (2007) is a major achievement of historical scholarship).

4   Ib Bondebjerg (2006) has recently written illuminatingly about the idea of 'backstage' in relation to documentaries about politics.

5      Among the most celebrated films are *In the Year of the Pig* (1968) and *Milhouse – A White Comedy* (1971).

6      Morris's method famously uses the Interrotron, a kind of adapted teleprompter that allows interviewees to appear to address the camera (and thereby the viewer) directly by gazing at a monitor just beneath it on which the interviewer is seen asking questions. For his own account see the interview at www.errolmorris.com/content/eyecontact/interrotron .html (accessed 15 August 2009).

7      Directorial statements on these points are often loose and contradictory, but assertions of rhetorical, and indeed authorial, minimalism are common.

8      Emotionality is a key aspect of the debate about the gender profile of documentary work and about what feminist alternatives look like, or might look like, when set alongside dominant male practice. Again, it has been a factor in some of the more positive assessments of reality television formats.

9      This issue is widely debated. But see Rhoads (2004) for a sharply focused treatment.

10     The question of what given viewers will 'get' from an account when a high degree of interpretive openness is offered, or when devices of irony and implicit contrast are central to the design, is another issue confronting the ambition to be politically effective. Despite their own moments of openness, neither *Fahrenheit* nor *Nightmares* risks having their fundamentally critical and sharply focused intentions go unrecognised.

11     Among the many critical accounts, the perceptive discussions of it in Bruzzi (2006) and Wayne (2008) are notable.

12     The idea of 'cinema of attractions' comes from Gunning (1990). Its sense of a sequence or even an entire film made compelling by the variety and intensity of the discrete spectacles it offers rather than any dominant principle of continuity is applicable to aspects of contemporary documentary design. Beattie (2008) provides an illuminating account of modes of documentary 'display'.

13     Among accounts questioning anti-realist perspectives, Juhasz (1994) is deservedly much-cited.

14     The 'propositional' is a mode of documentary discourse, generated by speech but including the management of what is seen, that has sometimes been under-recognised recently as a result of an emphasis on observationalism that reality television has served to reinforce. I am exploring propositionality more fully in my current writing.

15     Substantive, rather than essentially speculative, ideas of audience interpretation have made a belated arrival in documentary studies. Austin (2007) and Amaya (2008) give suggestive examples and discussion.

# 9

## 'Critical social optics' and the transformations of audio-visual culture

### PRELIMINARY NOTE

*I wanted to focus here on a particular form of photography, the prize-winning press image, but to go beyond the terms of analysis appropriate to exploring professional work of this kind and to look at the ways in which such images circulated on the web and became the subject of intensive and varied critical commentary. It seemed to me that the range and detail of some of this commentary contributed to an unprecedented situation in international visual culture. It made an image 'discussable' and 'debatable' in new ways, sometimes setting up terms of dialogue in which the person who took the images would also contribute, partly perhaps as a matter of professional self-publicity but also in response to criticism and to questions which had been raised about meanings and the terms of their production. Thus, the sphere of the technical and aesthetic production of the image was brought into closer and richer alignment with the sphere of diverse subjectivities in ways which might register the impact of an image (confirming its power) but also question the meanings and purposes at work through it and behind it.*

*There is at the moment an extensive literature, some of which I have cited on earlier pages, about just how much, and in what directions, digital mediations and digital culture might change the present conditions of political and social life. Both in Chapter 2 and in Chapter 7 I have also looked at aspects of photographic form. My concern here was primarily with the placing of photographic work in new contexts of public space which seem to reposition the relationships between images and their meanings in quite decisive ways, whatever the arguments about the broader consequences.*

*As well as having an interest in the shape of the emerging audio-visual landscape, I am engaged by the question of how photo-journalism (for which a number of obituaries have already been written) might survive as an irreplaceable way of learning about the world through looking steadily at images of selected parts of it, reduced to stillness. Here, an increased flow of amateur rather than professional images looks like being part of the pattern.*

In this chapter I want to raise some questions about the ways in which images are encountered, perceived, understood and (often) questioned as a result of the radical transformation of visual culture within digital contexts. This will involve attention to aspects of the changing culture of photography, since it seems to me that, in engaging with the implications of the digital, media scholarship can benefit considerably from a closer, comparative attention to what has happened to photography as it has become transformed over the last fifteen years or so. This transformation has clearly affected its practices of production and has completely reconfigured its modes of distribution, display and consumption. More broadly, it has generated what I think can be seen as a new, critical appreciation of how images mean and of the complexity of the processes both of production and of consumption involved. Along with other developments, without directly 'subverting' the use of images, it has brought about a degree of *instability* in visual meaning. It has served to 'unstick' the image from the world a little – not detaching it completely, but pulling it over into the more openly contentious realms of culture and of politics. It is this process I want to highlight in my title term 'critical social optics', with its emphases on critical engagement and the sociality (both in awareness and in the terms of their distribution) of emerging modes of the image.

Television remains, in most countries, the dominant public medium. Its versions of mobile visibility, its kinetic (and sonically supported) renderings of the world, have been given expanded reach through the diverse applications that other chapters in this book explore. Whatever the changes it undergoes, its semiotic commitments to flow, sequence, process, action, and narrative design are likely to continue, albeit with modifications. However, within this context I want to open up some questions about the revived public profile of the still and silent image, whose distinctive, provocative ways of setting up relationships of seeing, of brokering between world and subjectivity, of 'holding' time and 'giving' time, provide, as I have suggested, a useful comparison with television's characteristic modes of 'capturing' the real and of promising knowledge to viewers.

The new Routledge journal *Photographies* provides just one indication of the kind of revised agenda of theory and enquiry generated around digital change and the culture of the image. The editorial to its first issue noted that:

> One thing seems certain: there is now more photography, possibly of more kinds, than ever before. We are dealing with a truly

expanded field where deep continuities run alongside unforeseen
and radical transformation. (Editorial, 2008)

Over the last two decades, photography, far from being dispatched into
a more marginal, residual position within media culture by the developments of new technology, has become a more dominant and influential
feature of the mediascape. Most dramatically, it has wholly reconfigured
the character of self-documentation in the private sphere, its digital possibilities and applications bringing about a shift in private visual culture
that has continued with accelerated pace the revolution in 'seeing ourselves' (and, of course, 'seeing others') that popular photography first
introduced in the late nineteenth and early twentieth centuries.

How have the new shifts impacted upon the character of photography as a mode of public communication, as a mode of 'seeing the social'
and 'seeing the political'? First of all, it is immediately clear that the radical changes to photography in what I have called private visual culture
have often had direct implications for public visual culture. This is most
obviously true in respect of the use of photography within photoblog-
ging, where the private/public fusions that are defining of 'blogs' as a
genre are given an open articulation.[1] It is also clearly true in respect of
the important role photographs play within social networking sights such
as *Myspace* and *Facebook*, where precisely the uncertain borderlines
between 'private' and 'public' have been the source of pleasure, insight,
embarrassment and even legal prosecution.[2]

But what of more direct uses of the photograph as an agency of
public and political knowledge? With its widely discussed characteristics
of silence and stillness, characteristics imparting both its semiotic
strength and its limitations, how does the photograph figure within a
public culture that might be thought to be moving ever more emphatically towards a commitment to the semiotics of sound and to movement,
to the hectic modalities of representation characterised, for instance, in
'reality television' and in the new modes of 'infotainment'?[3] In what
ways has its significatory and ideological profile shifted, revealing new
possibilities both for deception and for knowledge, within the emerging
terms of technological application? How far does that 'critique of
photography' (and especially of documentary photography) developed
in the 1970s and 1980s transfer to the newer modes of production and
display?[4]

I want to pursue some of these questions by looking at examples of
recent high-profile 'public photography' and exploring how digital
applications have worked to thicken and extend the exchange of

viewer's critical discourse around the still image at the same time as providing photographers with a new platform for displaying their images and for telling stories about them and about the contexts of their taking. Images have thus become more thickly 'narrated' both by those who produce them and those who view them. Following up on the point made earlier, by using the phrase 'critical social optics' I mean to signal both a concern with the construction of the image as an aesthetic, artefactual object of engagement and perhaps of pleasure and a broader address to the political and cultural consequences of connecting viewers to the world photographically. As photography takes its myriad digitalised routes through political, social, institutional and psychological space, it has become newly 'foregrounded', more sharply marked as a social practice.

## CASE STUDY: THE WORLD PRESS PHOTO OF THE YEAR AWARD

In 2007, the World Press Photo of the Year Award for the best news picture of the previous year was given to the American photo-journalist Spencer Platt of Getty Images for a photograph taken on 15 August 2006 in Beirut. ('World Press Photo of Year Award 2006' brings up a number of options on a Google 'images' search, involving over 50 websites in June 2009. Worldpressphoto.org itself includes an opportunity both to see the image and to hear Spencer Platt talking about it.) 15 August was the day after the ceasefire in the conflict between Israel and Hezbollah forces in the Lebanon, a conflict that had resulted in the Israeli shelling of parts of Beirut.

The photograph shows five young people, four women and one man, seated in a moving red convertible against a background of devastated buildings and heaped debris from the shelling. The bottom half of the frame is tightly around the group in the car, running from the windscreen along to the folded canopy at the rear. The upper half of the frame is dominated by the damage on the far side of the street, down which the car is driving left to right. A few standing figures can be seen in front of the debris, some apparently speaking on mobile phones. The picture cuts off the visible foreground after revealing only the first few inches of the car's nearside, but a strong perception of the out-of-frame foreground is signalled by the fact that four of the car's occupants, all but the man driving, are looking towards this foreground, two at an angle to the line of the camera and two looking directly in its direction.

One of the women on the back seat is holding a handkerchief to her face, one appears to be taking a photo (or perhaps sending a text) on a camera phone. Four of the car's occupants are wearing sunglasses.

The shiny red colour of the car, the resonance of open-topped driving and the sense of youthful style conveyed by the clean, neat appearance of those seated inside, with the woman on the front seat in a white T-shirt, and two of those in the back in black dresses, all are in striking contrast with the setting. Crucially, the position of the photographer is higher than road level, allowing a perspective that gives the car's interior a depth from nearside to offside within which its occupants can be more clearly and fully seen. We look into the car as well as perceive it against its background.

The caption initially given to the picture was 'Affluent Lebanese drive down the street to look at a destroyed neighbourhood in southern Beirut' with an added date. However, the contrastive force of the image was picked up and amplified more explicitly by other users (one Dutch newspaper used the caption 'The Cool People VS. Hezbollah'). A website writer noted, more critically still and elaborating on the caption:

> The 'Young Lebanese' happen to be a sports car full of women who have clearly devoted a lot of energy to trying to look sexy in a global-celbutard sort of way. It's like they were hoping to be hounded by paparazzi, but ended up instead in a war photographer's viewfinder. ('One Photograph That Sums it All Up', Veryshortlist.com, 22 February 2007)

When it was awarded the top prize in February 2007 by World Press Photo (an independent, non-profit foundation supporting international photojournalism and based in Amsterdam), the chairwomen of the panel offered a more nuanced reading, noting how it was 'a picture you can keep looking at. It has the complexity and contradiction of real life, amidst chaos. The photograph makes you look beyond the obvious' (cited in www. lensculture.com. 'World Press Photo Winners for 2006'). On the website OpenDemocracy.net ('Beirut and Contradiction', 13 Feb. 2007, www.opendemocracy.net/conflict-Literature/world press photo 4342.jsp) the writer Mai Ghoussoub picked up the theme of contradiction after having the image emailed to her by a friend. She observed how the picture 'looked disturbing and even repellent to most viewers' but went on to note her own fascination with it and the way its meaning for her centred on 'the metaphor it creates about war photography', about 'voyeurism' and 'the act of taking photos in tragic situations'. She also mentioned another friend's suggestive comments about how the image of these young people together in a convertible seemed to connect connotatively with a classic Hollywood iconography of youth, glamour and fate. To many viewers of the image, this will be seen as a plausible pick-up on the cultural echoes (even down to the Monroe-like profile of the woman in the white top and dark glasses at the front of the car).

Negative readings of the image as showing 'disaster tourism' circulated alongside more complex, or positive ones, with controversy surrounding the award in a number of countries, both among professional and amateur photographers and more widely. For example, Lebanese photographer Samer Mohdad claimed that the giving of the prize was 'an insult to all news photographers who have risked their lives to cover this horrible war' (cited in 'Award Winning Photograph Puts Subjects on the Defensive' mesarabies.blog, 22 Feb. 2007). A Toronto gallery-owner and photography festival organiser posted a note on the site of the Canadian magazine *Walrus* raising questions not only about the values of the people in the photograph but, by metaphoric extension, about those of society in general:

> At first glance, this photograph is an indictment of the five youths in the car. Clearly the children of privilege, they seem to be on an innocuous Sunday drive. Their bright red sports car and fashions show them as the 'in crowd'. What is it that shields them from the devastation that surrounds them? Is it the shiny car, their money, or their attitude? It is the latter notion which troubles me the most because it isn't the attitudes of these five that disturbs me, but our own. Although we are informed of the world's problems and hold opinions for solutions, or at the very least we express exasperation at the improbability of finding answers to many specific issues from regions with systemic hatred, we are sheltered in our own islands of affluence. (Stephen Bulger, *Walrus*, 28 August 2007)

Questions were inevitably raised about the conditions of the photograph's taking, and Platt was quite quick to establish its 'authenticity' and his own relationship of integrity towards what it depicted. His account, in interview, was posted on a number of websites, and a crucial passage went as follows:

> This was the first morning that we were able to really survey what had happened here. And I saw out of the corner of my eye, coming

at me at a fairly decent speed, a car that really stood out from everything else. It was clean. Nothing in the neighborhood was clean. It was like 9/11, the day after ... I had very little time to focus, to compose. I snapped, I suppose, about five images, four of which were completely and totally ruined because there was a gentleman standing in front of me and his arm was in the picture. ('Through The Looking Glass', www.onthemedia.org, 4 May 2007)

He went on to note that he took 400 images that day, editing it down in his hotel room to 30, which he sent through and which included the car photo. Reflecting on the difficulties in making sense of the image, he commented:

There's a lot of ambiguity to the image, who the women are, what they're thinking, what kind of background do they come from? I hear a different interpretation of it every day, and I'm somewhat sympathetic with them all. ('Through The Looking Glass', www.onthemedia.org, 4 May 2007)

Speaking on a short presentation placed on the World Press Photo website after the award had been made, he elaborated on the range and scale of interpretations:

You go online and there are 12, 15, 20 different interpretations from 20 different nationalities and backgrounds, about what they think about it, what they feel about it, what they think the photographer was trying to say. (worldpressphoto.org, 2007)

In further comment during a telephone interview with the BBC, reported on the BBC website, Platt moved to a slightly different take on the people in the car from the dominant concern with whether or not they were 'disaster tourists'. He placed them as possible victims, but victims seen in a new way:

The picture challenges our notion of what a victim is meant to look like. These people are not victims, they look strong, they're full of youth. (Cited in Kim Ghattas, 'Lebanon War Image Causes Controversy', bbc.co.uk, 8 March 2007)

Few published interpretations had taken the 'victim' route, even in speculation or as a perceived challenge to stereotypical readings. In the context of the developing controversy around the image, Platt elaborated on this view (complicating it with some further, rather revealing, judgements aligning political power and spending power) in an interview with Getty Images CEO Jonathan Klein (posted on You Tube):

> In the media ... you are used to seeing people from the Middle East that are not empowered. And these people have power. These are beautiful, sexy looking people that look like they have some spending power. And these people represent a dynamic in a very important part of the Middle East. ('Jonathan Klein interviews Getty Photographer Spencer Platt', posted 22 July 2007, www.youtube.com/watch?v=iQQIp2PEr-s)

In a development that is not too surprising, given the level of international media interest, the people in the car were found and interviewed by the press (German and Belgian journalists were involved initially, with the account rapidly being distributed to other news outlets and websites). In the process they gave their own story of the background to the image. Four of them were actually residents in the area depicted, who had had to flee because of the shelling. This was their first trip back, to check on their apartment and belongings. The car itself had been previously used to transport medication to refugees taking shelter in central Beirut. One of them noted of the image:

> It's an interesting picture, but there were so many more that reflected what really happened here ...
>
> But it's true that there were people who did come to the area just to have a look at the destruction ...
>
> It's the caption that went with the picture that made it famous and that's what's upsetting, the caption reinforces the cliché.

Another commented:

> I understand why the picture won. It's about the contrast between destruction and glamour. But it's the wrong image of the war and it sanitizes it. (Both quotations from bbc.co.uk, 'Lebanon War Image Causes Controversy', full reference as cited above)

The implication from these interviews is also that none of the people in the car had any idea that the picture had been taken until its publication in *Paris Match* in September 2006. They had not noticed Platt at all.

What this example highlights is that familiar capacity of photography to be both powerful and indeterminate. This combination can be found in other media, but photography's lack of propositionality, its much-discussed status as an apparent representation of a given moment rather than an explicit discourse about that moment, gives its way of being 'open to interpretation' a very distinctive character. The circuits of the web are providing both a new and prominent platform for the display of photographic practice, for its special ways of bringing us close to the 'look of things', and at the same time an active critical forum, a space of exchange, for debating the photograph's problematic and contestable 'iconicity', its often implicit (sometimes beguiling, sometimes deeply objectionable) ways of producing knowledge and encouraging judgements.

While not having the space to develop a second case study at comparable length, I would like to mention here the World Press Photo of the Year Award winner for the following year, taken in 2007 and awarded in 2008 (as with the Beirut photo, there are many website carrying this image as 'World Press Photo of Year Award 2007', with worldpressphoto.org itself an obvious choice). Once again, the critical social optics of 'seeing conflict' are involved. This image, taken by the British photographer Tim Hetherington, working for *Vanity Fair*, shows a young US soldier leaning back against the earth wall of a darkened military bunker in Afghanistan. His upturned helmet is cradled against his chest by his left hand and his right hand diagonally covers his upper face, leaving the left eye visible, in a gesture of exhaustion and stress. The background details of the image (military equipment, netting etc.) are reduced in definition by the overall darkness of the scene, giving the soldier (and especially his face) strong focus. The official caption was 'American soldier resting at bunker, Korengal Valley, Afghanistan, 16 September', but other websites have variations on this, for instance the BBC website reproduces it with the slightly more interpretative caption 'An exhausted American soldier in Afghanistan's Korengal Valley'. Hetherington was working at the time with the writer/reporter Sebastian Junger (author, among things, of the 'faction' bestseller and then film, *The Perfect Storm*). He has noted how the image was taken spontaneously (in his acceptance speech, available on rethink.dispatches.com – details and date below, he described it as 'a snatched moment ... I had no idea what the soldier was thinking or feeling'). He and Junger were resting in the bunker at the time and using its protection against the possibility of further Taleban fire on what had been an 'intense day'. Hetherington also comments:

At the time I took the picture, I remember seeing the image on the
back of the digital camera, showing it to Sebastian. I knew it was
good. ('Picture Power: Tim Hetherington', bbc.co.uk, 14 February
2008)

The idea of 'exhaustion' was carried further, into an implicitly political
interpretation, by the Chairman of the jury, Gary Knight, who observed
that 'this image shows the exhaustion of a man – and the exhaustion of
a nation' – worldpressphoto.org). The broader view stops short of offering a more precise reading of the terms of 'national exhaustion', leaving
the specific attitude taken towards America and the war as relatively
open. In his acceptance speech, Hetherington commented: 'It's said
the man portrayed shows the exhaustion of a nation. Some people see it
as propaganda for the war, others as an indictment of the war. But it
doesn't need to be either ... it's about a young man stuck on the side of
a mountain in Afghanistan'. Hetherington went on to say how the
soldier in the picture was now 'proud of it', as were his family, although
the soldier was unhappy with the news that it had been used on placards
at an anti-war protest in Nashville (rethink-dispatches.com/world-press-
photo-acceptance-speech, dated 27April 2008).

Clearly, keeping the meanings of the image contained around the soldier himself, rather than playing them into frameworks for assessing the
war, is virtually impossible, as I found when I showed this image to my
students and asked for their immediate interpretations. The iconicity of
a sole human figure in a posture of fatigue against a darkened background immediately works symbolically as well as naturalistically.
Similarly, the photograph has sufficient figurative ambiguity to afford a
resource both for pro-war and anti-war readings, as student opinion also
showed.[5] It is a photograph that one might imagine the US Army being
quite comfortable with, as well as the anti-war movement. Since
Hetherington was working at the time as an embedded journalist, this is
not at all surprising.

Aesthetically, the very darkness of the image was central to critical
responses, for some critics the indication of a technical/compositional
flaw, but for others quite the reverse, conveying the enriching suggestions of chiaroscuro. In a detailed and perceptive posting on the
photo website Foto8 (Adam Broomberg and Oliver Chanarin,
'Unconcerned but not Indifferent, 5 March 2008), the writer noted how
the 'blurred focus and pixelated JPEG compression make this image
feel accidental and urgent ... for some members of the jury it was also
"painterly"'.

Unlike the 'Beirut' image, the Afghanistan photograph, although deeply ambivalent, did not become strongly controversial for what it depicted, but only formally, for its choice as the winner against more sharply defined, attractively composed images on the shortlist.

## TEMPORALITY, INSTABILITY, RELOCATION

Just where the routine professional work of photojournalism and photo-documentary is now placed within these newer circuits of distribution, promotion, commentary and critique, within the emerging digital spaces and times, is uncertain. This is particularly so since the power and centrality of television journalism is in most countries defining for visual public knowledge. Nevertheless, the single image remains one dominant, media mode, both realist and expansively symbolic, for engaging with the world, perhaps most notably in the traditional form of the front-page photograph. Disasters, wars, domestic political affairs and various kinds of 'scoop' are given a focalising, condensing and often figurative projection through this practice. Web photography continues and then extends the practice, not only in relation to the scale of image availability and its subsequent informal distribution, but also in relation to the huge increase in representational scope, including image–text combinations, given by the use of site-based 'gallery' folders containing multiple images and perhaps involving slideshow formats. These widely used formats permit the control of individual image engagement by the viewer or they can be clicked to provide a time-sequenced route determined by the photographer with opportunities for narrative development and voiced-over commentary that allow closer proximity to television-video.[6] The emerging forms of web publication take place in what is still a 'second tier' of mediation, below that of mainstream television, newspapers and magazines. The attention they receive is therefore demographically skewed, although we know that the social profile of web use, including its relation to mainstream media, is now rapidly changing and that mainstream media themselves are sensitive to this, as they are to the wider circulation of images brought about by digital photography.[7] A much wider take-up of what had become 'newsworthy' images clearly happened with the World Press Photo Award images, carrying them digitally well beyond their first, selective print publication.[8]

I have suggested that the new contexts for photography include thickened possibilities both for explanation, commentary and critique. In that sense, they not only give added projection to the distinctive qualities of the still image as a mode of mediated perception and knowledge, but also create a broader and more varied forum for debating the image in both highly specific and also more general terms and according to a number of criteria, both substantive-realist and formal. The photograph as 'public document' thus itself becomes the object of a certain (constrained but significant) public discourse and the *debatability* of photography, not just photographic practice, is given a novel, expanded scope.

Moreover, I believe that the long-running and intensive debate about the 'adequacy to the real', the social sufficiency, of television's news and documentary portrayals is given a further, instructive point of reference by the photographic practices and the discourses of photographic comment that have been encouraged by digital platforms.[9] What is beyond dispute is that these practices and discourses require attention in any proper assessment of digital culture's character and direction, including the directions now being taken by television, and of the impact upon the shifting conditions of 'public seeing'.

## Notes

All cited web materials checked for access in June 2010 unless otherwise indicated.

1    Chris Cohen (2005) provides an illuminating account of the aesthetic and social drives at work here. See the *New York Times*' new photoblog 'Lens' (lens.blog.nytimes.com) for an indication of how mainstream media can work to relay elements of the photographic blogosphere as well as contribute to it.

2    As I write, the latest British narrative of public embarrassment here follows the appearance on Facebook of details of the family life, accompanied by photographs, of the next head of the Secret Intelligence Service. They were placed there by his wife, using her own page, and then quickly removed by authorities following discovery by the press. Photographs of him playing football on a beach, in swimming trunks, make a dramatic contrast with the fact that his predecessor began his period of office publically unnamed and with no public images of him allowed.

3    As well as the formative discussions of photography's semiotics contained in the work of Barthes and Sontag (notably Barthes, 1984 and Sontag, 1979), there are many illuminating studies of photographic temporality. A recent, important collection is Green and Lowry (2006).

4    An influential example of this would be Martha Rosler's classic essay (1981; revised and expanded 1989).

5    Some students found reading the soldier's primary circumstances (routine tiredness after being on watch, total fatigue, utter despair?) difficult, quite apart from making the move from this particularity to a broader symbolic level (the war, America etc.). Quite a few read the image as showing a soldier showing the physical toll of 'doing his duty', a reading that could move into patriotic, affirmative directions at least as easily as critical ones.

6    See Langton (2009) for a very recent account of the continuing possibilities and constraints for photo-journalism, written from the perspective of a practitioner.

7    Here, one example would be the routine use made by television news programmes of images sent in by 'eye-witnesses', now including video images captured on phone cameras. Another, broader, example of this expansion and multi-layering of visual culture would be the regular call by some popular television magazine programmes, including holiday series and even the weather slots of regional news, for viewers to send in their own images as part of an informal 'competition' to get a possible showing on the programme.

8    Of course, the most important and widely discussed instance of a photo-digital record (here, a private one) receiving major public circulation is the Abu Ghraib 'prisoner abuse' photographs of 2004. Among the commentaries and critical literature, Susan Sontag's 'Regarding the torture of others', first published in the *New York Times*, (Sontag, 2004) and widely reprinted, is an essential point of reference. A very recent discussion is Andre Gunthert's (2008). This includes attention to the issue of why, in an age of supposed scepticism towards the integrity of the digital image, these images were read immediately and widely as 'true'. For a suggestive analysis of the paradoxes of veracity at work in digital culture, see Fetveit (1999).

9    I have recently discussed the history of debate about documentary 'adequacy' in Corner (2008).

# References

Allen, R. and Hill, A. (eds) (2004). *The Television Studies Reader*. London: Routledge.

Alpers, S. (1993). 'Picturing Dutch Culture', pp. 57–67 in Wayne Franits (ed.) *Looking at Seventeenth Century Dutch Art: Realism Reconsidered*. Cambridge: Cambridge University Press.

Althusser, L. (1971). 'Ideology and the State', pp. 123–73 in *Lenin and Philosophy and Other Essays*. London: New Left Books.

Altman, R. (1999). *Film/Genre*. London: British Film Institute.

Amaya, H. (2008*)*. 'Racialized documentary: Reception of Ken Burns' *Jazz*', *Television and New Media* 9.2, 111–30.

Andrews, J. (2006). 'Spin from tactic to tabloid', *Journal of Public Affairs* 6.1., 31–45.

Arendt, H. (1973). 'Lying in Politics', pp. 9–42 in H. Arendt *Crises of the Republic*. Harmondsworth: Penguin Books.

Arendt, H. (1993/1961). 'Truth and Politics', first published in 1961 and reprinted in H. Arendt, *Between Past and Future*. Harmondsworth: Penguin.

Aristotle (1872). *Treatise on Rhetoric* (ed.) Theodore Buckley. London: Bell and Daldy.

Atton, C. (2001). *Alternative Media*. London: Sage.

Austin, T. (2007). *Watching the World: Screen Documentary and Audiences*. Manchester: Manchester University Press.

Bainbridge, C., Rustin, M., Radstone, S. and Yates, C. (eds) (2007). *Culture and the Unconscious*. Basingstoke: Palgrave Macmillan.

Baker, C. E. (2002). *Media, Markets and Democracy*. Cambridge: Cambridge University Press.

Baker. C. E. (2006). *Media Concentration and Democracy*. Cambridge: Cambridge University Press.

Barnhurst, K. (1998). 'Politics in the fine meshes: young citizens, power and media', *Media, Culture and Society* 20.2, 201–18.

Barnhust, K. and Nerone., R. (2001). *The Form of News*. New York: The Guilford Press.

Baron, N. S. (2008). *Always On*. New York: Oxford University Press.

Barthes, R. (1973). 'Myth today', in R. Barthes *Mythologies* (tr. Annette Lavers), London: Paladin.

Barthes, R. (1975). *S/Z*. New York: Hill and Wang.

Barthes, R. (1977). 'Rhetoric of the Image' (reprinted from 1964), pp. 32–51 in S. Heath (trans.) *Image, Music Text*. London: Fontana.

Barthes, R. (1984). *Camera Lucida*. London: Fontana.

Bassett, C. (2007). *The Arc and the Machine*. Manchester: Manchester University Press.

Baudrillard, J. (1988). *Selected Writings* (ed. M. Poster) Cambridge: Polity.

Baudrillard, J. (1995). *The Gulf War Did Not Take Place*. Bloomington: Indiana University Press.

Beattie, K. (2008). *Documentary Display: Re-Viewing Nonfiction Film and Video*. London and New York: Wallflower.

Bell, E. and Gray, A. (eds) (2010). *Televising History*. Basingstoke: Palgrave Macmillan.

Bellamy, R. (2008). *Citizenship: A Very Short Introduction*. Oxford: Oxford University Press.

Benjamin, W. (1980). 'A short history of photography', in A. Trachtenberg (ed.) *Classic Essays in Photography*. New Haven, Conn: Leete's Island Books.

Bennett, T., Emmison, M. and Frow, J. (1999) *Accounting for Tastes: Australian Everyday Cultures*. Cambridge: Cambridge University Press.

Bennett, T., Savage, M., Silva, E., Warde, A., Gayo-Cal, M. and Wright, D. (2009). *Culture, Class and Distinction*. London: Routledge.

Bennett, W. L. and Entman, R. (2001). *Mediated Democracy*. Cambridge: Cambridge University Press.

Benson, R. D. and Neveu, R. (eds) (2005). *Bourdieu and the Journalistic Field*. Cambridge: Polity.

Bignall, J. (2002). *Media Semiotics* (2nd edn). Manchester: Manchester University Press.

Bignall, J. (2007). *An Introduction to Television Studies* (2nd edn). London: Routledge.

Biressi, A. and Nunn, H. (2004). *Reality Television: Realism and Revelation*. London: Wallflower.

Blain, N. (2002). 'Sport as dispersed symbolic activity', *Culture, Sport and Society* 5.3, 227–54.

Boltanski, L. (1999). *Distant Suffering: Politics, Morality and the Media*. Cambridge: Cambridge University Press.

Bondebjerg, I. (2006). 'Politics backstage: TV documentaries, politics and politicians', *Politik and Mediekultur* 2.

Born, G. (2004). *Uncertain Vision: Birt, Dyke and the Reinvention of the BBC*. London: Martin, Secker & Warburg.

Bourdieu, P. (1984). *Distinction: A Social Critique of the Judgement of Taste*. Cambridge, Mass.: Harvard University Press.

Bourdieu, P. (1992). *Language and Symbolic Power*. Cambridge: Polity Press.

Bourdieu, P. (1993). 'Outline of a sociological theory of art perception', pp. 215–37 in Bourdieu, P., *The Field of Cultural Production*. Cambridge: Polity.

Bourdieu, P. (1999). *On Television*. New York: The New Press.

Bourdieu, P. and Passeron, J. C. (1977). *Reproduction in Education, Society and Culture* (tr. Richard Nice). London: Sage.

Boyle, R. and Haines, R. (2004). *Football in the New Media Age*. London: Routledge.

Brants, K. and Voltmer, K. (eds) (2010). *Political Communication in Postmodern Democracy*. Basingstoke: Palgrave.

Briggs, A. (1985). *The BBC: The First Fifty Years*. Oxford: Oxford University Press.

Brugger, N. (2009). 'Website history and the website as an object of study', *New Media and Society* 11.1–2, 115–32.

Bruun, H. (2010). 'Genre and interpretation in production: a theoretical approach', *Media, Culture and Society* 32.5, 723–37.

Bruzzi, S. (2006). *New Documentary* (2nd edn). London: Routledge.

Butler, J. (1990). *Gender Trouble*. London: Routledge.

Butler, J. (2009). *Frames of War*. London: Verso.

Caldwell, J.T. (2008). *Production Culture*. Durham, NC: Duke University Press.

Calhoun, C. (1993). *Habermas and the Public Sphere*. Cambridge, Mass: MIT Press.

Calhoun, C. (1994). *Social Theory and the Politics of Identity*. Oxford: Wiley-Blackwell.

Calhoun, C. and Sennett, R. (2007). *Practicing Culture (Taking Culture Seriously)*. London: Routledge.

Cammaerts, B. (2008). 'Critiques on the Participatory Potentials of Web 2.0.', *Communication, Culture & Critique* 1.4, 358–77.

Carey, J. (1989). *Communication as Culture: Essays on Media and Society*. Boston Mass. and London: Unwin Hyman.

Carroll, N. (1998). *A Philosophy of Mass Art*. Oxford: Oxford University Press.

Chan, T.W. and Goldthorpe, J. (2007). 'Social stratification and cultural consumption: music in England', *European Sociological Review* 23.1, 1–19.

Chanan, M. (1995). *Repeated Takes: A Short History of Recording and Its Effects on Music*. London: Verso.

Chanan, M. (2007). *The Politics of Documentary*. London: British Film Institute.

Chouliaraki, L. (2006). *The Spectatorship of Suffering*. London: Sage.

Chouliaraki, L. (2008). 'The Media as Moral Education: Mediation and Action', *Media, Culture and Society* 30.6, 831–52.

Cobley, P. (ed.) (2009). *The Routledge Companion to Semiotics*. London: Routledge.

Cohen, C. (2005). 'What does the Photoblog Want?, *Media, Culture and Society* 27.6, 883–901.

Coleman, S. (forthcoming). *Voting: The Feeling of Being Counted*. Cambridge: Cambridge University Press.

Coleman, S. and Blumler, J. (2009). *The Internet and Democratic Citizenship*. Cambridge: Cambridge University Press.

Collins, J. (2010) 'Imaginary Fraternities', *New Left Review* 64, 131–8.

Corey, A. and Peterson, V.V. (2003). 'Who said what: subject positions, rhetorical strategies and good faith', *Communication Studies* 54.4, 403–19.

Corner, J. (1979). ' "Mass" in communication research', *Journal of Communication* 29.1, 26–32.

Corner, J. (1980). 'Codes and Cultural Analysis', *Media, Culture and Society* 2.1, 73–86.

Corner, J. (1991). 'Meaning, genre and context: the problematics of knowledge in the new audience studies', pp. 267–84 in J. Curran and M. Gurevitch (eds) *Mass Media and Society*. London: Arnold.

Corner, J. (1996). *The Art of Record*. Manchester: Manchester University Press.

Corner, J. (1999). *Critical Ideas in Television Studies*. Oxford: Oxford University Press.

Corner, J. (2000). 'Influence: the contest core of media research', pp. 376–97 in J. Curran and M. Gurevitch (eds) *Mass Media and Society* (3rd edn). London: Arnold.

Corner, J. (2002). 'Sounds Real: Documentary and Music', *Popular Music* 21.3, 357–66.

Corner, J. (2003) 'The Model in Question'. *European Journal of Communication* 18.3, 367–75.

Corner, J. (2008). 'Documentary Studies: Dimensions of Transition and Continuity' in T. Austin and W. de Jong (eds) *Rethinking Documentary*. Maidenhead: Open University Press/McGraw-Hill, 13–28.

Corner, J. (2010a). 'Promotion as Institutionalized Deception' in M. Aronczyk and D. Power (eds) *Blowing up the Brand: Critical Perspectives on Promotional Culture*. New York: Peter Lang.

Corner, J. (2010b). ' "Politicality" and the inter-generic settings of reality television', pp. 22–39 in L. Baruh and J. Hoon Park (eds) *Reel Politics*. Newcastle upon Tyne: Cambridge Scholars Press.

Corner, J. (forthcoming). 'Confronting Value' in Bailey, M. (ed.) *Richard Hoggart: Culture and Critique*. Critical, Cultural and Communication Press.

Corner, J. and Pels, D. (2003). *Media and the Restyling of Politics*. London: Sage.

Cottle, S. (2006). 'Mediatized Rituals: A Reply to Couldry and Rothenbuhler', *Media Culture and Society* 30.1, 135–40.

Cottle, S. (2008). *Global Crisis Reporting*. Maidenhead: Open University Press.

Cotton, C. (2009). *The Photograph as Contemporary Art* (2nd edn). London: Thames & Hudson.

Couldry, N. (2000). *The Place of Media Power: Pilgrims and Witnesses of the Media Age*. London: Routledge.

Couldry, N. (2003). *Media Rituals: A Critical Approach*. London: Routledge.

Couldry, N. (2006a). *Listening Beyond the Echoes: Media, Ethics and Agency in an Uncertain World*. Boulder, Col.: Paradigm Press.

Couldry, N. (2006b). 'Culture and Citizenship', *European Journal of Cultural Studies* 93, 321–39.

Couldry, N. (2007). 'Bourdieu and the media: the promise and limits of field theory' (review), *Theory, Culture and Society* 36.2, 209–13.

Couldry, N. (2008). 'Form and power in an age of continuous spectacle', pp. 161–76 in D. Hesmondhalgh and J. Toynbee (eds) *The Media and Social Theory*. London: Routledge.

Couldry, N. (2009). 'Does "the Media" have a Future?', *European Journal of Communication* 24.2, 437–49.

Couldry, N. (2010). *Why Voice Matters: Politics and Culture After Neoliberalism.* London: Sage.

Couldry, N. and Rothenbuhler, E. (2007). 'Simon Cottle on "mediatized rituals": a response' *Media, Culture and Society* 29.4, 691–5.

Couldry, N., Livingstone, S. and Markham, T. (2007/2010). *Media Consumption and Political Engagement: Beyond the Presumption of Attention.* Basingstoke: Palgrave Macmillan.

Creeber, G., Tulloch, J, and Miller, T. (eds) (2008). *The Television Genre Book* (2nd edn). London: British Film Institute.

Crick, B. (1980). *George Orwell: A Life.* London: Secker & Warburg.

Curran, J. and Seaton, J. (2009). *Power without Responsibility: The Press and Broadcasting in Britain* (7th edn). London: Routledge.

Curtis, A. (2004). *The Power of Nightmares.* London: BBC.

Dahlgren, P. (2003). 'Reconfiguring Civic Culture in the New Media Milieu' pp. 151–70 in J. Corner and D. Pels (eds) *Media and the Restyling of Politics.* London: Sage.

Dahlgren, P. (2009). *Media and Political Engagement.* Cambridge: Cambridge University Press.

Danner, M. (2006). *The Secret Way to War.* New York: New York Review Books.

Dant, T. (2003). *Critical Social Theory: Culture, Society and Critique.* London: Sage.

Davis, A. (2010). 'Forms of Capital and Mobility in the Political Field: Applying Bourdieu's Conceptual Framework to UK Party Politics', *British Politics* 5.2, 202–23.

Dayan, D. (2009). 'Sharing and Showing: Television as Monstration' *Annals of the American Academy of Political and Social Science* 625.1, 19–31.

Deacon, D., Pickering, M., Golding, M. and Murdock, G. (2007). *Researching Communications.* London: Hodder Education.

Deinst, R. (1994). *Still Life In Real Time.* Durham, N.C.: Duke University Press.

Deuze, M. (2005). 'Popular Journalism and Professional Ideology: Tabloid Reporters and Editors Speak Out', *Media, Culture and Society* 27.6, 861–82.

Dovey, J. and Kennedy, H. (2006). *Game Cultures: Computer Games as New Media.* Maidenhead: Open University Press.

Downey, J. (2008). 'Recognition and the Renewal of Ideology Critique', pp. 59–74 in D. Hesmondhalgh and J. Toynbee (eds) *The Media and Social Theory.* London: Routledge.

Downey, J. and Fenton, N. (2003). 'New Media, Counter Publicity and the Public Sphere', *New Media and Society* 5.2, 185–202.

Downing, J. and Husband, C. (2005). *Representing Race.* London: Sage.

Durkheim, E. (1995/1912). *The Elementary Forms of Religious Life* (tr. K. Fields). Glencoe, Ill.: Free Press.

Eagleton, T. (1991). *Ideology: an Introduction.* London: Verso.

Edmundson, M. (1994). 'Ideology, Energy and Cultural Criticism', pp. 220–36 in M. Torgovnick (ed.) *Eloquent Obsessions: Writing Cultural Criticism.* Durham, N.C.: Duke University Press.

Eldridge, J. (ed.) (1995). *News Content, Language and Visuals: Glasgow University Media Group Reader* vol. 1. London: Routledge.

Ellis, J. (1982). *Visible Fictions.* London: Routledge.

Ellis, J. (2005). 'Documentary and Truth on Television: The Crisis of 1999', pp. 342–60 in A. Rosenthal and J. Corner (eds) *New Challenges For Documentary.* Manchester: Manchester University Press.

Ellis, J. (2009). 'What are we Expected to Feel? Witness, Textuality and the Audiovisual', *Screen* 50.1, 67–76.

Elster, J. (2007). *Explaining Social Behaviour.* Cambridge: Cambridge University Press.

Fairclough, N. (1995). *Media Discourse.* London: Edward Arnold.

Fetveit, A. (1999). 'Reality TV in the digital era: a paradox in visual culture', *Media, Culture and Society.* 21.6, 787–804.

Fetveit, A. (2001). 'Anti-essentialism and reception studies: in defence of the text'. *International Journal of Cultural Studies* 4.2, 173–99.

Fisk, R. (2010). 'Fighting Talk: The New Propaganda'. *The Independent.* 21 June.

Fiske, J. (1987). *Television Culture.* London: Routledge.

Flavian. C., Gurrea, R. and Orus, C. (2009). Website Design: a Key Factor for Website Success', *Journal of Systems and Information Technology* 11.2, 168–84.

Foucault, M. (2002). *Power: The Essential Works of Michel Foucault 1954–1984 vol. Three* (ed. J. Faubion). London: Allen Lane.

Foucault, M. and Gordon, C. (1980). *Power/Knowledge: Selected Interviews and other Writings 1972–77.* New York: Pantheon Books.

Fraser, N. (1992). 'Rethinking the Public Sphere – A Contribution to Actually Existing Democracy', pp. 109–41 in C. Calhoun (ed.) *Habermas and the Public Sphere.* Cambridge Mass.: MIT Press, 109–41.

Frus, P. (1994). *The Politics and Poetics of Journalistic Narrative.* Cambridge: Cambridge University Press.

Frow, J. (1987). 'Accounting for tastes: some problems with Bourdieu's sociology of culture', *Cultural Studies* 1.1, 59–73.

Frow, J. (1995). *Cultural Studies and Cultural Value.* Oxford: Clarendon Press.

Gaines, J. (1999). 'Political Mimesis', pp. 84–102 in J. Gaines and M. Renov (eds) *Collecting Visible Evidence.* Minneapolis: University of Minnesota Press.

Garnham, N. (2000). *Emancipation, the Media and Modernity.* Oxford: Oxford University Press.

Gidden, A. (1991). *Modernity and Self-Identity.* Cambridge: Polity.

Gill, R. (2006). *Gender and the Media.* London: Polity.

Goddard, P., Corner, J. and Richardson, K. (2007). *Public Issue Television.* Manchester: Manchester University Press.

Green, D. and Lowry, J. (eds) (2006). *Stillness and Time: Photography and the Moving Image.* London: Photoforum/Photoworks.

Gripsrud, J. (ed.) (2010). *Relocating Television.* London: Comedia/Routledge.

228 REFERENCES

Gunning, T. (1990). 'The Cinema of Attractions: Early Film, Its Spectator and the Avant Garde'; pp. 50–62 in T. Elsaesser and A. Barker (eds) *Early Film: Space, Frame, Narrative.* London: British Film Institute.

Gunthert, A. (2008). Digital Imaging Goes to War: The Abu Ghraib Photographs', *Photographies.* 1.1, 103–12.

Habermas, J. (1985). *The Theory of Communicative Action* vol. 2. Boston, Mass.: Beacon Press.

Habermas, J. (1989). *Structural Transformation of the Public Sphere.* Cambridge: Polity.

Habermas, J. (1992). *Moral Consciousness and Communicative Action.* Cambridge: Polity.

Habermas, J. (1997). *Between Facts and Norms.* Cambridge: Polity.

Hall, S. (1973). 'Encoding and Decoding in the Television Discourse', University of Birmingham, CCCS Stencilled Occasional Paper (Media Series Number 7).

Hall, S. (1981). 'Notes on Deconstructing the Popular', pp. 227–40 in R. Samuel (ed.) *People's History and Socialist Theory.* London: Routledge.

Hall, S. (1981/1973). 'Encoding and Decoding in the Television Discourse', pp. 128–38 in Hall, S., Hobson, D., Lowe, A. and Willis, P. (eds) *Culture, Media, Language.* London: Hutchinson.

Hall, S. (1983). 'The Problem of Ideology: Marxism without Guarantees', pp. 57–84 in B. Matthews (ed.) *Marx: 100 Years On.* London: Lawrence & Wishart. Also reprinted in Morley and Chen (1996).

Hallin, D. and Mancini, P. (2004). *Comparing Media Systems.* Cambridge: Cambridge University Press.

Hariman, R. and Lucaites, J.L. (2007). *No Caption Needed: Iconic Photographs, Public Culture and Liberal Democracy.* Chicago: University of Chicago Press.

Hartley, J. (1999). *Uses of Television.* London: Routledge.

Hearn, A. (2008). 'Variations of the Branded Self', pp. 194–210 in Hesmondhalgh, D. and Toybee, J. *The Media and Social Theory.* London: Routledge.

Herman, D. (ed.) (2007). *The Cambridge Companion to Narrative.* Cambridge: Cambridge University Press.

Herman, E. and Chomsky, N. (1988). *Manufacturing Consent.* New York: Pantheon Books.

Hermes, J. (2006). 'Citizenship in the Age of the Internet', *European Journal of Communication* 2.1.3, 295–309.

Hesk, J. (2000). *Deception and Democracy in Classical Athens.* Cambridge: Cambridge University Press.

Hesmondhalgh, D. (2007a). *The Cultural Industries* (2nd edn). London: Sage.

Hesmondhalgh, D. (2007b). 'Audiences and Everyday Aesthetics: Talking about Good and Bad Music'. *European Journal of Cultural Studies* 10.4, 507–27.

Hill, A. (2005). *Reality TV: Audiences and Popular Factual Television.* London: Routledge.

Hill, A. (2007). *Re-Styling Factual Television.* Abingdon: Routledge.

Hill, A. (2010). *Paranormal Media.* Abingdon: Routledge.

Hodge, R. and Kress, G. (1979). *Language as Ideology*. London: Routledge.

Hodge, R. and Kress, G. (1988). *Social Semiotics*. Cambridge: Polity Press.

Hoggart, R. (1957). *The Uses of Literacy*. London: Chatto and Windus.

Hoggart, R. (1958). *The Uses of Literacy*. Harmondsworth: Pelican Books.

Hoggart, R. (1970). *Speaking To Each Other*, Vol 1: *About Society*, Vol 2: *About Literature*. London: Chatto & Windus.

Holmes, S. and Jermyn, D. (2008). 'Why not Wife Swap?' pp. 232–45 in T. Austin and W. De Jong (eds) *Rethinking Documentary*, Maidenhead: Open University Press/McGraw-Hill.

Holmes, S. and Jermyn, D. (eds) (2004). *Understanding Reality Television*. London: Routledge.

Honneth, A. (1995). *The Struggle for Recognition: The Moral Grammar of Social Conflicts*. Cambridge: Polity.

Horton, D. and Wohl, R. (1956). 'Mass Communication and Para-Social Interaction: Observations on Intimacy at a Distance', *Psychiatry* 19, 215–29.

Jackall, R. (ed.) (1995). *Propaganda*. New York: New York University Press.

Jones, J. (2010). *Entertaining Politics* (2nd edn). Lanham, Md.: AltaMira Press.

Jones, P. (2007). 'Why there is no such thing as 'Critical Discourse Analysis', *Language and Communication* 27.4, 337–68.

Jowett, G. and O'Donnell, V. (1992). *Propaganda and Persuasion* (2nd edn). Newbury Park, Cal. and London: Sage.

Juhasz, A. (1994). '"They said we were trying to show reality – all I want is to show my video": The Politics of the Realist Feminist Documentary', *Screen* 35.2, 171–90.

Junger, S. (1997). *The Perfect Storm*. London: Fourth Estate.

Kaplan, A. (1990). *Psychoanalysis and Cinema*. London: Routledge.

Katz, M. (2004). *Capturing Sound: How Technology Has Changed Music*. Berkeley, Cal.: California University Press.

Klaehn, J. (2002). 'A Critical Review and Assessment of Herman and Chomsky's 'Propaganda Model", *European Journal of Communication* 17.2, 147–82.

Kress, G. (2010). *Multimodality: A Social Semiotic Approach to Contemporary Communication*. Abingdon, Oxon: Routledge.

Krippendorff, K. (2004). *Content Analysis: An Introduction to its Methodology* (second edition). Thousand Oaks Ca.: Sage.

Lang, K. and Lang, G. (2010) 'Mass Society, Mass Culture and Mass Communication: The Meaning of Mass', *International Journal of Communication* vol. 3. Online journal accessed at http://ijoc.org/ojs /index.php/ijoc.

Langton, L. (2009). *Photojournalism and Today's News*. Malden, Mass.: Wiley-Blackwell.

Larrain, J. (1979). *The Concept of Ideology*. London: Hutchinson.

Larrain, J. (1996). 'Stuart Hall and the Marxist Concept of Ideology', pp. 47–70 in D. Morley and K. Chen (eds) *Stuart Hall: Critical Dialogues in Cultural Studies*. London: Routledge.

Lasswell, H. (1934). In Seligman, and Johnson, (ed.) *Encylopaedia of the Social Sciences*, vol. XII. London: Macmillan, reprinted in Jackall (ed.) (1995) *Propaganda*. New York: New York Press.

Le Bon, G. (1896). *The Crowd: A Study of the Popular Mind*. London: T. Fisher Unwin.

Lewis, J. (2001). *Constructing Public Opinion*. New York: Columbia University Press.

Livingstone, S. (2005). 'On the Relation between Audiences and Publics', pp. 17–41 in S. Livingstone (ed.) *Audiences and Publics: When Cultural Engagement Matters For the Public Sphere*. London: Intellect.

Livingstone, S. (2009). *Children and the Internet*. Cambridge: Polity.

Lloyd, J. (2004). *What the Media Do to Our Politics*. London: Constable and Robinson.

Lovell, T. (1980). *Pictures of Reality*. London: British Film Institute.

Lukes, S. (1974). *Power: A Radical View* (1st edn). London: Macmillan Press.

Lukes, S. (2005). *Power: A Radical View* (2nd Edition). London: Palgrave Macmillan.

Lury, K. (2005). *Interpreting Television*. London: Hodder.

MacCabe, C. (1974). 'Realism and Cinema: Notes on some Brechtian Theses', *Screen* 15.2, 7–27.

McCarney, J. (1976). 'The Theory of Ideology: Some Comments on Mepham', *Radical Philosophy* 13, 28–31.

McFall, L. (2004). *Advertising: A Cultural Economy*. London: Sage.

McGuigan, J. (1992). *Cultural Populism*. London: Routledge.

McKee, A. (2005). *The Public Sphere: An Introduction*. Cambridge: Cambridge University Press.

McLuhan, M. (1973). *Understanding Media* (first published London: Routledge and Kegan Paul, 1964, page references to London: Abacus edition).

McRobbie, A. (2004). 'Post-feminism and Popular Culture', *Feminist Media Studies* 4.3, 255–65.

Manovich, L. (2001). *The Language of New Media*. Cambridge, Mass.: MIT Press.

Marr, A. (2004). *My Trade: A Short History of British Journalism*. London: Pan Books.

Marshall, P.D. (ed.) (2006). *The Celebrity Culture Reader*. London: Routledge.

Marshall, T.H. (1950). *Citizenship and Social Class and Other Essays*. Cambridge: Cambridge University Press.

Mayhew, L. (1997). *The New Public: Professional Communication and the Means of Social Influence*. Cambridge: Cambridge University Press.

Mepham, J. (1972). 'The Theory of Ideology in Capital', *Radical Philosophy* 2.

Merck, M. (2004). 'Fast Train Coming: The Political Pedagogy of *Fahrenheit 9/11*', *Radical Philosophy*, Issue 128. November/December, 2–5.

Miller, D. (2001). *Themes and Issues in the Study of Consumption*. London: Routledge.

Miller, D. and Philo, G. (1996). 'Against orthodoxy: the media do influence us', *Sight and Sound*. December. 18–20.

Miller, T. (2007). *Cultural Citizenship: Cosmopolitanism, Consumerism and Television in a Neoliberal Age*. Philadelphia, Penn.: Temple University Press.

Montogomery, M. (2007). *The Discourse of Broadcast News*. Abingdon: Routledge.

Moore, M. (2004). *Fahrenheit 9/11*, Dog Eat Dog Films.

Morley, D. (1980). *The 'Nationwide Audience': Structure and Decoding*. London: British Film Institute.

Morley, D. (1981). 'The "Nationwide Audience": A Critical Postscript', *Screen Education* 39, 3–14.

Morley, D. (2006). 'Unanswered questions in audience research', *The Communication Review* 9 February, 101–21.

Morley, D. and Chen, K. (eds) (1996). *Stuart Hall: Critical Dialogues in Cultural Studies*. London: Routledge.

Morris, E. (2003). *The Fog of War*. Senart Films/@Radical Media.

Morton, D. (2006). *Sound Recording: The Life Story of a Technology*. Baltimore, Md.: Johns Hopkins University Press.

Mosco, V. (1996). *The Political Economy of Communication*. London: Sage.

Mulvey, L. (1989). *Visual and Other Pleasures*. Basingstoke: Palgrave Macmillan.

Mulvey, L. (2005). *Death 24x a Second*. London: Reaktion Books.

Murdock, G. and Golding, P. (1977). 'Capitalism, Communication and Class Relations', pp. 12–43 in J. Curran, M. Gurevitch and J. Woollacott (eds) *Mass Communication and Society*. London: Arnold.

Murdock, G., Lister, R. and Kellard, K. (2010). *Digital Citizenship: Participation and Exclusion in the e-society*. London: Policy Press.

Murray, S. and Ouellette, L. (2004). *Reality TV: Remaking Television Culture*. New York: New York University Press.

Murray, S. and Ouellette, L. (eds) (2009). *Reality TV: Remaking Television Culture* (2nd edn). New York: New York University Press.

Nead, L. (2008). *The Haunted Gallery: Painting, Photography, Film c.1900*. New Haven, Conn.: Yale University Press.

Neale, S. (1990). 'Questions of genre', *Screen* 31.1, 45–66.

Nelson, R. (2007). *State of Play*. Manchester: Manchester University Press.

Newey, G. (2009). 'The People Versus The Truth: Democratic Illusions', pp. 81–98 in Geenen, R. and Tinnevelt, R. (eds) *Does Truth Matter?* New York and Berlin: Springer.

Nichols, B. (1976). 'Documentary Theory and Practice', in *Screen*, 17.4, 34–48.

Nichols, B. (1991). *Representing Reality*, Bloomington and Indianapolis: Indiana University Press.

Nichols, B. (1994). *Blurred Boundaries: Questions of Meaning in Contemporary Culture*. Indianapolis: Indiana University Press.

O'Shaughnessy, N. (2004). *Politics and Propaganda: Weapons of Mass Seduction*. Manchester: Manchester University Press.

Orwell, G. (1962). *The Road to Wigan Pier*. Harmondsworth: Penguin. First published 1937.

Orwell, G. (1968). 'The Road to Wigan Pier Diary', dated 1936, previously unpublished. Item 74 in S. Orwell and I. Angus (eds) *The Collected Essays and Journalism of George Orwell Volume One 1920–1940*. Harmondsworth: Penguin.

Paget, D. (1998). *No Other Way To Tell It*. Manchester: Manchester University Press.

Panofsky, E. (1955). *Meaning In the Visual Arts: Papers in and on Art History*. Garden City, NY: Doubleday Anchor Books.

Paras, E. (2006). *Foucault 2.0: Beyond Power and Knowledge*. New York: Other Press.

Pickering, M. (2008). 'Experience and the social world', in M. Pickering (ed.) *Research Methods in Cultural Studies*. Edinburgh: Edinburgh University Press.

Postman, N. (1985). *Amusing Ourselves to Death: Public Discourse in the Age of Show Business*. New York: Penguin Books.

Press, A. (1991). *Women Watching Television*. Philadelphia, Penn.: University of Pennsylvania Press.

Propp, V. (1958/1928). *Morphology of the Folktale*. The Hague: Mouton.

Putnam, D. (2000). *Bowling Alone: The Collapse and Revival of American Community*. New York: Simon and Schuster.

Raban, J. (2009). 'Trouble at the Fees Office', *London Review of Books* 31.11, 11–12.

Rawls, J. (1996). *Political Liberalism*. New York: Columbia University Press.

Ranciere, J. (2009). *The Emancipated Spectator*. London: Verso.

Rawnsley, G. (2005). *Political Communication and Democracy*. Basingstoke: Palgrave.

Renov, M. (2004). *The Subject of Documentary*, Minneapolis: University of Minnesota Press.

Rhoads, K. (2004). 'Propaganda tactics and *Fahrenheit 9/11*', at www.working-psychology.com/download_folder/Propaganda_And_Fahrenheit.pdf (accessed 15 August 2009).

Richardson, K. and Corner, J. (1986). 'Reading reception: mediation and transparency in viewers' accounts of a TV programme', *Media, Culture and Society* 8.4, 485–508.

Robinson, P. (2002). *The CNN Effect: The Myth of News, Foreign Policy and Intervention*. London: Routledge.

Robinson, P., Goddard, P., Parry, K., Murray, C. and Taylor, P. (2010). *Pockets of Resistance: British News Media, War and Theory*. Manchester: Manchester University Press.

Rosler, M. (1981, rev. 1989). 'In, around, and afterthoughts on documentary photography', pp. 303–41 in R. Bolton (ed.) *The Contest of Meaning*. Boston, Mass.: MIT Press.

Runciman, D. (2008). *Political Hypocrisy: The Mask of Power from Hobbes to Orwell and Beyond*. Princeton, NJ: Princeton University Press.

Scannell, P. (1986). '"The Stuff of Radio": Developments in Radio Features and Documentaries before The War', pp. 1–26 in J. Corner (ed.) *Documentary and the Mass Media*. London: Arnold.

Scannell, P. (1996). *Radio, Television and Modern Life*. London: Wiley-Blackwell.

Scannell, P. (2000). 'For-anyone-as-someone Structures', *Media, Culture and Society* 22.1, 5–24.

Scannell, P. (2009). 'The Dialectic of Time and Television', *Annals of the American Academy of Political and Social Science* 625.1, 19–35.

Scannell, P. and Cardiff, D. (1991). *A Social History of British Broadcasting*. vol. 1: 1922–1939. London: Blackwell.

Schlesinger, P. (2006). 'Is there a Crisis in British Journalism', *Media, Culture and Society* 28.2, 299–307.

Schlesinger, P., Dinan, W. and Miller, D. (2001) *Open Scotland?: Journalists, Spin Doctors and Lobbyists*. Edinburgh: Edinburgh University Press.

Schudson, M. (1998). *The Good Citizen: A History of American Civic Life*. New York: The Free Press.

Schudson, M. (2007). 'Citizens, consumers and the good society', *Annals of the American Academy of Political and Social Science*. 611.1, 236–49.

Silverstone, R. (1994). *Television and Everyday Life*. London: Routledge.

Sim, S. (ed.) (2004). *Routledge Companion to Postmodernism*. London: Routledge.

Sontag, S. (1979). *On Photography*. Harmondsworth: Penguin.

Sontag, S. (2004). 'Regarding the Torture of Others'. *New York Times*, 23 May.

Sparks, C. (1996). 'Stuart Hall, Cultural Studies and Marxism', pp. 71–101 in Morley, D. and Chen, K. (eds) *Stuart Hall: Critical Dialogues in Cultural Studies*. London: Routledge.

Sparks, C. and Reading. A (1998). *Communism, Capitalism and the Mass Media*. London: Sage.

Splichal, S. (2002). *Principles of Publicity and Press Freedom*. Lanham, Md.: Rowman and Littlefield.

Staiger, J. (2005). *Media Reception Studies*. New York: NY University Press.

Stallabrass, J. (1997). 'Sebatiao Salgado and Fine Art Photojournalism', *New Left Review* 223, May-June, 131–60.

Stein, L. (2008). 'Speech without Rights: the Status of Public Space on the Internet', *The Communication Review* 11.1, 1–23.

Taylor, P. (1992).'Propaganda from Thucydides to Thatcher', address to the annual conference of the Social History Society of Great Britain, 1992. Text accessed at http://ics.leeds/papers/vp01.cfm.

Thompson, J. (1990). *Ideology and Modern Culture*. Cambridge: Polity Press.

Thompson, J. (2000). *Political Scandal: Power and Visibility in the Media Age*. Cambridge: Polity Press.

Thompson, P. and Sacks, G. (eds) (2006). *The Cambridge Companion to Brecht* (2nd edn). Cambridge: Cambridge University Press.

Tilt, B. and Xiao, Q. (2010). 'Media coverage of environmental pollution in the People's Republic of China', *Media, Culture and Society* 32.2, 225–45.

Todorov, T. (1969). 'Structural Analysis of Narrative' (tr. A. Weinstein) *Novel: A Forum on Fiction* 3.1, 70–6.

Tong, J. (2010). 'The crisis of the centralized media control theory: how local power controls media in China', *Media, Culture and Society* 32.6.

Trachtenberg, A. (1980). *Classic Essays on Photography*. Stony Creek, Conn.: Leete's Island Books.

Van Bauwel, S. and Carpentier, N. (2010). *Trans-Reality Television*. Lanham, Maryland: Lexington Books.

van Dijk, T. (1998). *Ideology: A Multidisciplinary Approach*. London: Sage.

Van Zoonen, L. (2006). *Entertaining the Citizen*. Lanham, Md.: Rowman and Littlefield.

Vincent, D. (2000). *The Rise of Mass Literacy*. Cambridge: Polity Press.

Walton, Douglas (1997). 'What is Propaganda and What Exactly is Wrong with It?', *Public Affairs Quarterly* 11.4, 383–413.

Wayne, M. (2008). 'Documentary as critical and creative research', pp. 82–94 in T. Austin and W. De Jong (eds), *Rethinking Documentary*. Maidenhead: Open University Press/McGraw Hill.

Wells, L. (2003). *The Photography Reader*. London: Routledge.

Wernick, A. (1991). *Promotional Culture: Advertising, Ideology and Symbolic Expression*. London: Sage.

Williams, C. (1994). 'After the Classic, the Classical and 'Ideology'. *Screen* 35.3, 275–92.

Williams, R. (1974). *Television: Technology and Cultural Form*. London: Fontana.

Williams, R. (1976). *Keywords*. London: Fontana.

Williams, R. (1989/1958). 'Culture is Ordinary', first published 1958, reprinted pp. 3–18 in Williams, R. *Resources of Hope*. London: Verso.

Williams, R. (1989/1974). 'Drama in a dramatized society', inaugural lecture at the University of Cambridge, 1974, reprinted in O'Connor, A. (ed.) *Raymond Williams on Television*. London: Routledge.

Willis, J. (2000). 'Breaking the boundaries', pp. 97–102 in J. Izod, R. Kilborn and M. Hibberd (eds) *From Grierson to the Docusoap*. Luton: Luton University Press.

Winston, B. (1995; 2nd edn 2009). *Claiming the Real: The Documentary Film Revisited*. London: British Film Institute.

Winston, B. (2000). *Lies, Damn Lies and Documentaries*. London: British Film Institute.

Zizek, S. (2010). 'A Permanent Economic Emergency', *New Left Review* 64 (accessed online).

# Index

Note: Literary works can be found under authors' names